IN THE NAME OF LOVE

The Movement for Marriage
Equality in Ireland

An Oral History

IN THE NAME OF LOVE

The Movement for Marriage Equality in Ireland

An Oral History

Una Mullally

The
History
Press
Ireland

This book is dedicated to my parents for all their love and support

First published 2014

The History Press Ireland
50 City Quay
Dublin 2
Ireland
www.thehistorypress.ie

© Una Mullally, 2014

The right of Una Mullally to be identified as the Author
of this work has been asserted in accordance with the
Copyright, Designs and Patents Act 1988.

British Library Cataloguing in Publication Data.
A catalogue record for this book is available from the British Library.

ISBN 978 1 84588 830 5

Typesetting and origination by The History Press

CONTENTS

ACKNOWLEDGEMENTS

Documenting a social history is always open-ended. There is no such thing as a definitive history, and it would have been an impossible task to fit everyone who partook in a movement centrally or peripherally into one book, but to the hundred or so people I spoke to in researching this topic, and the seventy plus I've included, I am endlessly grateful for your time, honesty and insight. Many of you were patient enough to allow me to interview you multiple times, thank you for that.

In 2012, Moninne Griffith approached me about writing an oral history, so this book is essentially her idea. Ronan Colgan at the History Press Ireland believed that idea could make a book, so this book is essentially his vision. Thank you to Beth Amphlett for overseeing its production. Thanks to Sarah Fox for her design magic. Thanks to Marie Redmond for the office. Cheers to my family and friends who listened throughout, especially Etain Kidney, Vickey 'Ragin' Curtis, Sonya Donnelly, Aoibhinn Ní Shúilleabháin, Roisin Ingle, Dash, Fionn and Larry, and The Birds: Isabel 'Izzy' Hayes, Sarah 'Meadzer' Meade, Roisin 'Ro' O'Dea, Elaine 'Lainey' O'Meara. Thanks to my colleagues and editors at *The Irish Times* for your advice and patience. Most of all, I would like to thank Sarah Francis for all of her help and general brilliance – there is no way I could have even started this without her, never mind finish it. Nobody owns history, and nobody owns the movement for marriage equality. A social movement is as much the property of a legislator as it is a kid who got on a bus to go to a march. Never doubt that a small group of thoughtful, committed citizens can change the world, and never doubt that everyone together can either – the named and unnamed, the prominent and the anonymous. To those who fought for equality who are no longer with us, thank you.

INTRODUCTION

I was born on International Women's Day, on the morning of 8 March 1983, in the Coombe Hospital in the south inner city of Dublin. Later that day, across the Liffey, four teenagers were sentenced for the killing of Declan Flynn, a 31-year-old man, perceived by his attackers to be gay, who had been beaten to death the previous September. The park is just 3 kilometres away from the courts. Dublin is a small place. The young men arrived in court assuming that the afternoon would end with them in prison, but they were given suspended sentences. In the gay community, a righteous anger was born.

I was born into an Ireland where gay men having sex carried a maximum punishment of life in prison, where gay women were so invisible they weren't even written into the law, and where upon killing a person in an act of hate, you could get away with murder. There are a lot of dark corners in Irish history, but there are always opportunities for brave people to emerge from the shadows.

This book is about brave people.

'History needs people to participate in it.'

– Katherine Zappone

'I think it was Míne Bean Uí Chribín, who was a rather interesting woman but very vehement. And at the end of one of these meetings where we were debating in one of the universities, in Trinity, I think, she said, "Oh, I know all about you and the gay agenda! You're not going to be satisfied until you have gay marriage!" And I said, "Well, how terribly interesting! What a good suggestion. I must make a note of that. Do you have any other ideas?"'

– David Norris

INTERVIEWEES

DERMOT AHERN: Former Minister for Justice and Law Reform, former Minister for Foreign Affairs, former Minister for Communications, former Minister for Social, Community and Family Affairs, Fianna Fáil TD (1987-2011).

IVANA BACIK: Senator, Deputy Leader of the Irish Senate, barrister, lecturer at Trinity College, Junior Counsel for the KAL case.

MICHAEL BARRON: Head of BeLonGTo Youth Services.

DAN BOYLE: Former Green Party Senator and Deputy Leader.

TIERNAN BRADY: Director of Gay HIV Strategies at GLEN, former Donegal County Councillor (Fianna Fáil).

DECLAN BUCKLEY: Drag artist at Shirley Temple Bar.

JERRY BUTTIMER: Fine Gael TD.

SUZY BYRNE: Blogger, Maman Poulet.

DENISE CHARLTON: Founding member of Marriage Equality, Chief Executive of the Immigrant Council of Ireland, former Director of Women's Aid.

EOIN COLLINS: Director of Policy Change at GLEN.

STEPHEN COLLINS: Political editor of *The Irish Times*.

LISA CONNELL: Founding member of LGBT Noise, founding member of Equals.

MATT COOPER: Presenter of *The Last Word* on Today FM, *Sunday Times* columnist.

BRENDAN COURTNEY: Television presenter and fashion designer.

MICHAEL CRONIN: Lecturer in NUI Maynooth, former *GCN* writer.

NIALL CROWLEY: Former head of the Equality Authority.

HAZEL CULLEN: Filmmaker, writer.

LINDA CULLEN: Board member of Marriage Equality, Head of Television and co-owner of COCO TV.

SUSAN DALY: Editor of *TheJournal*.

FIONA DE LONDRAS: Lawyer, academic.

BORIS DITTRICH: Human rights activist, former leader of the Dutch political party D66, first openly gay member of the Dutch parliament.

DIARMUID DOYLE: Former deputy editor of the *Sunday Tribune*, producer of *Savage Sunday*, Today FM.

JEFFREY DUDGEON MBE: Northern Ireland gay rights campaigner, author.

DAVID FARRELL: Political scientist.

BRIAN FINNEGAN: Author, editor of *GCN*.

CHARLIE FLANAGAN: Minister for Foreign Affairs and Trade.

SARAH FRANCIS: Writer, board member of the GAZE International LGBT Film Festival.

BRODEN GIAMBRONE: Director of Transgender Equality Network Ireland.

MARGARET GILL: Mother of Barbara Gill.

DR ANN LOUISE GILLIGAN: Lecturer, academic, former chair of the National Education Welfare Board, plaintiff in the KAL case.

ROSS GOLDEN BANNON: Board member of Marriage Equality.

JOHN GORMLEY: Former Minister for the Environment and former Green Party leader.

MONINNE GRIFFITH: Co-Director of Marriage Equality.

JOHN HANAFIN: Former Fianna Fáil Senator.

ANNIE HANLON: Founder of LGBT Noise.

GRÁINNE HEALY: Chair and co-founder of Marriage Equality.

NÓIRÍN HEGARTY: Former editor of the *Sunday Tribune*.

GERARD HOWLIN: Former senior Fianna Fáil advisor, columnist with the *Irish Examiner*, public affairs consultant.

ANDREW HYLAND: Co-director of Marriage Equality.

SANDRA IRWIN-GOWRAN: Direction of Education Policy, at GLEN.

IZZY KAMIKAZE: LGBT rights campaigner.

MAX KRZYZANOWSKI: LGBT Noise member, former Mr Gay World.

EDMUND LYNCH: Gay historian and filmmaker.

JOHN LYONS: Labour Party TD, Deputy Labour Party Whip.

SENATOR FIACH MAC CONGHAIL: Senator, Director of the Abbey Theatre.

ANNA MCCARTHY: Member of LGBT Noise.

ELOISE MCINERNEY: Founding member of LGBT Noise.

UNA MCKEVITT: Early member of LGBT Noise, theatre-maker.

PHILLY MCMAHON: Theatre-maker.

MARIE MULHOLLAND: Formerly of Equality Authority and ICCL.

AOIBHINN NÍ SHÚILLEABHÁIN: Broadcaster.

DAVID NORRIS: Senator, gay rights campaigner, civil rights activist, first openly gay person elected to public office in Ireland.

EOIN Ó BROIN: Sinn Féin Ard Comhairle member, South Dublin County Councillor.

BREDA O'BRIEN: Iona Institute patron and columnist.

CIARÁN Ó CUINN: Former advisor to Dermot Ahern.

KATHERINE O'DONNELL: Director of the Women's Studies Centre, UCD.

COLM O'GORMAN: Executive Director of Amnesty International Ireland, Founder of One In Four, former Senator.

CONOR O'MAHONY: Senior lecturer in constitutional and child law, UCC.

BUZZ O'NEILL: PR and event manager, club promoter, member of Sinn Féin.

RORY O'NEILL: Drag artist Panti Bliss.

AVERIL POWER: Fianna Fáil Senator.

CONOR PRENDERGAST: Children of same-sex parents, campaigner.

BERNARDINE QUINN: Project Coordinator, Dundalk Outcomers.

KIERAN ROSE: GLEN board chairperson, former board member of the Equality Authority, Senior Planner with Dublin City Council.

EAMON RYAN: Former Minister for Communications, leader of the Green Party.

BRIAN SHEEHAN: Director of GLEN, former co-chair of the NLGF.

KATHY SHERIDAN: Author, *Irish Times* journalist.

AILBHE SMYTH: Former chair of the NLGF, board member of Marriage Equality, academic, LGBT rights activist.

MARC SOLOMON: National Campaign Director of Freedom to Marry (USA), former Executive Director of MassEquality, former Marriage Director of Equality California.

WILL ST LEGER: Founding member of Equals, artist.

JILLIAN VAN TURNHOUT: Senator, chair of Early Childhood Ireland, vice-chairperson of the European Movement Ireland, director of the Irish Girl Guides Trust Corporation Ltd.

MURIEL WALLS: Family lawyer, board member of GLEN.

TONIE WALSH: LGBT rights activist, founder of the Irish Queer Archive, former president of the NLGF, founding editor of *GCN*.

NOEL WHELAN: Political analyst, lawyer, *Irish Times* columnist.

SENATOR KATHERINE ZAPPONE: Senator, plaintiff in the KAL case, first openly lesbian member of the Oireachtas, member of the Irish Human Rights Commission.

1

THE PAST IS PROLOGUE

'We were the people who organised the Fairview Park march
after the killing, which is the thing that people say was
"The Irish Stonewall". And perhaps it was.'

– Izzy Kamikaze

*It was 1982 and the acronym for 'grotesque, unbelievable, bizarre, unprecedented'
was coined by journalist Conor Cruise O'Brien, and paraphrased by the Taoiseach
Charlie Haughey. 'GUBU' was the reaction to the astounding events surrounding the
double killing by Malcolm MacArthur, which culminated in him being arrested at
the Attorney General Patrick Connolly's house, where he had been staying as a guest.
The government was dissolved twice, and there were two general elections. One saw elected
Haughey as Taoiseach. Another government was led by Garret FitzGerald. On RTÉ
radio, an uninterrupted thirty-hour dramatised performance of Ulysses was broadcast
to mark Bloomsday. Hilton Edwards, an icon of the Dublin gay scene who founded the
Gate Theatre along with his partner Micheál MacLiammóir, died in November.*

*In 1982, three separate killings had a profound impact on the gay community.
On 21 January 1982, Charles Self, an RTÉ set designer, left a pub on Duke Street
and returned to his home in south Dublin. There, he was stabbed to death. He was 33.
His killer was never identified. On 8 September, John Roche, 29, was stabbed to
death in room twenty-six at the Munster Hotel in Cork. The hotel porter who killed
him, Michael O'Connor, 26, said, 'Your gay days are over', as he stabbed him. 'I had
to kill him,' he told Gardaí. 'He would have ruined my life. He wanted me to become
a gay. I said no way, and I killed him.' The jury found O'Connor not guilty of murder,
but guilty of manslaughter. On 9 September that year, Declan Flynn, 31, left a pub
in Donnycarney for Fairview Park, a popular cruising spot. The events that unfolded
on that night changed Irish history.*

On 22 April 1983, a Supreme Court judgement was about to be delivered in a case taken by David Norris against the Attorney General of Ireland. Norris sought to challenge the constitutionality of sections 61 and 62 of the Offences Against the Person Act, 1861, and section 11 of the Criminal Law Amendment Act, 1885. His initial claim to the High Court was rejected. Section 61 dealt with the act of buggery, which was punishable under Irish law by a maximum penalty of life in prison. Section 62 dealt with attempts and assaults for the purpose of committing buggery on a man. That crime held a maximum penalty of two years' imprisonment. Section 11 related to the public or private commission of or attempts to procure the commission of any man for an act of gross indecency with another man. The maximum penalty was imprisonment for two years. In 1983, David Norris was 38. If he won the case, male homosexuality would be virtually decriminalised in Irish law by removing the criminal charges and penalties for the sexual acts of gay men.

DAVID NORRIS: My objective from the very beginning in the early '70s was to get equality. I realised that step number one, if we were to make any progress, was to remove the criminal law. So that was the first objective … My view was that you did it in stages. First of all, you couldn't build civil rights without removing the criminal law.

Chief Justice O'Higgins delivered his judgement, rejecting Norris' appeal. The second Supreme Court judge, Finlay, agreed with O'Higgins' judgement. Then the third, Henchy, threw a spanner in the works, and sided with Norris. A fourth judge, Griffin, agreed with the judgement of the Chief Justice. A fifth judge, McCarthy, sided in parts with Henchy. David Norris lost the appeal three judges to two.

Justice Henchy referenced Dudgeon v. United Kingdom, the first European Court of Human Rights case to decide in favour of gay rights, taken by Jeffrey Dudgeon. Dudgeon filed a complaint with the European Commission of Human Rights in 1975. A hearing in 1979 declared his complaint should be heard by the European Court of Human Rights. The court sat in April 1981 before nineteen judges. In October, the court ruled, fifteen votes to four, that the criminalisation of homosexual acts in Northern Ireland was a violation of Article 8 of the European Convention on Human Rights, with regard to the right to respect for one's private life without interference by a public authority. Male homosexual sex in Northern Ireland was decriminalised a year later, October 1982.

JEFFREY DUDGEON: Our group, the Northern Ireland Gay Rights Association, was a direct take on the Northern Ireland Civil Rights

Association. We capitalised on the mood at the time, particularly coming from America: the civil rights organisations; the black organisations; by '71, '72, Stonewall, the beginnings of gay liberation and the emancipation notions that were developed. One thing always led from the other. And obviously in Northern Ireland then, unexpectedly the whole thing descended into war very rapidly from '69 onwards. That destroyed the early gay scene in a sense. It was put on hold for a number of years. But it gave us the opportunity to think new thoughts.

Outside the Supreme Court where Norris lost his appeal, exactly 3 kilometres away, and eight months previously, Declan Flynn, was on his way to Fairview Park around midnight. That evening, 9 September 1982, he'd been in Belton's Pub in Donnycarney. Waiting in the park were 17-year-old Colm Donovan from Lower Buckingham Street, 18-year-old Pat Kavanagh from the North Strand, 18-year-old Robert Armstrong from Finglas, and 19-year-old Tony Maher from the Poplar Row flats. They were joined by a 14-year-old boy on his bicycle. For six weeks, they had attacked around twenty men they perceived to be gay in the park. Queer-bashing, they called it. That night, they would do the same. They chased Flynn and beat him to death with sticks. As he lay choking on his own blood, they stole his watch and £4 from his pocket.

Nineteen-eighty-three, it turned out, would be another GUBU year in Irish history. In January, the government confirmed the Gardaí had bugged the phones of journalists and politicians. The racehorse, Shergar, was kidnapped. A referendum on a constitutional amendment on abortion was carried. Over three dozen Provisional IRA prisoners escaped Maze Prison in Antrim. U2 promoted the album War with a huge concert in the Phoenix Park, a place where the previous year, MacArthur killed his first victim, a young nurse.

In the aftermath of the Stonewall riots in New York, gay people and their allies were meeting in Ireland in small numbers. In October 1973, a group of ten men and women – Ruth Ridderick, Mary Dorcey, Margaret McWilliam, Irene Brady, Michael Kerrigan, Gerry McNamara, Hugo McManus, Peter Bradley, David Norris, and Edmund Lynch – met in a room in Trinity College to form the Sexual Liberation Movement.

EDMUND LYNCH: I think the moment for me was the first seminar that was held in Trinity College on a Saturday. It was organised and we were expecting [only] so many, but it was packed out. I had succeeded in getting the Liam Nolan show [*The Liam Nolan Hour*] to interview the late Margaret McWilliams and Hugo McManus on the Friday, so that was the first time on Radió Éireann. And then convinced Gay Byrne to pay for Rose Robinson, the founder of Parents Enquiry in England, to help parents understand children being gay, to bring her over for *The Late Late Show*. So he paid for her over and everything else. And she was successful on the show, just an ordinary kind of grandmotherly person, who was interested in her kids being looked after.

In 1975, the Campaign for Homosexual Law Reform began, with Mary McAleese on board as a legal advisor, and succeeded by Mary Robinson. Both women became Irish presidents. The judgement in Norris' case in April came in between two seminal moments of gathering. In March of 1983, the young men charged with Flynn's death escaped with suspended sentences, returning to family celebrations at their non-incarceration. The gay and lesbian community and their allies reacted with an unprecedented march on Fairview Park where people showed up in their hundreds. And in June, the first Gay Pride march was held.

IZZY KAMIKAZE: We were the people who organised the Fairview Park march after the killing, which is the thing that people say was 'the Irish Stonewall'. And perhaps it was.

In 1979, the Hirschfield Centre opened in a rundown area of Dublin. Named after the German physician, sexologist, writer, feminist, and gay and transgender rights advocate who died in 1935, it became the heart of the Irish gay scene. The centre on Found Street was the home of the National Gay Federation, which would later become the National Lesbian and Gay Federation (NLGF), and later still, NXF. The NGF was a membership organisation, funded by the gay community. The Hirschfield became a hub for gay activism, solidarity and socialising. Dublin was a grim place then. Between 1979 and 1986, the unemployment rate would balloon from 7 per cent to 17 per cent. By the end of the '80s, nearly half a million people had emigrated, a huge number for a country with a then population of around 3.5 million. Amongst the endless stream of emigrants was a large percentage of gays and lesbians, moving to London, New York and San Francisco, where they could live more openly gay lives. Elsewhere in Dublin, some gay bars emerged, covert and small. Bartley Dunne's, Rice's, and the 'gay-friendly' The Bailey on Duke Street on Saturdays.

Later, Hooray Henry's on South William Street, and The George on South Great Georges Street would emerge. As dance music hit Ireland, Sides nightclub became a focal point. And later still, the club nights HAM, GAG, and PowderBubble. For lesbians, the nights out were in dingy premises such as upstairs in the Trinity Inn or JJ Smyth's, before The Salon created a more sophisticated vibe at the Chameleon restaurant near Found Street.

IZZY KAMIKAZE: In those days nobody was calling Temple Bar 'Temple Bar'; it was just this sort of area between the quays and Dame Street that was going to be redeveloped for a bus station. They realised they were going to run into planning difficulties around it and there wasn't really the money for the massive redevelopment they wanted, so they started letting them out on caretakers' agreements to all kinds of fringe groups. The origins of the now much debased Temple Bar area concept lie in that.

EDMUND LYNCH: In my time, people were sneaking around. I was lucky enough that back forty-one years ago I told my mother and father that I was gay – or 'homosexual' was the word then – for the simple reason that I couldn't be honest with myself if I was telling everyone else to be themselves and I wasn't. My mother and father didn't understand homosexuality, but they knew one thing: that I was their son.

BILL HUGHES: I came out in 1972. It was coming up on my seventeenth birthday, and I told my parents that I was bisexual, because at the time I was sleeping with girls and with guys. The fact that I was having sex at all was the biggest shock to my parents, but then the fact that I was having it Betty Bothways was really upsetting to my mother. My father was so much older. So in 1972, he would have been mid-60s and he said, 'I'll tell you something', because he had travelled a lot as a young man. He had travelled all over North America. He had hitched, he had worked on trains, worked on boats, he had worked on logging camps. And he ended up having learned how to cook, and he became a really good cook. He ended up working at the Waldorf Astoria on the cold-salad buffet table. That was part of his thing, roasting the meats and preparing the salads. He said to me straight away, 'I met a lot of guys like that on my travels, and the one thing they had in common was that they were lonely, and I hope you never have to come and tell me that you're lonely. I would feel sad then that I failed as a dad.' Not so much in those lovely words, but close to those words. And that was it. There was never any judgement after that.

TONIE WALSH: I'll take you back to when I first became politically involved. It stemmed from a couple of things. I came out, I finished a relationship with a woman who turned out to be a lesbian – it was like the blind leading the blind – and she went back to France. This was 1979. I was almost 19. I came out in Amsterdam, I just had to deal with it.

And then I discovered the Hirschfield Centre which had been open about six months. Within a couple of months I realised I needed to focus my energies and use my loud mouth for something, and also use my – I suppose, my sense of indignant outrage, focus it and challenge it into something tangible, practical.

EDMUND LYNCH: What I first heard about was men would go down the quays, pick up other men in the toilets. I would have heard the pubs that people would go to: Rice's, and also Bartley Dunne's, and that sort of thing. And I must admit when I went to one of them I was delighted! You ended up going to private parties. There were always parties or something afterwards. It was a different world. Totally different world. I suppose we knew that there was something different about [Micheál] MacLiammóir and Hilton Edwards, things like that, but we wouldn't realise there were gay people all over the place.

BILL HUGHES: I went off to college in Birmingham, and I did my coming out there where I was completely anonymous on the wildest gay scene that could ever have been in my imagination. Birmingham in the mid-'70s. Jesus! It was completely crazy. It was the beginning of the disco era, and it was just wild. It was completely promiscuous. It was completely bohemian. It was crazy. And I came out in that and qualified from college and moved back to Ireland in '79 and found the scene here completely dead, whereas I could go to gay clubs in Birmingham, and go down on the train to London and go to Heaven and go to Bang and go to these clubs and have a drink. And I came back to Dublin and I could only go to the Hirshfield and they only served tea or coffee with cream cakes. And that was it. Because the queens couldn't be allowed to drink by the cops. I became great friends with Vincent Hanley at the time and he would travel all the time to New York, and subsequently I became his producer on *MT-USA* and he would say, 'Oh, we're in a backwater, darling! We are in such a back-water!' The only place that struck me where gays could have a drink was on Saturday afternoon in The Bailey, which became gay for Saturday after-noons, or in Bartley Dunne's, but everybody said, 'Don't go in there. It's dirty aul fellas and the smell of piss, and it's vile.' Then there was Rice's on the Green, 'Don't go in there because the aul fellas will offer you money for sex.' And that was the gay scene, but then all these little clubs started springing up. You could go to the Hirschfield for a fantastic dance and hear the best music ever, or you could go to the South Lotts and that was where there were great underground clubs. They were like New York, and it was bring-your-own-booze, and you could be as wild as you wanted. I'd go to New York working with Vincent over there, and we'd go down to the Village and all the bars, and we'd go to the big clubs. We'd go to The Saint on a Saturday night where a thousand gay men with their tops off would look up at the ceiling because it was a planetarium. Every Saturday night at 1 a.m., a box on the side of the wall would open and an electronic arm would come out, and the biggest star in the world would be standing on that electronic arm and do one song and leave. So I was there for Grace Jones the night she premiered 'Pull Up to the Bumper'. I was there for Diana Ross when she premiered 'Chain Reaction', and Laura Brannigan and 'Self Control'. And this was camp! This was high! And then they were gone, and then it was, 'Were you there? Were you in The Saint that night?' Yes, I was in The Saint that night! And people around me, the drug culture, everybody was doing cocaine. Everybody was having the fun, the fun, the fun. This is all early '80s stuff. And it was just at the tail end of Studio 54. So I got to stick my toe in that, and then come back to Dublin and have a cream cake and a cup of tea at the Hirshfield! So you know, it was quite ridiculous. Everybody was just like, 'Jaysus, are we never going to get our act together here? Is nothing ever going to happen in Ireland that's gay?'

JEFFREY DUDGEON: [The Dublin scene] was bigger and more relaxed. I think people were more mixed in a sense. There were more classes and religions. The Belfast gay scene was fairly Protestant and it was fairly working class, I suppose you could say. I was from a middle-class background. People in Belfast didn't have places to live. They all lived with their parents. Whereas Dublin was a bigger city, more freedom, students had their own place sometimes. There were more in terms of class; there were middle-class people, people who were well off and had their own houses and that sort of thing. So it was quite relaxed, actually, Dublin. I was there for a couple of years, '66 to '68. It was a very relaxed operation for those who were on the scene.

KATHY SHERIDAN: My father was a politician way back in the '60s and '70s, and I remember at the time, I think he held the casting vote for a short period in the Dáil, and he held that Fianna Fáil government in the palm of his hand. The saying around Longford-Westmeath was that Joe

Sheridan had such clout with that government that if there was a gay couple living in the town, when one of them died he would be able to get the other the widow's pension. That was a joke that went around, and it was 'hilarious' because it was deemed so unlikely. It was almost like the idea of a gay person getting a widow's pension when somebody died was like we could all fly to Mars or something.

IZZY KAMIKAZE: I'm 51 years old now and I came out when I was 19. The whole scene was very politicised in those days, so I was involved in the National Gay Federation, which it then was, I was involved in Liberation for Irish Lesbians, and I was also involved in the one that I'm proud of, which was the Dublin Lesbian and Gay Collective … In criminalised days when very, very few people were out, the guards turning up at people's places of work to interview them about a murder in a gay club was pretty serious stuff. So there was an element of protest around that, but basically a selection of various kind of left-wing backgrounds came together and that included Christopher Robson, Bill Foley, Melissa Murray, Ursula Barry, Maura Molloy and her partner, Cathal O'Kerrigan who was Sinn Féin, Mick Quinlan who in those days was Sinn Féin, me who was kind of non-aligned, a woman called Amanda Harvey who has gone on to do a lot of work in the domestic violence movement. A lot of people who went on to do a lot of really good stuff kind of cut their teeth in that.

TONIE WALSH: I spent ten years, all of my twenties, involved either with the Hirschfield Centre or as various official functions in NLGF; general secretary for years and then later on David Norris was the first president. In '84 I was elected president. The NLGF would have had around 3,500 members around the country at the time. In a way it was like a big sailing ship that was difficult to steer sometimes, compared to smaller agitprop groups and the single-issues campaigns like the Dublin Lesbian and Gay Collective, Cork Lesbian Collective. NLGF was bound by standing orders, elections, accountability, transparency. It wasn't always perfect, but from the get-go it had to be also running a resource – real estate – it was very important to have all those protocols in place. I then became president and spent five years being president and took the organisation through very turbulent times with where we were addressing things like various elements of the equality conversation.

By the early '80s the Hirschfeld Centre became the focal point of the scene. From there, services and organisations grew, such as Tel-A-Friend, a gay helpline. It also housed the nightclub Flikkers where DJs including Tonie Walsh, Paul Webb and Liam Fitzpatrick cut their teeth.

EDMUND LYNCH: I never saw myself as the front person because David Norris is much more articulate than I am. He had three good things going for him: one, he was articulate; two, he was Church of Ireland, minority religion; and three, both his parents were dead. So he had that sort of freedom. And that was important.

There was also a separate woman's centre nearby.

IZZY KAMIKAZE: There was a group of feminist women – there was no funding from the State whatsoever for a women's centre – but a lot of women weren't working, and they volunteered and kept it going, and the women who were working paid a standing order to pay the rent. The overheads were very low because of this caretaker's rent. It was the corner of Dame Street and Temple Lane – Nico's restaurant, the building above – the entrance was on Temple Lane. Nico's was already there; it must be one of the oldest restaurants in Dublin. That's where we were. We had four floors there. LIL, which was Liberation for Irish Lesbians, had one room in it. It was a bit ghettoised. It was largely dykes who were running the centre and staffing the centre, but there was always a bit of tension with the straight women that they felt we were putting straight women off coming in, you know? But things like the Women's Right to Choose campaign – we're talking about the first abortion amendment here – things like that ran out of that building. It was a bit like Youth Defense and all those things now these days! You know the way they're all run out of one building? We were like that back in the day! There was a library in there, a bookshop, there was what we called a coffee shop but it was a very amateur-hour kind of operation, but people would take it in turns to go in. Somebody would cook a meal every day. If you were working, you could go in and get your lunch and catch up with other women. It was a very good environment in a sort of activist era. Maybe something like Seomra Spraoi* would be an equivalent now.

*Seomra Spraoi is a non-hierarchical social space operating in Dublin.

In 1987, a fire badly damaged the Hirshfield, closing the centre. Aside from running the centre, the NGF had been publishing magazines; Ireland's first gay magazine, Identity, from 1982 to 1984, and Out from 1984 to 1988, featuring contributions from Tonie Walsh, Thom 'The Diceman' McGinty, Nell McCafferty and Nuala O'Faolain. On 10 February 1988, the first copy of Gay Community News (GCN) was published with Tonie Walsh and Catherine Glendon as the founders.

Another group that emerged was GLEN, the Gay and Lesbian Equality Network founded in 1988 as a voluntary organisation to progress legislative change around equality for gays and lesbians. For most gays and lesbians in Ireland, legislative change in terms of relationship recognition wasn't even conceivable and most campaigning in the late 1980s and early '90s was taken up with the HIV and AIDS crisis.

TONIE WALSH: GLEN claim the middle ground in LGBT agitation. When it was set up in '88, it was a response to a lot of people being individually burnt out, emigration – the campaigning movement had been decimated by AIDS, and there was a real need to focus the energies of all the disparate organisations under an umbrella group and just specifically focus on law change and then beyond law change, but I cannot remember the early days throughout the early '90s. I really think discussion around marriage equality really only came into play after '93, much later on. I was partying and clubbing a lot from the mid-'90s onwards, so my recollections are a bit hazy.

BILL HUGHES: Sadly my awareness of the need for couples being acknowledged and for rights and for, in some sense, access was through the AIDS plague. In the '80s, AIDS swept through Dublin. It didn't sweep through Dublin to the same extent as it swept through New York and London and San Francisco; however, an awful lot of Irish people were in New York and London and San Francisco, and they died during that period. But for people who had stayed here, and gays who were living in Dublin and living open gay lives, going to the Hirschfield and in relationships, suddenly one would get sick and it was sick with AIDS, so everybody knew then it was the death sentence, because that's what it was. I started to become aware of the sadness because the families started to move in. People who had come to Dublin and made a career for themselves and had a nice flat, and had nice belongings, and were going on nice holidays, and the family hadn't wanted anything to do with them. But as soon as they got sick and there was a sense of 'oh well'; they just moved in and the partners got pushed aside and the partners had no recourse and had no access. And in some cases even the final wishes of the person were not observed because the partner wasn't able to enforce them, and the family decided for whatever reason if they requested cremation, 'No, no, no, they're having the full funeral and their coffin is going to go up the main street of our country town because that's the way.' It was at a time like that where I just thought, 'Jesus, this is messed up, this is fucked up.' I wasn't in a relationship at that stage, but I thought if I was in a relationship, I would need to be certain that the law in some way protected me, but then the law couldn't protect me, because we weren't decriminalised until 1993. So you were caught in an illegal limbo where: tough shit, you got AIDS; tough shit, you have no recourse to the law; tough shit, your family can do what they want – estranged brothers, estranged sisters, estranged parents who had cast aside people who had come out as gay suddenly were taking control of their assets, their homes, their prized possessions, and they were marching off with them before the body was cold. The partner was left grieving with nothing, sometimes was thrown out of the home that they shared because it wasn't written down anywhere. There was no contract that could be enforced. So it was around then, the mid-'80s in particular, where I started to realise there is so much unevenness in society, and particularly with regard to gay people and gay relationships that, Jesus, something needs to be done.

CHARLIE FLANAGAN: I can tell you there was one gay guy in Mountmellick when we were growing up and, I mean, the reality was that there was one known gay guy and everything else was swept firmly under the carpet, which was a really sad indictment of society. I know gay people who emigrated, contemporaries of mine who emigrated because they didn't feel they could survive or they didn't feel they could embark on any meaningful career or achieve either professional or personal satisfaction living here. I find that actually shameful.

IZZY KAMIKAZE: I was involved in the AIDS helpline back in the late '80s and then Dublin AIDS Alliance. In those days, the Dublin AIDS Alliance ran on a FÁS* scheme, pretty much. But it was big. There might have been twenty people on the FÁS scheme, and there might

*FÁS is a State agency which runs courses and placements for people seeking employment.

have been another twenty or thirty volunteers who worked pretty much daily, because there was a huge unemployed pool of activists at that time. The AIDS crisis was unfolding very immediately and urgently around us and there were no services really. Nothing. So it was up to volunteer efforts to pull together whatever they did. We had two flag days a year, which is basically what that was funded from: Irish AIDS Day and World AIDS Day. We went out and shook buckets on the street.

BUZZ O'NEILL: What got a lot of people agitated was late '80s, '90s, the HIV epidemic. That's where gay men particularly felt completely isolated legally. So I would have had a lot of friends, a lot of casualties lost along the way. It was always horrible. You're hearing all the stories of them pretending to be his brother, if the family were cool with it, saying to a nurse, 'Yeah, this is his brother', so he could get into the hospital to someone dying in a bed. So I suppose that's where it was kind of at the time in the '90s two strata: gay men dying of AIDS wanting legal recognition and a lot of lesbians that were secretly bringing up children.

IZZY KAMIKAZE: The Hirshfield Centre burnt down. That was the end of the NGF as anything meaningful in my view, because the centre wasn't there anymore. I mean, they continued to publish *GCN* and so on, but as a membership organisation it was finished. It used to have 2,000 members back in the day, but that evaporated when there was no facility for members to use and by that time there had started to be a bit of a commercial gay scene so they didn't have the monopoly that they once had anyway. So that more or less died. The women's centre had closed down. Basically Temple Bar was getting redeveloped and a lot of people got diverted into the AIDS crisis, which was obviously the next big thing that came along.

GCN continued to publish, and for many LGBT people, it became a touchstone.

JERRY BUTTIMER: *GCN* was probably the one periodical, the one paper that I remember in Cork, once the co-op store in O'Sullivans came together. And, you know, you bundled it under your jacket and you brought it home.

The Declan Flynn protest in Fairview Park in 1983 is frequently cited as the birth of LGBT protest in Ireland, but there were others before that.

TONIE WALSH: 'Gay rights are human rights, gay rights are your rights.' That was even on Pride banners at the time that was used. Walking down Grafton Street on Dublin's first Pride with that banner leading the parade: gay rights are your rights … Well, obviously it was addressing us, the LGBT community, and reminding us that gay rights are human rights – part of a wider discourse that was also being addressed by ICCL, by Amnesty International or whatever, the Women's Council … I'm talking about the early '80s – politically it was a horrible time to be lesbian or gay in Ireland, and of course transgender people didn't even get a look-in. It was a horrible time. Paradoxically, creatively it was really interesting. The very oppressive nature of Irish society actually acted in a paradoxical way; it gave us something to push against. There's something enormously liberating about being a sexual outlaw. You're not defined by any rules. There are no rules. You're outside the pale. So in fact, the whole world is there to create. How we imagine a new world is there for the taking as far as I'm concerned – and that seemed to me quite clear in my mind. Now how you articulated the need for change to get to that – attain to that new world – was something else. And that was also of course quite an engaging process. But I do remember making a very conscious decision. I looked around me and I thought, I don't see many voices, LGBT voices, that represented my political and cultural and social sensibility. There were very few. You had David Norris. And I'm not being ungenerous, but in a sense [he] was hogging the limelight, for good or bad reasons. He was a big person, but he was fifteen years older than me. To me, somebody in their twenties, he was just some old guy, even though he was only 35 or whatever! We were all these bright young things in our early twenties advancing towards whatever, advancing towards creating a wonderful, new Ireland! Not just for ourselves, but for wider society. You know, full of the innocence and anger of youth I suppose, that's what it really is.

IZZY KAMIKAZE: I had been involved in some of the early Dublin Prides, and they fizzled out – let's see, when was the last one? I think 1987. We had a really big one in 1983, right after the Fairview Park march. The Fairview Park march was in March I think, so in June there was still good energy around about that. The anti-amendment campaign was going on at the time. There was lots of allies. Four or five hundred people got out, which in those days was remarkable to get 400 or 500 people. That was like getting 30,000 now. Huge success. But in the subsequent years, because the anti-amendment campaign, for anyone doing social history in Ireland, it was such a divisive, difficult time. People were so worn out by that struggle, which dragged on for years. As I say, the AIDS thing was developing, the gay community lost its community centre in those years. All those things happened and everything kind of fell apart. There were 400 attended that year. I have a picture the following year, there was maybe fifty, which was still pretty ok. The year after that there was maybe thirty. The year after that there was twelve, and serious fucking harassment on the street. The year after that it didn't happen. So it hadn't happened for seven years. In 1991, I was also involved in a thing called ACT UP, which was the AIDS Coalition To Unleash Power, a local chapter of that. We did one action a month for thirteen months. Things like going in and occupying offices in the Department of Health and whatever. There was a little crew of us who went out and did these direct-action type of things together. We did some quite nice stuff. Three of the people from that went on to form Dublin Pride. Belfast had a Pride parade – 'Dander', they called it. In 1991, their first one, we went up in the back of a van to take part in that as Dublin ACT UP. All the way back we were going, 'Oh, we have to do a Pride in Dublin next year! We have to do a Pride in Dublin next year!' That enthusiasm made us do that in 1992.

Another protest in 1992 was held by Irish gays and lesbians who went to New York to protest the exclusion of gays and lesbians from the St Patrick's Day Parade there by the Ancient Order of Hibernians.

SARAH FRANCIS: But the same year, the first gay float took part in the St Patrick's Day Parade in Cork. Under a banner that I think said 'Hello New York', it was thirty lesbians!

IZZY KAMIKAZE: These things are connected with each other, that's how it happens. Pride had never stopped happening in Dublin, but there had stopped being a parade. So it had stopped being a public thing really. I think without the parade it doesn't really count. There still used to be a Pride picnic in Merrion Square; there would be movies and various social events, but there was no public thing. And I think what Pride counts as is a visibility exercise, so that part of it had stopped happening and this little bunch of people – and we were pretty fringe people in the community, we weren't people that would be regarded as suitable leadership material maybe, which is always the issue! We decided to do that and Pride is a very suitable thing for fringe people to do, because what Pride is about is all of us have a right to be seen. I'm mentioning this now because this comes into the marriage equality thing. Just like decriminalisation: the whole fight for decriminalisation was about presenting a certain kind of picture or a respectable picture of gay people … The decriminalisation thing depended on a particular kind of respectable image of the community being marketed. There was tremendous trouble at times. Very few people were prepared to speak publicly as gay people at that time. But if you did and you didn't toe the party line, you'd have been pretty much fucking burnt as a witch. I feel it's not as intense now because a lot more people are out and there basically isn't the central control anymore. Anybody could say anything. That isn't quite as strong an issue as it used to be; that nobody got to speak in public about gay rights who wasn't sort of middle-class, employed, respectably partnered, you know? Scrubbed up well, and who was saying, 'We're exactly the same as straight people aside from this one tiny little difference.'

Having failed in the Supreme Court, David Norris had taken his case to the European Court of Human Rights in 1983. Five years later, the court found that Irish law was in breach of the Convention for the Protection of Human Rights and Fundamental Freedoms, with regards to a right respect one's private life. Norris, supported by the Campaign for Homosexual Law Reform, had won Norris v. Ireland. However, the government failed to act on the ruling until 1993 when the Minister for Justice Máire Geoghegan-Quinn brought through a bill that dealt with equal age of consent and the decriminalisation of male homosexual activity. The bill went through the Oireachtas and on to the President, who now, in an occasion of synchronicity, was Mary Robinson, the woman who had represented Norris as barrister and senior counsel in his European Court of Human Rights case.

STEPHEN COLLINS: Albert Reynolds would have been traditional, middle-of-the-road Catholic. But he wasn't an 'anti'; he didn't have strong views one way or the other. If Fianna Fáil opposed divorce, he would have opposed divorce, but they did that for political tactics. So Albert was Taoiseach and Máire Geoghegan-Quinn was the minister. Now, Máire Geoghegan-Quinn was personally in favour of it, and quite strongly committed to it. The fact that she was the Minister for Justice I think did have an impact.

TONIE WALSH: I think in the early days, lesbians were really generous about fighting that battle when you know they weren't specifically legally affected by it. But of course they were in a double bind. Most lesbians were invisible in the '80s actually.

BRENDAN COURTNEY: When homosexuality was decriminalised, I remember my aunt showed me the newspaper cutting. I would have been 18 or 19. Now going back to the age of 14 or 15, I remember I had the Bronski Beat record 'Age of Consent' and in Ireland on the back it said 'illegal'. I remember that the decriminalisation felt very otherworldly to me because, to be honest, I didn't feel oppressed by it, or that's what I thought. I was from a liberal background, and not a very religious background, so not your average Irish family. My older cousin was gay, my aunts were gay, and so even though we were quite working class, it wasn't a big deal … I was bullied in school for being gay, but I always thought that was them and this was me, and I felt I had a protected but probably naive upbringing. As I got older, I realised how judged I was by my sexuality, and how deeply entrenched some of the institutions I still work for were in their homophobia.

BRIAN FINNEGAN: Almost immediately what happened in Dublin after decriminalisation was the scene went from having two tiny pokey little bars to just basically exploding into something that was unheard of in this city. The bars, you used to have to knock on the door, and they'd pull a little thing inside and if you looked gay, they'd let you in – that kind of thing. The Front Lounge opened, the George expanded, Powderbubble, HAM – all of these things started becoming the thing that people were caring about, because they never had it. This idea that we were free and we were visible. So I don't think people were really thinking about drilling down to the next thing at that stage… I worked in *GCN* on a FÁS scheme in 1993-94 and decriminalisation was 'the thing'. That's what everyone talked about during that time until July '93 when it was repealed. So after that there was a kind of tailoring off in political activity for about a year. If you look back at *GCN*s it's a bit boring; there was nothing, no news, nothing, no political news. And then Gráinne Healy is on the cover of one in about '95, and I remember that. I remember reading that. It was the first I heard of the idea that we would be striving for marriage equality. There's a picture of Gráinne on the cover and she's calling for partnership rights.

Around northern Europe, the idea of partnership rights or relationship recognition was brewing. In 1989, Denmark became the first country in the world to legalise same-sex unions. In 1993, Norway introduced rights for registered partnerships. In 1994, Sweden introduced partnership rights. In 1996, Greenland and Iceland introduced partnership rights. That year, Bill Clinton enacted the Defense of Marriage Act, pre-empting the movement for marriage equality. The Act allowed for individual states to not recognise the potential partnership rights of couples secured in other states. At the time it was a hypothetical. Although a court case was being taken in Hawaii (Baehr v. Lewin) by three same-sex couples who were arguing that the state's ban on same-sex marriage was against the constitution of the state, it wouldn't be until 2004, eighteen years after the Defense of Marriage Act, that the first provisions would be made by two US states – New Jersey and Maine – for same-sex partners, the same year that Massachusetts would leap ahead and declare same-sex marriage legal.

KATHERINE O'DONNELL: I was very interested in the legal mechanisms of the marriage movement in Hawaii and how the federation of the United States went to shut that down. I suppose part of where I've done activism has been in the East Coast of the US. I lived in Boston for three years and was involved in ACT UP and an Irish lesbian and gay organisation – you know, in small ways – and Queer Nation in Boston. So it was fascinating to me to see the legal arguments used, but also how the people who would have been my mentors – a lot of them would have been academic – felt that this was kind of a 'Friends of Bill' movement, that it was a movement for assimilation into a culture and a politic that we were very critical of. Again we had a certain amount of privilege in that most of the people I was hanging out with were Jewish or otherwise white intellectual people with jobs, so while we could experience marginalisation due to being out as lesbians and gays, we also had quite a privileged class position, and I think we really valued the critique we were able to launch from a more marginal position into the centre, and the vantage point it gave us and how power worked in cultures and societies. So the people that I would have been mentored by were suspicious of this movement, and later the whole Don't Ask Don't Tell debacle of gays in the military, which was never a mainstream LGBT issue. And I would have been thinking of the marriage movement in that light, arguing for assimilation to an idealised notion of heterosexuality and that in the movement I find it kind of problematic in that I saw a lot of people asking for assimilation on grounds that were not recognising the heritage, culture and specificity of LGBT lives, culture and family formation. So from the very beginning way back then in the early '90s, I would have been rather critical of that marriage movement.

In 1997, the Netherlands, which would later become the first country in the world to legalise same-sex marriage, introduced partnership rights. And back in Ireland, a key piece of equality legislation, the Employment Equality Act, was progressing.

BORIS DITTRICH, UCC MARRIAGE EQUALITY CONFERENCE, 28 MARCH 2014: My political party asked me to run for national parliament and at that time in the Netherlands there was no registered partnership, there was no same-sex marriage. I was an openly gay man and when I was asked to run for parliament in 1993, several people I talked to said, 'Well, you know, the country is not ready yet for an openly gay member of parliament, so don't emphasise your lifestyle and your personal life.' I always thought that was really crazy. I mean, how can you ask somebody to be a people's representative if he cannot represent himself? So it irritated me so much that during the election campaign I started to talk about LGBT rights and I talked about civil unions and Scandinavia, where registered partnerships could take place, and we didn't have them in the Netherlands. Because I was so visible in the campaign talking about these issues, a lot of journalists started to ask me, 'What else do you want to achieve for the LGBT community?' And I thought, well, I really need to have something we can really work on, and something very important, something clear, something a lot of people would find interesting. And so, after some conversations with a lot of people, I said, 'Well, actually, I want to introduce marriage equality to the Netherlands.' At the time, because [there was] nowhere in the world same-sex couples could get married, this was a really far-fetched idea. I had a lot of opponents – [including] surprisingly enough, the LGBT movement in the Netherlands. The board consisted of some older people and they came to parliament and said, 'What are you doing? You are reinforcing this old-fashioned institution of marriage with new blood. We actually want to get rid of marriage as an institution and now you are trying to reinforce it. So we are against.' Of course, that didn't really strengthen my position in parliament because if the LGBT movement is vocally against your proposal, it doesn't really lead to anything. So at the same time, there were some members of parliament, members of the government, who said, 'Well, maybe legally you might be right that it's feasible to introduce marriage equality, but why don't we just take this registered partnerships, civil unions like they have in Scandinavia, and let's do that?' In the back of their minds it was: once the gays have that, they will stop talking about marriage equality. Fortunately it didn't happen that way. Because we talked about marriage equality, the whole idea of civil unions or a registered partnership was something very boring and nobody really discussed that, so it was actually fairly easy in 1998 to introduce the act of registered partnership, and it's open for same-sex couples and different sex couples, but it was not really very popular because the whole debate was about marriage equality … I introduced a motion, a resolution in parliament, which was adopted by the majority, asking for the government to introduce legislation on marriage equality. And then the prime minister said to me, 'Although we have a majority in parliament, we cannot do that, because nowhere in the world same-sex couples can get married and people will really mark us. They will laugh at us, because the Netherlands is known for its coffee shops where you can smoke pot, marijuana, and now you come with same-sex marriage. No, this is not good for our reputation.' So although we had a majority in parliament, our own government and my political party, in spite of the government, they didn't want to introduce this legislation. We had elections afterwards and in 1998 I became the leader of our negotiations team, and two other political parties because we were going to form a coalition government, they really wanted us to be there, to be part of the new government. And so, I had a very good, strong position, and I said, ok, we'll join the new government if we will get euthanasia, if we will get same-sex marriage, and some other issues. And although they informally supported and actually didn't really care about same-sex marriage, they said, 'Ok, if that's what you want, you can get it.' And so actually it was relatively easy in 1998 to convince the government to start the law process, the legal process. However, in government there were a lot of people who said because marriage equality doesn't exist in the world, it's probably legally very difficult. So first the government installed a State committee, and the State committee had to see if it was legally possible for two men or two women to get married. The outcome of that committee took one year to study, it was exactly what we had always said: yes, it's possible, it's a political choice. Because it was in our coalition contract, it was actually very smooth, the whole process, and people started to get married on 1 April 2001.

It's hard to pinpoint when legal relationship recognition for gays and lesbians emerged as a pertinent conversation. In fact, for many gays and lesbians, because marriage was so unavailable, critiques were developed about the institution itself, and alternative relationship structures that would be less conformist, less heteronormative and less patriarchal were moulded by gays simply getting on with their lives. While European nations were the first to introduce partnership rights for lesbian and gay couples, the more branded marriage equality movement that emerged later was influenced by activism in the US.

TONIE WALSH: I'm 53. I'm of a generation not just of gay activists, but of a generation that just grew up with this idea that actually, as sexual outlaws, the type of relationships we wanted were there to be claimed in whatever form we wanted. Whether we wanted to live with three partners, whether we wanted to be serially monogamous, whether we wanted a multiplicity of partners in all sorts of domestic or non-domestic arrangements – that was all there to be claimed. It's dreadful trying to sort of revisit the past actually and not be revisionist, sort of tiptoe around one's memory of the past, but I imagine that actually, most of us weren't particularly interested in marriage. The reason we weren't interested in marriage was deep down we imagined it was unattainable and maybe that's indicative of how simply oppressive and repressive society was that just simply nobody could actually imagine that. There was such an enormous societal shift required that it seemed insurmountable. As a result of it being insurmountable, we just simply didn't care about it. We just got on with the business of going, 'Ok, let's see what all the other options available are.'

GRÁINNE HEALY: The first couple I met who were married was a couple from the Netherlands, and I suppose I was surprised then because I was thinking, 'Oh, two women getting married, I'm not sure about that, I have a whole lot of issues about marriage.' I remember meeting that lesbian couple from the Netherlands and it started me thinking about not being too sure about marriage – feminist views of marriage, very critical of marriage. And then I suppose I started to develop from there on.

IZZY KAMIKAZE: I do remember very early on, about 1984, Irish people didn't travel – they emigrated. People would disappear and you'd never see them again, but otherwise you were here. One of the first women

I met when I came out – she was maybe ten years older than me – fell in love with a passing American and went to America with her. The next thing was, people started getting letters and postcards from her, and they had got married in the Metropolitan Community Church. And that was the first person I had ever heard of, a gay person, getting married. There was probably an element of amusement about it more than anything else, but I mean, we were all very happy for her. It was definitely a good thing for them personally, but was it something we felt we had to go out and campaign for in the streets to be able to do? No. You're also talking about the early '80s in Ireland, which was very much the spirit of the '70s in terms of what was happening anywhere else. Marriage was on the decline for straight people as well. The kind of straight people that I mixed with – left-wing activists, feminist activists – most of them didn't get married. They cohabited and stuff. They serially cohabited! But they didn't get married. Most of the children I knew were born outside of marriages, whether they were born to straight people or gay people. In that particular era – it wasn't called polyamory in those days – but a lot of people were experimenting with non-monogamy, non-traditional sorts of relationships, gay and straight people. And the notion that gay people would be out in the streets demanding the right to marry would have seemed ludicrous, I think. So was anybody talking about that? No.

COLM O'GORMAN: The first time I became aware of it was when I was living in the UK. I lived in the UK from '86 to 2003 and I can remember when Ken Livingstone, as Mayor of London, brought in a form of ceremony as opposed to any kind of recognition whereby people could go along to City Hall and have an event where they in some form, I suppose, solemnised their relationship, because civil partnership wasn't even on the books then. And two friends of mine – two women I had known for years – did that … I always wanted to get married. Paul asked me to marry him two weeks after we met. He loves reminding me of that! I also said yes two weeks after we met. At that time, there was no possibility of that happening. We met in 1999.

EOIN COLLINS: There was a kind of view from a – I don't know if you'd even call it progressive, non-serious progressive side – saying, 'Well why do you want marriage anyway? Marriage is a patriarchal institution, a failed institution', whatever. See this was usually people who were married and had all what it had to offer, and just didn't grasp the issue which we were talking about, which was an equality argument. So there was an argument like that around, that some people had; that we didn't want to replicate a heterosexual institution, a patriarchal institution and so forth. I don't think it really grasped the kind of key issue for lesbian and gay people – it really didn't – which was we were in a battle in a sense to have our relationships recognised as equal to others, and that was the big issue for us … There was that argument around the place and I think it was strong at the time.

As gays and lesbians grappled with these hypothetical options that could potentially be available at some stage in the future, it was clear that relationship recognition was going to be The Next Big Thing in the gay rights movement, which, to generalise, had overcome criminalisation, was beginning to overcome the worst of the HIV/AIDS crisis as new treatments were coming online, and had created social spaces to build a community.

BILL HUGHES: Then as the decriminalisation came about and people started to use the words 'gay marriage' or 'civil partnership', I just thought, 'Wow, this is the chapter'. In the same way that the people who had died of AIDS had missed the life-saving cocktail, they had also missed the life-saving legislation. Because to me, it's live-saving. My partner and I are together now since the summer of 1997, so that's seventeen years this year, and I have done everything I can to protect us legally, but we're both holding out for marriage.

AILBHE SMYTH: I felt there had been such an evolution in attitudes towards lesbians and gays at that stage in Irish society back in the mid-2000s that really it was time to move on to tackle the remaining areas of rights, and certainly children is still quite a challenging and difficult issue. But it was perfectly clear we were going to have to do something about this issue. You just couldn't ignore it. As there began to be older generations of lesbians and gay men, we would – most of us, not all of us, not everybody – but we would tend to be in more settled relationships, and both want and need to have those relationships recognised. We need to have them publicly recognised because of issues to do with children, because of things to do with succession and inheritance, because of ownership, the death of a partner, that it just simply couldn't go on like that. How were people to live their lives? What was to become of us as we grow older unless we grasp society by the scruff of the neck and say,

'You know, we're not prepared to lurk on the outside of the major social institutions in this country or any country? If you're telling us we're equal, we're telling you we're definitely equal and we therefore have access to and participate in everything that's going.' And indeed, if we have criticisms of that and critiques – fine, so do straight people. I have so many friends who have been together for a good number of years now and why on earth can't they have their relationship recognised in the ways that are available to straight people if that's what they would like to do, if that's what they need to do? Why not? And I always found that the onus was on heterosexual society to answer that question. Not me. I don't have to answer that question. It is for the straight person who says, 'Why on earth would you want to be getting married?' I'll say, 'Why on earth can't we?' What is it that's so precious about your heterosexual marriage that you can't share that?

BILL HUGHES: At that stage I would've known so many elderly gays where one partner was dying, and the other partner was losing their home. So that was happening too … Jesus, is nobody going to look after us? Is nobody going to protect us? Can we not be? We're fully paid-up members of society but how come we're not being looked after like the rest of society is? How come the same rules aren't being applied to our lives because we're every bit as valid and relevant? The law is an elastic band, and at some stage can it not be stretched to wrap around us as well? I suppose the big thing too was initially there was a lot of anger about it. Initially there were a lot of people who said, 'I don't want the straight curse of marriage, and I don't want to have my relationship evaluated as heterosexuals are evaluated. I don't know many happy marriages. Why would I want one?' And that was the knee-jerk reaction.

ANNA MCCARTHY: I don't think there was much discussion here. It struck me that we weren't having those discussions. We weren't in that place yet. And even when the UK were talking about introducing civil unions, that discussion wasn't really starting here. And to be honest it wasn't really until – I think it was probably when Canada introduced marriage equality and people started travelling over and so then you actually had Irish people, a cohort of people that had marriage from a different country and could because they didn't have any residency requirements. Then it was like, 'Oh, well this could be possible here.'

AILBHE SMYTH: It didn't really strike consciousness here I think in a major way until Ann Louise Gilligan and Katherine Zappone decided to take their case … And I do think of all the various other arrangements both here and elsewhere – civil union in the UK or the pacts in France or whatever – as fobbing-off arrangements which are a very poor kind of second best. I find that very insulting actually.

BILL HUGHES: Conversations would happen in the pub. They'd happen over dinner. You'd go to parties … And there'd be massive discussions going on. We've had seventy guys here at a party. Cocktails flowing, everybody yap yap yap and the roof would be lifting off with conversation. And it would be everything from art to social studies to right across the board, to gay rights. There would also be big rows about football and all the things people don't assume gays know about. And in among that would be peppered every now and again: what about getting married? What about gay rights? And there was huge cynicism about people who needed to do that. 'Are you that insecure?' There would be a question, 'Do you really need the ring that much to validate how much you feel for your partner?' Then it didn't take long for the discussion to then get about: well, we want to be protected. We want our rights protected.

2

EARLY LEGISLATION ON THE ROAD TO EQUALITY

''93 created at least a mood change where people could at least be more open in their lives, and the Employment Equality and Equal Status Acts created more freedom to be open.'

– Brian Sheehan

EOIN COLLINS: I'll backtrack a little bit. We had done a study in '95, which was the first big study on lesbian and gay people in Ireland. It was funded by the Combat Poverty Agency and it was called 'Poverty, Lesbians and Gay Men'. Now the poverty focus was partly because it was funded by them, but it really was just a study of people over the life cycle, so looking at people's experience in education, looking at coming out, looking at their experiences in employment, looking at their relationships – all those aspects.

EOIN O BROIN: The first policy document I was ever involved in coordinating was the first written LGB equality document, which was passed in the Sinn Féin Ard Fheis in 1996. In 1995 I had proposed to the party that we should develop a written policy on LGB rights, as it was then called. While we had good statements and good instincts on it, we didn't have a written policy document. The party agreed. I was tasked with putting together a working group. There was a small group of us, Sinn Féin activists, north and south, and what we did was met with pretty much all of the LGB groups as they were then; Belfast, Derry and Dublin. We did a range of meetings. GLEN, NILGA in the north, the Rainbow Project in Belfast, Lesbian Line in Belfast, and a range of others, probably about fifteen organisations that we met. We said, 'Ok, look, we want to develop this policy; tell us what you would like to see in it.' The idea was rather than us drafting a policy, we wanted the advocacy organisations themselves to outline what were their priorities, what did they think political parties should be doing. The interesting thing about that was very little of it was actually formal policy … A lot of what the groups were asking us to do, which made sense but which we didn't anticipate, was about how do we make sure that our own house was in order, that we were combatting whatever prejudice existed inside the party. Where we had influence, particularly at a community level and in working-class communities north and south, how we could use that influence to address issues that would be affecting LGB folks in those communities. It wasn't that we got this big long list of policy demands for legislation; it was much more about what can you actually effect and do to improve people's day-to-day lives. When you read the document, it kind of reflects that.

BUZZ O'NEILL: For Sinn Féin it was them getting their house in order, lining up post-Good Friday Agreement … So somebody was sent off to form a committee and figure out where we were at. Sinn Féin at the very, very start said full equal marriage, end of. And then there's – I suppose Ivana would have been next to have stepped it up, where she was coming to the fore for Labour. Because, you know, Labour didn't really have anyone that strong on it either. They certainly had no high-profile gay-rights activists. Sadly the rest of the political parties were 'just ignore it'. They had nothing to say.

NIALL CROWLEY: I suppose the introduction of the Employment Equality Act and the Equal Status Act and the naming of a sexual orientation ground was an important step on that road, although it wasn't necessarily obviously so at the start. But looking back on it, it was a crucial foundation to move towards same-sex marriage … The key bit was the move from decriminalisation to an actual protection against discrimination, which was a much more positive move in terms of just removing an oppressive piece of legislation. Here was putting in a progressive piece of legislation to protect people on the grounds of sexual orientation from discrimination at work and the provision of goods and services. So it was a milestone in terms of the positioning of lesbian and gay people in society. It was a marker of a new status in society, and I think that actually served as a launching pad.

The Employment Equality Act 1998 and the Equal Status Act 2000 set out rights and specifically outlawed discrimination in employment, vocational training, advertising, collective agreements and the provision of goods and services. However, Section 37 of the Employment Equality Act set out an exemption, 'A religious, educational or medical institution which is under the direction or control of a body established for religious purposes or whose objectives include the provision of services in an environment which promotes certain religious values shall not be taken to discriminate against a person … if it gives more favourable treatment, on the religion ground, to an employee or a prospective employee over that person where it is reasonable to do so in order to maintain the religious ethos of the institution.' This section effectively closeted gay and lesbian Irish teachers, considering over 90 per cent of Irish schools are under the patronage of the Catholic Church. A test case to challenge the legislation has never been taken.

NIALL CROWLEY: It's a sting in its tail. I think there has always been a problem of under-reporting by lesbian and gay people for loads of reasons, and Section 37 was a chilling factor, without a doubt. So in that sense it's problematic. I would have loved somebody to have taken the case. It was very hard for people to take the case, because we were never able to prove just how damaging it was in fact. But was it used to discriminate? I think it certainly was. And it has to go. We had recommended a long time ago that it should be revised to clarify that it could not be used to discriminate on a family status ground or the sexual orientation ground.

Under the Employment Equality Act 1998, the Equality Authority was set up, established in 1999 with Niall Crowley as CEO. The statutory body had a mandate to combat discrimination and promote equality.

EOIN COLLINS: So when we went into the Equality Authority that time, Niall Crowley was just phenomenal. Great guy. And he was always opening up these spaces, very proactive on the sexual orientation issue and on the transgender one as well.

MARIE MULHOLLAND: In the Equality Authority, I had the sexual orientation brief and I had two things that were done. One was I produced a report on lesbian, gay and bisexual equality and we also commissioned an academic to do a trawl through how legislation in the Republic of Ireland differed from other progressive legislation in Europe *vis-à-vis* everything to do with sexual orientation. In that it came up the whole issue about same-sex partnerships, both in terms of partnership rights and in terms of marriage. That was way back in 2000.

The Equality Authority embarked on producing a landmark report on lesbian and gay partnership rights.

NIALL CROWLEY: It was about a year after the EA was set up that we established the advisory committee and it worked over a year and a half. It was clear to me that the nub of the issue was around partnership rights. And the nub of the partnership rights issue was around marriage and same-sex marriage because if you took equality just purely as a resources issue and equal access to resources, it is a partnership rights issue, but if you see equality as encompassing resources, power, influence, status, standing, it had to be same-sex marriage. But it was on the committee quite a controversial issue in that it clearly hadn't been worked out. It was clearly sort of a burning issue but one that hadn't been thought through. And I think that's why the committee took so long to report … We also organised with the lesbian, gay and bisexual organisations some kind of consultation around it to get people talking about it and to see what the views were in relation to it. And it captured in many ways that, at that point, a lot of people had worked out clearly what they were against, but hadn't quite worked out where it was all heading in a way. It was a really interesting period in terms of generating that agenda. It wasn't our agenda; it was a shared agenda. And that report came up with the idea that you did need a form of partnership rights that were required for both same-sex relationships and also heterosexual relationships, but you also need to open up marriage to same-sex relationships and that was in the report. At the time we thought that could be quite controversial in a way. We also went for adoption; that it was important to resolve the right to adopt as part of the same package. It was just taken sensibly in the media and discussed seriously. You suddenly had this significant, I think, social policy recommendation being discussed sensibly in the media and I thought that was a really powerful sign. The sort of tone of it was, 'Well, marriage is alright, but adoption, surely that's going a bit far.' And that was kind of interesting. It did mark I felt a real possibility for change in a way. Ten years later and we're still waiting. But it was an important milestone, that report.

GRÁINNE HEALY: A report had come from the Equality Authority so I had gotten sort of involved, talking to Niall quite deeply about that and how that report could actually lead to something kind of substantial around LGBT issues.

EOIN COLLINS: I think Niall deserves great credit for pushing things through, lifting everyone's expectations around it. I think Niall kept the bar very high.

MURIEL WALLS: The Equality Authority did their report in the early 2000s and the fact that they seemed to have as much political support for it as they said they had – they said they had interviewed so many politicians and they were all in favour of this – was a bit of an eye-opener. You sort of felt, 'Well actually maybe this isn't such a mountain to climb.'

The National Economic and Social Forum also published a report titled 'Equality Policies for Lesbian, Gay and Bisexual People: Implementation Issues' in April 2003.

EOIN COLLINS: The Equality Authority one was the first one where marriage had actually been put in a document. But again, it was just so far out there, no one was thinking it at that time. And in the NESF document, there was no focus on marriage. Then it just started happening. I think it happened in the Netherlands, it happened in Massachusetts.

MURIEL WALLS: The other big thing, which in fairness to Charlie McCreevy – this would have been back in the early 2000s – he brought in a tax provision to say that if somebody died and their cohabiting partner inherited the house, provided they lived in the house for three years before the death and remained living in it for a number of years after the death, then they wouldn't pay inheritance tax. That was a huge issue; that even if you wanted to provide for your partner, the government was going to take an absolute big slice of whatever was given.

COLM O'GORMAN: In some ways, I don't know if this is fair or reasonable so I could be completely wrong about it, but whether or not the community was kind of caught on the hop a little bit by what was happening internationally, and by the fact that people from outside the community, including the Archbishop of Dublin and Michael McDowell as Minister for Justice, were saying things about legal recognition for same-sex couples. And the community hadn't said or come to any particular position, so I think there was a fair old bit of catching up to do.

IZZY KAMIKAZE: I think we committed too early without proper debate, and to be honest just sort of slavishly following what was going on in other countries that maybe had a different legislative background and cultural background and historical background. I'd have rather see us ploughing our own furrow on this one.

In 2003, David Norris began working on a Civil Unions Bill which he tabled in 2004, and which was debated in 2005.

DAVID NORRIS: My view was for the time being to forget about the word 'marriage' because that raised people's heckles and you would have to have quite a substantial discussion because it was a shift and people are concerned about new ideas – they're frightened of them. The thing to do was to examine the tangible practical benefits conferred on two citizens by the act of marriage and deconstruct them or disassemble them and then put them all into a bill which avoided the word 'marriage' because what I was interested in was the practical advantages, and I didn't want to waste a whole lot of time arguing over language at that point … Then about the end of 2002, beginning of 2003, I put a little committee together, which included people like Chris Robson from GLEN, who died recently, and Ivana Bacik. There were other people I can't quite remember. And I managed to get help from Dr Mary Lyons in Trinity, who was a legal person, and we made quite a complicated bill, which was very largely technical things and inheritance and money and all the rest of it. And we looked at that and that wasn't comprehensive enough, even though it was very big. So we designed what I thought was quite a clever one; I think it was Section 6 of the bill that said, 'Notwithstanding anything else, any advantages conferred upon the citizen by the act of marriage shall be held to be conferred upon two persons of the same-sex who go through this thing.' So it was effectively marriage, but it wasn't going to be called marriage in the legislation.

IVANA BACIK: David and I were working together on his bill. I helped him draft it; he introduced it in the Seanad.

DAVID NORRIS: The bill – I had it down and I understood it was going to be let through to the second stage. That was my understanding with the government. And they suddenly changed their mind for some reason. So I was furious. I got on to Michael McDowell, the Minister for Justice and a very decent man, but I got on to his office and I said, 'Look, I'm going to cause a scandal for this. I am not turning up for my own debate.' This is my two-hour debate that you get about twice a year as an independent. They're every Wednesday for two hours, and they're the big debate of the week. I said, 'I'm going to issue a statement saying that because the government have reneged on their promise, I'm not turning up. You can turn up, anybody else who wants to turn up, but I am not proposing a motion so you'll be there for nothing.' So there was a big to-do and all the rest of it. And they came up with this idea which since then has been used quite a lot: you leave two minutes remaining in the debate. So it's still effectively on the order paper and can be moved and you can extend the time if you want. And it was on that basis that I went in and we made the arguments. That was the introduction of the bill, which I think was 2004, and it raised the ideas and made them current. And I think it to a certain extent lit a fuse under the liberal elements in government, in particular the Labour Party.

BRIAN SHEEHAN: Chris Robson was involved with a working group with David Norris which was trying to work towards a civil unions bill. Michael McDowell as Minister for Justice in effect demolished it in the Seanad, basically saying it's unconstitutional. That was the first time there had been a debate on the rights. In effect the bill was all the rights of marriage, and there's a balance between the enumerative thing – you start at zero and enumerate upwards all the rights that are there – or you start at marriage – you can have all the rights 'except'. I think McDowell's thing was Norris' final bill was all the rights 'except', but that was the first time the thing was debated in the Oireachtas at that point and that was really good I think, a very important moment about naming an aspiration. But the aspiration was still civil unions.

MARIE MULHOLLAND: I was asked by the Irish Council of Civil Liberties to coordinate a working group on equality for all families – that was our brief. Our brief was looking at how would you ensure that no family, no matter its composition, was discriminated against and obviously it was looking at same-sex families, it was looking at extended families, it was looking at generational stuff, because the whole idea of family is changing rapidly in the last twenty years, particularly the fact that we have immigrants coming into the country and people's ideas and cultures are very different. So therefore it's shaking up our very view of 2.2 and a dog. Also, it was our understanding and our experience that there were gay families out there. Reconstituted families, women getting involved and bringing children into that relationship – all of those kinds of things were happening. So we were looking at the concept for equality for all families and totally inclusively. It took two years to do that. I don't want to be underplaying it, but I don't recall there being any great call for gay marriage. What there was was some form of partnership rights that would be equivalent to marriage that would give people rights and protections, and particularly children of those relationships. That was very much what was going on, and it was around things like fostering and adopting and all those kinds of things. We wanted to get the report right, we wanted it to be as inclusive as possible and [for there] to be as many possible options for people. The idea would be no one family is the same, and therefore there needs to be a menu of choice and the choices that you make should not be a cause for you to be discriminated against, so we looked at a menu of options that would bring equality to various types of families. Clearly we had to change the social welfare system – that was one of the most discriminatory elements – so there was a lot of work done on social welfare on that end of it. There was a lot of work done on children's rights and for me, as someone who was co-ordinating that and chairing that, I really felt that we had to put children's rights firmly at the top of the list in the sense that whatever else we sought for it, children's rights must be supreme over all else. This argument that everybody has a right to be a parent – well, personally I think every child has the right to decent parents, so we put the child first and everything else follows onwards. So that was key. The menu of choice we came up with [included] people's rights not to get married and to cohabit, and for cohabitation to be recognised and for people not to be discriminated against in the social welfare and legal system because of cohabitation. We came up with civil partnership. And we also came up with gay marriage. So we gave a whole range of choice.

BRIAN SHEEHAN: At the same time, around 2003, 2004, Fine Gael [with Sheila Terry] were developing a partnership policy. And they were the first party that came out with anything, which was funny when you think of it, and it was launched with Olivia Mitchell, Fergus O'Dowd in the Fitzwilliam Hotel. We strongly welcomed that because this was the first time a political party had come out with a policy.

3

THE KAL
CASE

'I think one of the most exciting things I ever witnessed was
Katherine and Ann Louise outside the High Court talking
about their love for each other ... Even now, thinking
about it, I think, "Jesus, what fucking incredible women."'

– Gráinne Healy

*As the conversation about relationship recognition was emerging in Ireland, couples in
long-term relationships were examining their own personal circumstances.*

MURIEL WALLS: I'm a family lawyer for over thirty-five years and a campaigning one as well. So the campaigns we would have had were abolishing
illegitimacy back in the '80s, the first divorce referendum in the mid-'80s,
and losing it, the second divorce referendum then in the mid-'90s. But one
of the by-products, if you like, of no divorce was that there were loads of
couples living together: so they got married, the whole marriage was a bit
of a disaster, separated, and now they were in a loving stable relationship
but it wasn't a marriage. So I was very focused on the rights and needs
of cohabiting couples and I was a bit of a campaigner on that. And that
brought me then in touch with another group of cohabiting couples, who
were lesbian and gay couples. So a lot of the advice I gave to heterosexual
cohabiting couples was: put the house in joint names, make wills, take out
life assurance cover. All of that was equally good advice for lesbian and gay
couples. Within my practice, I sort of had a bit of a reputation for trying
to understand the problems and trying to give practical tips. To be honest,
I didn't think there was going to be marriage coming down the tracks anytime soon. We didn't. It was more a practical solution.

One couple considering their options was Katherine Zappone, from Spokane, Washington, and Ann Louise Gilligan. A public policy consultant and educator, Zappone was the former CEO of the National Women's Council and had lectured in practical theology at Trinity College and elsewhere. In 2001, she was appointed a Commissioner on the Irish Human Rights Commission. Her partner worked at St Patrick's College, Drumcondra, establishing the Educational Disadvantage Centre. In 2001, she established and chaired the National Education Welfare Board. Their relationship was private, but it was about to become very public. Katherine and Ann Louise wanted to get married.

KATHERINE ZAPPONE: We did go and travel a bit to some other European countries where there was some form of legal recognition to see if that was possible… But there wasn't any place where it – at least at that point – where we could travel to and actually get some form of ceremony unless you were a citizen or a resident of that country.

ANN LOUISE GILLIGAN: And we actually did go to fair lengths on this. I remember we were in Sweden at something, and we literally went along to know, if you weren't a resident, if you weren't a citizen [what the options were].

KATHERINE ZAPPONE: I think around late '99 or 2000 the conversation started going on here. Maybe there was some formalising of that with the Equality Authority putting out a report on partnership and same-sex couples, and so we certainly were aware of that. Some colleagues suggested that we go and speak with members of GLEN to see what they were doing, so we did, and I met with, over the course of two years, one or two people in GLEN to see what were they doing. And they had said that they were starting to put together a domestic partnership legislation bill.

KIERAN ROSE: We used to kind of meet them but then I think probably – obviously you get on with people and stuff like that, but there were very, very strong differences of opinion. I think there was a sense that at the time that all principle was on one side and what GLEN was doing was something like grubby or dealmaking or whatever, as opposed to the pure driven snow principle that other people seemed to project, or you got that sense that's what they thought.

KATHERINE ZAPPONE: So I would come back every couple of months and see what was the progress. And there wasn't a whole lot of progress. And when there was some kind of some initial drafts of a bill, it was very much in the form of a legislation for almost like a business partnership – well, a domestic partnership as distinct from something that was a recognition of the kind of lifelong relationship, love, family, etc., that we were experiencing. So anyhow, we did wait a couple of years in the meantime for that to maybe come on to the scene. It didn't … We were looking were there any other couples interested in taking a case with us. And I think we looked for a number of months, and basically nobody was. We got a little impatient and it was again other friends who said, 'Well, you know, if you just want to take a case, why don't you go start to talk to a couple of lawyers? Why don't you go talk to Ivana Bacik?'

IVANA BACIK: I remember the meeting very well, although I can't remember what year it was. Katherine and I met in a café upstairs in what was then that bookshop on the corner of Nassau Street – Easons – and Dawson Street. We had a discussion about it and she said, 'Would you be willing to take on the case?'

KATHERINE ZAPPONE: I knew her a little bit because I was teaching in Trinity at the time she was a student … I explained to her what was going on, that you [Ann Louise] and I were thinking that we really wanted to do something. We felt quite frustrated from our own perspective … We weren't exactly young. We weren't exactly older. But we felt that we were at a point in our lives that we were ready for it … And so Ivana said, 'Yeah, sure, that would be fantastic.'

AILBHE SMYTH: I had bronchitis and I was in bed and they rang me from some trip they were on, driving around the country, and I just remember laughing, thinking, 'This is brilliant, this is absolutely fantastic', actually thinking to myself, 'Oh my God, that's going to be such fun, such a challenge.'

IVANA BACIK: I think the solicitor would have rung me, Phil O'Hehir from Brophy Solicitors, who was the solicitor on the case … I remember thinking, 'This is just going to be a great case.' Legally you could just see all the arguments were being made in the US at the time, you know, in Canada. There had been such movements in other common-law jurisdictions towards recognition of marriage equality through the courts and it was just a really exciting thing to be part of. I asked Gerard Hogan to be the senior counsel on the case. He came on board. He's obviously now a judge of the High Court, a leading constitutional lawyer. So it was a really good case to launch.

Zappone and Gilligan sought advice from friends and people they thought would be interested, and others who could possibly offer financial assistance through a series of dinner parties.

KATHERINE ZAPPONE: We invited a number of people to three or four dinners. We probably would have had …

ANN LOUISE GILLIGAN: Twenty a dinner.

KATHERINE ZAPPONE: Probably, yeah, three or four dinners. One or two at our own home. One night it was snowing so they couldn't get out there, so we held it in An Cusán, which is the community organisation we founded in Jobstown. And our objective of that was to lay out: this is what we are doing, this is why we've done it, and if you're supportive of this kind of freedom and equality for gay and lesbian people, then are there ways in which you could begin to participate and also take the lead or whatever. I mean, we had fundraisers there, advocacy groups, and not just LGBT; friends, people who would have been business people, colleagues, human-rights folk.

GRÁINNE HEALY: I would have known Katherine and Ann Louise for many years through their work as feminist theologians, and also as Katherine was the director of the National Women's Council when I was chair. We worked together over many years. They invited a number of us to dinner one night to tell us they were taking the case. So there was maybe twenty people … My understanding was at first they had considered a number of people taking a case.

NIALL CROWLEY: I do remember meeting Katherine specifically about it to explore the potential in the equality legislation in relation to it and whether they should move the case through the Equality Authority and the equality legislation. Then I also do remember that bigger meeting in her house about the purpose of the case … Katherine and Ann Louise have always been clear about marriage. For me it's always been marriage as well, and that the real danger with civil partnership is that it enshrined an inferiority or a hierarchy of relationships with same-sex couples at a lower rung on the hierarchy. So I would have to say that I would have been against partnership rights and for civil marriage. And certainly, the big debate at the dinner, if I remember correctly, was around this issue of the importance of civil marriage, and not to get stuck on partnership rights.

GRÁINNE HEALY: Katherine and Ann Louise were laying out their vision for why they as a couple wanted their marriage recognised, what that recognition would mean to them, and how it was in their view a significant space for LGBT rights, before they had lodged the papers. So they were laying out the beginning of what became the case that they made when they went into the court. And I suppose they were looking for people – I felt anyway. I mean, we were simply invited to dinner, weren't necessarily told what the dinner was for – it was just a dinner. And they would do that from time to time; you'd arrive out and sometimes it would be about fundraising for the Shanty* or it might be just a group of women. I think some people were certainly surprised. My initial thought was here was a couple whom I knew were lesbian, but most other people didn't … It was like, 'We brought you here this evening because we're planning on doing this, and we wanted to share it with you, and maybe there's some way [you can help] or something you'd like to say.' So we did go around the table and people did say, 'Well, you know, I'm very supportive of this' or 'I'd have to think about this for a while.' But most people there were saying, 'We think it's very brave; we don't think it's going to be easy'.… They were fairly clear that there were European things that were being trod on, European Conventions that gave a right to privacy and a right to family and therefore the right to marry. And because Niall would be very up on that, he wasn't quite so sure that was necessarily the correct way to go. I've a feeling maybe there might have been a German or French case around the same time. There was the famous Kitzinger case in England where they had tried to do the same thing, where they had tried to basically force the UK to recognise their marriage because of the European Convention and it wasn't upheld and the European Court didn't uphold it either. So there was that kind of conversation – 'These are the arguments we're putting forward', and people around the table saying, 'I'm not sure if that one will work, but what about this?'

*Another name for An Cosán.

MARIE MULHOLLAND: I was invited to one of them. It was a very interesting experience. It was an unusual way of doing things. But also they had it out in that place they have out in Tallaght – you know, the education centre. I'll be honest with you, I found the whole thing disconcerting. They had all these little women who were dressed in black-and-white waitress gear serving the dinner, and it was all very much kind of like being in 'the Big House' – it felt like being invited to the Big House kind of thing, do you know what I mean? Anyway, certainly at the one I was at, there was quite a diverse group of people. And one of the things was we were all asked to introduce each other around the table and say why this was an area we were interested in. For me it was obvious because of the work I was doing at the ICCL and because of the Equality Authority.

GRÁINNE HEALY: Two things. One, I thought, 'Jaysus, aren't they very brave?' – in Ireland, you know – to be putting themselves in for what was definitely going to be a trial by fire, and just all of the prurient interest that there would be in these two well-known, very middle-class, middle-aged women coming out as lesbians and the whole interest in that. I remember thinking, 'Jaysus, I hope they've thought this through', concerned about them, really, and then thinking, 'Well, if they're going to do that, the rest of us are going to have to get behind them and support them. They're putting themselves personally out there.' That was the evening I decided, 'Ok, whatever this case requires', and that for me was the sparking point – I need to get behind this.

NIALL CROWLEY: I thought it was hugely important on the same basis that people taking the anti-discrimination cases was very important. This was bigger even, and riskier in terms of the cost and scale of it, and the courts that they were moving through in relation to it – the High Court – and so it was a very courageous move, a very strategic move, a very well-thought-out move, a very carefully planned move. It was very impressive in every way.

KATHERINE O'DONNELL: They were ideal poster girls, which is very important when you're going for a legal case. So they were perfect in that regard, and they were able to speak to Middle Ireland. They were able to speak in quite religious language as well, and spiritual language, and they've been together a very long time. They had led exemplary, good lives, so they were perfect as a test-case couple and they were robust and strong enough to carry the emotional demands, which are really significant in taking that kind of case. They were ideal. Just the tax case thing, I could never get very excited about that. I think it would have been more helpful to have taken on another kind of case.

In 2003, Ontario had opened up its marriage law to allow non-resident same-sex couples to marry in the jurisdiction. Katherine and Ann Louise travelled to Vancouver and got married.

IVANA BACIK: Then we started to put together the case. We had various meetings in the offices of Brophy Solicitors and we were trying to construct a way of challenging the prohibition of marriage between same-sex partners. Because at the time, the legislation was not yet in force – the '04 Civil Registration Act, provision of which specifically rules out same-sex couples from getting marriage – but there's no impediment in the constitution to define marriage as between gay couples or straight couples. It's simply that the family based on marriage is protected in Article 41. So we wanted to challenge that. For some time we looked at taking a very different sort of case, looking for recognition of the Canadian marriage, because, of course, Katherine and Ann Louise had got married in Canada, so they were already married, so the question was, 'Should we be looking at a recognition of marriage case?' So the case began. In a way it was launched on that basis, and on the refusal of the Revenue Commissioners to recognise their marriage for the purpose of the tax breaks for married couples. So ultimately we took a case against the Revenue Commissioners. So it was a somewhat sideways attempt to challenge the law. Just through the meetings we had, this seemed to be the best way at the time. The case has been relaunched since as a more direct challenge to the section, section 22(e) of the Civil Registration Act. And a more direct challenge, what's now seen as an implicit constitutional prohibition on same-sex marriage. In the meantime, of course, the political climate has changed completely.

GRÁINNE HEALY: Any legal advice we were getting even in those early days was saying it's not going to happen. The courts are not going to find for this. You're going to have to go another route. We couldn't get a senior counsel who was willing to go on record and say, 'We think this should be legislated for, there's nothing against the constitution.' All of them were saying, you know, 'There's too much statute law saying marriage is between a man and a woman.' The 2004 Civil Registration Act had actually put it in, which, as you know, their legal team had missed entirely.

Marriage is not defined as that between a man and a woman in the Irish constitution. However, in 2004, the Civil Registration Act was introduced, for the first time including a ban on same-sex marriage in legislation.

CIVIL REGISTRATION ACT, 2004: PART 1.2.2 (E): For the purposes of this Act there is an impediment to marriage if – (e) both parties are of the same sex.

IVANA BACIK: In retrospect, I suppose, we might have relaunched it as a more direct challenge. It became a direct challenge in any case because the conflict, the comparative law issue about whether the Irish State would recognise the Canadian marriage ultimately boiled down to: does the Irish State recognise same-sex marriage? So it became a direct challenge.

KATHERINE ZAPPONE: We were then looking to take the route that was taken in other jurisdictions, which was to apply for a marriage licence, to be told no, and to take a judicial review on the basis of that. But it was after we had gotten the legal team together and we were starting to plan that this possibility opened in Vancouver. So it became a different case, or slightly different. Basically not a different case, but a different strategy: to look for recognition as distinct from the right to marry here.

KIERAN ROSE: It's the right of every citizen to take a case, but there is equally the classic statement: don't ask a question if you don't know the answer. And this was a case where they knew the answer. The chances of success were minimal. Lawyers love taking cases – it's grist to their mill – but if 99 per cent of lawyers are telling you – other than your ones [on] your case – it hasn't a chance in hell, why would you take it? And equally, why would you take it when political change was possible? David Norris took his case when no political change was possible, when

Noël Browne was laughed out of the Dáil when he tried to raise gay law reform. Again, it was a kind of high-risk strategy because I think if you want to achieve legislative change, go through the Oireachtas. It's a safer route and the door was open. The door was not shut. Going the judicial route is very high risk because it can end up boomeranging on you. You can go there looking for change and a judgement can be delivered which makes change even more difficult, which in a sense happened.

DENISE CHARLTON: I thought, 'Fair dues to them, but it's not really a priority for me.' I don't think I quite understood the significance of it. I would have been a feminist – still am a feminist – and I wouldn't have thought 'marriage'. I worked in Women's Aid for years. The institution of marriage wasn't something that I would have strongly advocated for, but I became convinced. I listened to the arguments, listened to the debates and thought 'yeah'. For me it became much more around the right to parent. So I too was persuaded, and then obviously became a very strong advocate for it.

On 26 April, Katherine and Ann Louise's solicitors wrote to the Revenue Commissioners, with their marriage certificate enclosed, requesting that they be able to claim 'our allowances as a married couple under the Taxes Consolidation Acts'. On 28 April 2004, their solicitors wrote to the Registrar General's office seeking confirmation that their Canadian marriage was legally binding in Ireland. On 10 May, the Registrar General's office replied stating that it was not within their remit to make a declaration of validity of marriages occurring outside of the State, and said it was a matter for the courts. The Revenue Commissioners responded on 1 July, stating that the Taxes Consolidation Acts provided for a husband being assessed on his and his wife's total income. Saying the Taxes Act did not define husband or wife, they offered instead an Oxford English Dictionary definition, adding, 'Revenue's interpretation of tax law is that the provisions relating to married couples relate only to a husband and a wife. Therefore I cannot allow your clients for allowances as a married couple.'

On 9 November 2004, Katherine and Ann Louise went to the High Court to seek permission for a judicial review, in other words, permission to take the case.

BRIAN SHEEHAN: Chris [Robson] had been engaging with them beforehand. Chris's sense was you have to be very careful going to court because the risk is that you end up setting things back rather than moving them forward. And they talk in their book* about Chris actually saying quite strongly that a court case wasn't the way to do it, that all of the change had come through a political persuasive process, and that was the process that would deliver relationship recognition.

KATHERINE ZAPPONE: So I'm up in my study phoning a few people still to let them know this is about to happen, because we wanted to make sure we told all of our close friends so they didn't just hear it in the news. We weren't going to court until later in the afternoon. And I'm up there and all of a sudden Ann Louise runs up to me and says, 'It's breaking news this morning that there is a lesbian couple that is taking a case for their partnership.' But they didn't name us.

ANN LOUISE GILLIGAN: I'm chairing a State board at this time. So I have to ring the minister and say, 'Look, this is breaking. We didn't think it would have broken. We thought you better know.' … It broke in sixty-seven countries.

KATHERINE ZAPPONE: We met our solicitor and we were literally going into the courtroom to seek permission to actually run the case. As we went to the courthouse, there were tonnes of photographers because they wanted to know who the couple was.

ANN LOUISE GILLIGAN: I remember Mary Wilson sitting at the table on the way in.

KATHERINE ZAPPONE: Then word started to go out. We get upstairs, we wait to go in, we met sisters, relatives of friends of ours who are law-yers, and they saw us and they said, 'Oh, it's you!' And then we get into the courtroom. It's a packed courtroom, and this is a day where a judge comes in and he's just listening to one case after another and looking for permission. And it's usually about ten minutes. That's what Ger Hogan said to us, 'You'll be in and out.' There's a couple of cases before us saying, 'Yes, you've got permission.' Just before one o'clock or lunchtime, Ger Hogan stands up and he says something to the effect of, 'Your Honour,

*Our Lives Out Loud: In Pursuit of Justice and Equality (2008) by Katherine Zappone and Ann Louise Gilligan.

I'm here to outline the reasons why we're seeking permission for a recognition for my clients, who are a same-sex couple, of their Canadian marriage.' The judge was like this kind of, 'Uhhh?' He just looks up – 'WHAT?'

ANN LOUISE GILLIGAN: 'Clear the courtroom!'

KATHERINE ZAPPONE: So Ger continues just a little bit and it's lunchtime and the judge says, 'Ok, we have to pause for lunch, but actually I'm clearing the courtroom for the rest of the afternoon, and I just want you to come back.' That's effectively what happened. So we all go off and we get back in the courtroom and Ger then continues his whole hour of presenting why we should basically reach the criteria to get a judicial review. And the judge listens and listens and I'm not sure if this is the exact sequence, but basically he then says, 'Ok, yes', so he's considered this, and then he says, 'But I need until the morning to give my answer.' And again, we're like, 'What? You might not give us permission after all this!' Do you know what I mean? … Instead of going down the elevator because there are so many people there, Ger and Ivana and Phil, our solicitor, and ourselves go into the stairwell to have a little huddle to say, 'What is going on?' And Ger Hogan says he's never seen the like of it in his life; he has no idea why the judge needs the whole evening to come and give his view the next morning. We waited. And it was this next morning, and this was McKechnie – Liam McKechnie – who is now on the Supreme Court. He was in the High Court at that stage.

ANN LOUISE GILLIGAN: And we were very lucky to get him.

KATHERINE ZAPPONE: He gave this beautiful statement where he said, of course, ultimately you meet the bar, the criteria, yes, you can have the judicial review, but he had wanted to reflect in order to make the statement about how significant this case could potentially become.

ANN LOUISE GILLIGAN: In a European context.

KATHERINE ZAPPONE: And then we went off and that was the day.

ANN LOUISE GILLIGAN: I remember the next morning, waking early and there was this noise outside our gate. So we have a bit of a drive up to our house and I remember waking and just saying, 'Oh my God, is there somebody going to take down the gate?' Now, you might say, 'Jesus, that's over the top', but actually it's not over the top … Why I think that the notion of marriage equality is so resisted is that it is actually a profound disruption of patriarchy. Because if one reads as you would have read, the history of marriage – especially the last 400 years – you know it was one of the hinges in the way it was interpreted that upheld patriarchy. And so to suddenly see two women – which was way worse than two men – that two women are actually going to confront this institution because by owning marriage you are actually going to transform it foundationally. You also then have to recognise that there are people –and they're not that cracked, actually, in outward appearance – who would be so resistant to this. You wouldn't quite know what they'd do next. Anyway, our gate didn't come down.

The case came before the High Court on 3 October 2006.

ANN LOUISE GILLIGAN: I remember the first week in court with Ger. And he was positively magnificent. I don't know if you've ever seen him operate in court, but he puts his foot up on the chair and he was going for it. He was inspirational. Anyway, he was going for it and Ivana sitting behind him, feeding up stuff, and the excitement! And I, because I'm a philosopher by profession, was writing away, and noting the different philosophical kind of underpinnings. I was just fascinated because the law is absolutely underpinned by ideas, by concepts, by the history of philosophy. So I was kind of doing my thing. But it was so exciting. And every day after the case, Ger would come up to this little room in the courthouse and he'd talk. 'Well, how are you doing? How are you?' So I remember on the Friday of the first week, I said to him, 'That was just brilliant. There is nobody that could ever indent the arguments and the way you structured them.' And it reached this crescendo where you could say done and dusted, it's in the bag, they have to say. And he said, 'Ann Louise, I would hate to disillusion you, but wait until this day next week,' he said, 'there is going to be a very strong opposition to this. And you know, just wait to hear it.'

IVANA BACIK: It was very exciting. It was a case that I was really enthusiastic, really passionate about. Katherine and Ann Louise are brilliant people – I'm a huge admirer and fan of theirs. And so it was a great case, one of those cases where you feel 'this is why I'm practising law'; to try and be involved in constitutional change. I mean, I'd been involved in other constitutional cases before and since where you feel you're making a difference, but a lot of my work was very much bread-and-butter criminal work.

KATHERINE ZAPPONE: Our other Senior Counsel, Michael Collins, again also did brilliantly and he was spectacular. I was crying after his first opening, and he said to me … 'Katherine, there will be good days in court and there will be bad days.' And there were several bad days. The State, the two men who were against us, one of them also on the bench now – the Supreme Court – and the other one was Attorney General and was top senior counsel. It was big fight. Every day there was a big report coming out of it, and one of the days – the first day it broke, I think – it was probably Kathy Sheridan who wrote a piece and it was, 'Oh, love is in the air', and all this kind of stuff.

KATHY SHERIDAN: I remember going down to the High Court on the day. Now, I've covered many a case in the High Court and what struck me was that a lot of journalists turned up late. I'm generally not late for cases. What they [the plaintiffs] had done was the standing on the steps, and had been giving pre-court appearance interviews and having their picture taken. I always remember their good humour and serene authority. They came back and recreated their entrance for the media, gave the interviews. To me there was something about these women that was so warm and serene. This country has a terribly divisive history on these social agendas, and these two women were the furthest thing from divisive. As a journalist, you're treated as the scum of the earth in the High Court. No one will talk to you or give you documents or anything. But here were the plaintiffs, very happy to discuss it all with us in a grown-up fashion.

ANN LOUISE GILLIGAN: As the next week unfolded, I could see – not that I could agree with it – but I could absolutely see what was happening, which was: 'Society isn't ready. The definitional argument is what people understand to be marriage. Marriage is about complementarity. Marriage is about children.' All of which, of course, is false. I could have stood myself and given the counter-argument to every single point, but

I could see the judge above, and I just had that sinking feeling. You know, 'I think the people are probably ready, but I don't think the legal system is.' That's what I was thinking … My experience in that second week in the court is the lack of attention to the fact that the personal is legal and the legal is personal. And at times I felt there was such a lack of attention to the personal implications for Katherine and I of some of what was being said.

IVANA BACIK: I remember some of the witnesses we got being really elated to hear this evidence given in court for the first time. I remember Harry Kennedy, the director of the Central Mental Hospital, also a psychiatrist with a specialism in this. He was able to give us a really brilliant account of psychiatric history and how homosexuality had been regarded as a disorder and that was completely now refuted … It was a brilliant sort of exposition. We had some really great witnesses on the parenting issue and so on. So a lot of the witnesses we offered and the evidence they gave was hugely important to put on the public record about parenting. That was elating.

KATHY SHERIDAN: Michael Collins was the senior counsel, and I always remember one thing that stood out was a question he asked. He argued that these women were denied the right to marry each other while all sorts of people could marry whoever they like. I remember being so struck by the simplicity of that sentence. I've always believed it was a human right, but I felt it marked something new, because this is something that could have been a very divisive subject. I believe [their case] was hugely instrumental in making this issue accessible to ordinary people. I think those women accomplished something powerful just by their whole demeanour in the court case, and by Michael Collins arguing that marriage is more than just a tax exercise, or about a house after someone dies, and it wasn't about wearing a white wedding dress either. Also, a final question he asked was begging common sense: what was the interest of the State in preventing these people from marrying?

ANN LOUISE GILLIGAN: The day that we came out of the High Court was a day I went back to college because I was interviewing for a new doctoral programme we had created, and every time there was a knock at the door and it was actually another student coming in to be interviewed, or potential

student, I didn't know if it was the archbishop who had sent down somebody to indicate I had lost my job because of course, according to Article
37 [Section 37 of the Employment Equality Act], that was absolutely in his
remit. How am I going to pay the mortgage? How am I going to continue
to live financially? If you're going to live a belief to the ultimate of what that
actually calls for, well, you have to go for it. If you can go for it.

*A representative from Price Waterhouse Cooper outlined taxation matters. Professor
Henry Kennedy, a consultant forensic psychiatrist and the clinical director of the
Central Mental Hospital, gave evidence. He said homosexuality was an aspect of
normality, and outlined the stigma attached to homosexuality from a psychiatric and
rights perspective. Professor Daniel Maguire, a professor of moral theological ethics at
Marquette University in the US, gave evidence. Professor Richard Green, a psychiatrist and lawyer, gave evidence saying that there was no evidence to show that children
raised by same-sex couples are disadvantaged in terms of their psychological development, citing research he had conducted.*

BRIAN SHEEHAN: Introducing the issue around children was maybe
unwise in the context of they didn't have children, so the courts were
making an abstract decision rather than a concrete decision.

*Professor Patricia Casey, a Professor of Psychiatry at UCD and a patron of the Iona
Institute, gave evidence. She criticised the studies of Professor Green. During cross-
examination, Casey confirmed that she had not carried out or published any studies
on same-sex relationships. Professor Linda Waite, a professor in Urban Sociology
at the University of Chicago, gave evidence outlining a preference for heterosexual
marriage as a family form.*

*One of the things that the KAL case did do was bring the concept of a same-sex couple
getting married in Ireland out into the mainstream. It kickstarted conversations. And,
by and large, many of those conversations in the media were relatively well measured.
With the backdrop of the court case, Zappone and Gilligan had a new platform of
high-profile media appearances. Their visibility moved the conversation along a trajectory where winning the hearts and minds of people has always been key.*

KIERAN ROSE: Katherine Zappone and Ann Louise on *The Late Late Show*,
Pat Kenny; I remember watching that and thinking we've kind of won
now … on lots of issues. *The Late Late Show* is kind of the bellwether thing,

so it was hugely important. They were such a lovely couple, you know, they looked like your older sisters or your aunts or something like that.

GRÁINNE HEALY: I think one of the most exciting things I ever witnessed was Katherine and Ann Louise outside the High Court talking about their love for each other … Even now, thinking about it, I think, 'Jesus, what fucking incredible women.'

4

PLAYING POLITICS AT
THE FILM FESTIVAL

'Mulholland doesn't believe that there'll be any fruit or
vegetables thrown in the Irish Film Institute this Thursday.'

– Hugh Linehan, *The Irish Times*

*In the summer of 2005, a controversial move by Brian Sheehan caused a huge argument
within the LGBT community, but in a roundabout way, also ended up providing an
opportunity. At the centre of it was the then Minister for Justice, Michael McDowell.*

BRIAN SHEEHAN: I had been director of the [Lesbian and Guy] Film
Festival. We had decided the theme would be around families. It was
very clear to us that we were going to need political change. It was 2005,
we hadn't had the result from the [KAL] case yet, so I invited as director,
Michael McDowell [to open the event]. I didn't do it very well; I should
have gone through the committee. I think maybe instinctively I knew
I would have had a hard job persuading people, but look, the film festival was run on a voluntary basis. It was very clear he was the minister
with the responsibility to address this area. Whether we liked him or not,
we had to deal with him, and maybe this was a way of engaging him on
the issue. He responded immediately and said, 'I'd be delighted to do it.'
And all hell broke loose. It was a furore.

HUGH LINEHAN, 25 JULY 2005, *THE IRISH TIMES*: 'Look out!' is the catchy
new name of Dublin's 13th Lesbian and Gay Film Festival, which takes
place next weekend at the Irish Film Institute in Temple Bar, but Minister
for Justice Michael McDowell should perhaps take that title more literally than the organisers intended when he officially opens the event on

Thursday evening. The online bulletin boards and discussion forums of gay community groups have been buzzing with debate and argument over whether McDowell is an appropriate choice to launch this year's festival. There has been talk of egg and tomato throwing, organised protests and boycotts, while one member of the festival committee has resigned in protest at the invitation.

After the annual Gay Pride festival, the Lesbian and Gay Film Festival is the biggest social and cultural event in the calendar for gay men and women in Ireland. About 5,000 people will attend movies, themed this year around the subject of 'family values'. There's the French family farce *Cockles and Muscles*, the drama *Queer Parents* and the homoerotic *The Clan*, along with the documentary *Andrew & Jeremy Get Married*. The contro-versy over whether McDowell's role points up divisions within a section of society which is usually described (often by itself) as a 'community', but which is just as socially, politically and demographically diverse as the rest of Irish society.

The protesters are largely drawn from those who see the struggle for lesbian and gay rights as part of a broader political agenda which includes other minorities such as travellers, the disabled and refugees (all of whom are represented within the lesbian and gay communities as well, of course). Those who support the invitation argue that McDowell, as the government minister who will make the crucial decisions on issues such as legal partnerships and family rights for same-sex couples, is a completely appropriate choice. 'We were delighted and surprised he accepted,' says festival director Brian Sheehan. 'It's very significant that a lesbian and gay event can attract a senior minister's attention.'

Marie Mulholland, chair of the Irish Council for Civil Liberty's Partnership Rights and Family Diversity Initiative, disagrees strongly. 'I informed the board members of this, one of whom was very upset and has since resigned.' In an open letter to the festival board, Mulholland argued: 'To provide a platform at a lesbian and gay community event to an individual who has done more in a short time to ensure through his legislation, policies and statements that equality remains a privilege and not a right, is an extremely difficult and disturbing development.'

By the end of last week, according to Sheehan, the festival had received almost fifty letters and e-mails of protest. It responded with its own open letter, arguing: 'While there has been significant progress in equality leg-islation in the last decade in Ireland, implementation of equality remains a significant issue, and not just for LGBT people. Recognition and protection of our family relationships remain as key areas of inequality for us, particularly in relation to the lack of civil marriage or partnership provisions for same-sex couples and the lack of recognition of same-sex partnerships in immigration and residency regulations. There has been increasing public discussion on these subjects over the last year, and there is a growing consensus that change is required. The challenge for LGBT people is to ensure that policy and legislative changes in these areas are implemented on the basis of full equality. In this context, to open the festival, the DLGFF invited the minister charged by the government with the responsibility for Law Reform in the key areas of partnership and immigration. This minister has huge responsibilities to our community. The minister will be presenting on behalf of the government the bill to establish our civil rights to partnership and as such should meet a wide membership of our community, at a time when we can at least remind him of the urgency of our concerns.'

Marie Mulholland rejects the notion that the McDowell's appearance will represent some form of engagement with lesbians and gays. 'This is not engagement. I've put several options to the festival, that there should be some kind of Q&A or that somebody should be given equal time to him on the platform. None of these has been accepted. What we've got here is the hijacking of an event which up to now has been a celebration.'

Kieran Rose, chair and co-founder of the Gay & Lesbian Equality Network, accuses the protesters of practising 'more radical than thou' politics. 'I don't see disability or refugee groups calling for a boycott,' he says. 'It's an immature kind of politics, as if nobody else has opinions on immigration. You must engage with the democratically elected government. The only way not to be criticised is to do nothing. We think it's entirely appropriate to invite the minister to a festival around the theme of "family values". The festival has a right to invite him and there's no connection between sexual orientation and politics. Your social class has more to do with it.'

On the face of it, there is no particular reason why gays should be on the left. In other countries, particularly in the US, many have seen their interests as being more closely aligned with the libertarian right and with neo-liberalism, agrees Sheehan. 'Lesbians and gays don't fit into any particular political group,' he says. 'Maybe activism has tended to be of the left, but there are also many people who identify socially but not politically with the community. But a lesbian and gay film festival will always be a political event when a gay couple can't walk down a Dublin street hand in hand.'

Beneath the surface of the debate there are tensions surrounding the accountability of organisations such as the Gay & Lesbian Equality Network and the festival. 'Brian needs to take responsibility,' says Mulholland. 'There was no consultation with representative groups or with his own board. I think what's happened is indicative of a deeper malaise within the community's organisations, which are run by the same people all the time. They don't actually consult.' Rose retorts: 'The other words for "same old faces" are "long-term commitment". The whole question of representing the entire community is difficult. We see ourselves as accountable and transparent, with clear reporting structures.'

This controversy takes place against a backdrop of expectation of changes in the law as it pertains to same-sex partnerships. Rose believes that the Oireachtas committee on the Constitution is likely to come out in favour of civil partnerships. 'Although, as an equality organisation, our position was that there should be a right to marriage, with the same duties and responsibilities,' he says.

Last year, McDowell spoke in the debate in the Seanad on Senator David Norris's Civil Partnership Bill, which has been postponed pending the committee's deliberations. While drawing attention to what he said were 'major constitutional, philosophical and discriminatory issues', he acknowledged on behalf of the government 'that the position before the law of same-sex couples and others in caring relationships, including extending State recognition to civil partnerships between such persons, needs to be addressed. We cannot walk away from, ignore or postpone this issue.'

Rose believes the speech was a 'positive enough analysis of the need for change'. He also accepts that the gay community was extremely unhappy with changes introduced by the government last year, which excluded same-sex couples from recognition for social welfare purposes, and with Minister for Social and Family Affairs Mary Coughlan's comment that Ireland was not ready and 'may never be ready' for gay couples with children in a family unit. 'This is not our ideal government, but we'd be waiting around a long time for that,' he says.

Mulholland doesn't believe that there'll be any fruit or vegetables thrown in the Irish Film Institute this Thursday and is wary of the protest being hijacked by groups such as the Socialist Workers Party, but she points to a late fundraising drive by the festival as proof that 'people have spoken with their money' and will be staying away. There is also talk of a petition and of leaflets being circulated.

Michael Cronin, a former board member of the festival, is also opposed to the invitation, but reflective about what it means. 'To me, the festival has always been about openness and equality,' he says. 'Michael McDowell seems to me to be opposed to that. There's no doubt he's a divisive and controversial figure. The people who are involved in lobbying groups appear to think they always know best. But the reason I can be publicly critical of them is because they have helped create the conditions in which I, as a gay man of my generation, can do that. This may turn out to be a good thing, if it gets people like me thinking about these issues of accountability.'

BRIAN SHEEHAN: It was a horrible. People I knew, people I had worked with and everything, were voicing their very, very strong opposition to this; that it was 'outrageous and wrong', and that 'you're wrong', and to rescind the invitation. And 'it's a disaster and we should never engage with him'. 'You're supping with the devil.' I had a hugely instinctive feeling that it was absolutely the right thing to do, that the only way to win change is to win over people. You hear this over and over when you talk to GLEN – our job is not to be right but to win rights and to achieve real, serious change for LGBT people. And I think there was a clear sense that the only person with the power to deliver here is McDowell. Or the Taoiseach. We needed political engagement, so how the fuck do you do that?

SUZY BYRNE: You had the 'be nice to Michael McDowell' thing which was also going on … We protested him being asked. Some of us were involved in the protest because of what he was. He was anti-equality as a measure, as a political ideal. Not anti-LGBT equality, but anti-equality. Also, the stuff around immigration, asylum seekers, other things that were going on. There was a few of us who were uncomfortable that the gay community were getting close to him or trying to give him a platform.

BRIAN SHEEHAN: To be very fair to Suzy, [she was] politely very strong against it, but politely turned up and listened to him and was very respectful about it. But actually a lot of people weren't.

EOIN COLLINS: There was a lot of controversy around that because there was the referendum over citizenship. There were a lot of issues going on, but anyway the committee stuck to their guns and invited him and he got a very warm reception when he got there. And as a result – we found this out later from civil servants – he came away terribly pleased by his reception. Despite some of the things people say about him, he was supportive of gay rights. He was very supportive of decriminalisation. He was supportive. But he had a particular view at that time that gay people didn't want marriage and kept articulating that and re-articulating that.

BRIAN SHEEHAN: I knew it was controversial. I didn't think it would be divisive. Slight difference. I'd still have done the same thing though. I still profoundly think we have to engage. And just because we don't like a Taoiseach or a Prime Minister or a Minister for Justice or whoever, they are the ones whom we have to win over to deliver on essential change for lesbian and gay people.

KIERAN ROSE: I remember meeting Michael McDowell, and you know his position was that some people told him that gay people didn't want civil marriage and he was going to give us some small contract, not even some form of civil partnership, but some form of contract law. I always thought it was like signing your hire-purchase agreement for your car or something, contract law. He has a fierce reputation. In our meetings with him, this was then what he was going to be offering. I was saying that the GLEN position was for civil marriage – that's what we wanted, that's what we were going to campaign for, and that's it, and we're not going to put up with whatever he was talking about. He went on to say what he was saying and what his thinking was and civil marriage and divorce is just a way for lawyers to make money. And then I thought, 'He's going to have a go at me now if I repeat we're for civil marriage.' Anyway, he's not as fierce as his reputation. Those are the kind of things I suppose that people don't know, that even behind closed doors GLEN was arguing for civil marriage.

BRIAN SHEEHAN: That period around the film festival was very, very difficult. There were emails on a constant basis. The forums were all unpleasant about it. For the committee it was difficult. And actually the committee were brilliant. One member resigned, fair enough. Irene Hislop. Totally fair, and I certainly apologised to the committee for going ahead and doing it, but as I said to them 'I would have strongly tried to persuade you that it was the right thing to do anyway, to invite him' … There were long debates about whether we should withdraw the invitation. I said, 'Well, no. I go if we withdraw the invitation.'

5

THE COLLEY
GROUP

'All these guys from the Ancient Order of Hibernians
all were throwing copies of the constitution up at us.'

– Eoin Collins

In 2005, the first UK Civil Partnership was held on the island of Ireland in Belfast. The next day, Michael McDowell announced he was putting together a working group to look at various partnership options for relationship recognition. That group, led by Anne Colley, became known as The Colley Group, and their report, published in 2006, became known as The Colley Report. The members of the Colley Group were Anne Colley, Eilis Barry, Dervla Browne, Eoin Collins, Helen Faughnan, Kieran Feely, Joe Gavin, Laurence Band, Dr Finola Kennedy, John Kenny, Niall McCutcheon, Christine O'Rourke, Pat Patterson, Joe Cullen and Dr Vincent Palmer.

EOIN COLLINS: Finally, in December 2005 [McDowell] said he would set up a group to look at it. And the terms of reference were actually quite limited. The terms of reference were specifically something like 'looking at relationships outside of marriage'. It wasn't just same-sex relationships. So he set up the group. It was chaired by Anne Colley, former PD politician. It had a lot of civil servants from the Attorney General's office, from Revenue, from the Department of Social Protection, and then they had a few independent people: Eilis Barry, who is just a really wonderful person, really great and supportive and very strong on the committee; and then there was also Finola Kennedy. Finola had, I suppose, a reputation for being quite close to the Catholic Church and she was somebody who some people had considered a spoiler or something or was there to, you know, limit progress, but nothing could have been further than the case, because she turned out to be, I think, just thoroughly decent and really thoughtful in the true meaning of the word. I think our first meeting was in January or February [2006], and we had twenty-one meetings.

In May 2006, the Colley Group helped organise a conference on the topics they were examining at the Royal Academy of Physicians on Kildare Street in Dublin, just a few doors down from Government Buildings.

EOIN COLLINS: GLEN, the Equality Authority and the working group – we held a conference, a big international conference in 2006. McDowell launched it. And all these guys from the Ancient Order of Hibernians all were throwing copies of the constitution up at us. So it was kind of scary!

NIALL CROWLEY: We had a seminar on partnership rights with this Canadian judge over. She was really, really good. But Michael McDowell spoke at it and the Ancient Order of Hibernians were there and threw the constitution at him. It was really dramatic! He was very good at it, I must say. He was very good. But yet, this thing of five people standing up throwing the constitution at him, and it looked like he was going to be attacked! It was just me and him standing in front. Then another guy from the Equality Authority stood in front of him as well and I thought he was going to get involved in a fight. It was really tense. What was interesting about that one was we had a European speaker at it as well who wanted to set out a theory that the way to get civil marriage was to get civil partnership and then get civil marriage – and this in the build-up to the conference was a really tense issue [because] certainly we wanted to go for civil marriage and not go the torturous route through civil partnership and then maybe civil marriage. As it turns out, that's the route it looks like we're going to go.

EOIN COLLINS: We went for really top people. We got the former Supreme Court judge of the Canadian Supreme Court who gave a really strong, powerful statement around marriage and then also we had a Law Lord, the top woman Law Lord in Britain, Baroness Hale, so really strong people. But the real thing we were trying to do in Colley, and through that conference, was get marriage on to the agenda … At that time I think the Zappone-Gilligan case helped an awful lot because you had these two women articulating marriage as an equality goal. That was really very powerful at that time. I went on *The Late Late Show* with them – I was a person in the audience agreeing with them. So it was powerful. So we succeeded. What we got through Colley was that marriage was the equality option and that they also looked at two elements of it, that it had a status element and it had the legal consequences, and that the status element was really important, as I think it would underpin a wider equality for lesbian and gay people. The other thing I did was I prepared a paper for the group working with LINC in Cork, [with] Angela O'Connell, a paper on children of same-sex parents. So what we were trying to do there was get some kind of provision for children into it. We succeeded actually in getting a commitment to adoption, joint adoption. Marriage then got in as the equality option.

MURIEL WALLS: Eoin Collins of GLEN was able to constantly remind people that there was this whole cohort of people who were living together and could only live together. It's not that they had the option to get married like heterosexual couples. So they highlighted that with the committee. I appeared before the Colley committee, and I would know Anne Colley from other things. She was a very good chair.

BRIAN SHEEHAN: Eoin, Kieran and I used to meet maybe once or twice a week [to discuss] the gory details of it. There were an awful lot of meetings. They seemed to meet every Friday. Eoin managed to persuade them – brilliant – that because lesbian and gay couples are excluded from marriage, if you're talking about lesbian and gay couples, you can include marriage, you know, because it's not marriage as it is now, it's marriage as it could be. So they agreed to that. And winning them over to say that marriage is the only option that guarantees equality for lesbian and gay people and it'll underpin a wider equality in society. That was the magic phrase.

THE COLLEY REPORT: The introduction of civil marriage for same-sex couples would achieve equality of status with opposite-sex couples and such recognition that would underpin a wider equality for gay and lesbian people. Civil marriage offers legal certainty and predictability in terms of the consequences for each partner. It would be administratively straightforward as the registration arrangements already in place for marriage would apply and would also be straightforward in terms of recognition …

Full civil partnership falls short of full equality for same-sex couples as it excludes such families from the protection given to the family in the constitution. While there is a consensus on the granting of as full recognition as possible to same-sex couples, in the absence of civil marriage the full civil partnership option is seen by the Group as one which would address the majority of the issues encountered by same-sex couples.

KIERAN ROSE: Michael McDowell set up the Colley Working Group, and then it went native. The Colley Working Group ignored his parameters and came out for civil marriage.

6

THE KAL
JUDGEMENT

'To be honest, I didn't pay much attention to the
decision. I mean, it seemed to be going on forever.'

– Dermot Ahern

In 2006, Judge Dunne ruled against Zappone and Gilligan.

JUDGE ELIZABETH DUNNE, 14 DECEMBER 2006: I have difficulty in this case
in accepting the arguments of the plaintiffs to the effect that the definition of marriage as understood in 1937 requires to be reconsidered in
the light of now prevailing standards and conditions … Marriage was
understood under the 1937 constitution to be confined to persons of the
opposite sex … I accept that the constitution is a living instrument … but
I also accept the arguments of Mr O'Donnell to the effect that there is a
difference between an examination of the constitution in the context of
ascertaining unenumerated rights and redefining a right which is implicit
in the constitution and which is clearly understood. In this case the court
is being asked to redefine marriage to mean something which it has never
done to date … The definition of marriage to date has always been understood as being opposite-sex marriage. How then can it be argued that in
the light of prevailing ideas and concepts that definition be changed to
encompass same-sex marriage? Having regard to the clear understanding of the meaning of marriage as set out in the numerous authorities
opened to the court from this jurisdiction and elsewhere, I do not see
how marriage can be redefined by the court to encompass same-sex marriage. The plaintiffs referred frequently in the course of this case to the
'changing consensus' but I have to say the there is little evidence of that.

The consensus around the world does not support a widespread move towards same-sex marriage. There has been some limited support for the concept of same-sex marriage as in Canada, Massachusetts and South Africa, together with the three European countries previously referred to but, in truth, it is difficult to see that as a consensus, changing or otherwise … The final point I wish to make in relation to the definition of marriage as understood within the constitution is that I think one has to bear in mind all of the provisions of Article 41 and Article 42 in considering the definition of marriage. Read together, I find it very difficult to see how the definition of marriage could, having regard to the ordinary and natural meaning of the words used, relate to a same-sex couple … I have touched very briefly in the last paragraph on the fact that civil partnership legislation is not available in this jurisdiction. Early on, in the course of evidence in this case Dr Zappone noted that the plaintiffs were not seeking the introduction of civil partnership rights. She made it plain that the right sought by the plaintiffs was the right to marry. As I have explained above I do not think that it is a right which exists for same-sex couples either under the Irish constitution or under the European Convention. It is noteworthy that at the moment (and some reference has been made to this in the course of submissions) the topic of the rights and duties of co-habitees is very much in the news. Undoubtedly people in the position of the plaintiffs, be they same-sex couples or heterosexual couples, can suffer great difficulty or hardship in the event of the death or serious illness of their partners. Dr Zappone herself spoke eloquently on this difficulty in the course of her evidence. It is to be hoped that the legislative changes to ameliorate these difficulties will not be long in coming. Ultimately, it is for the legislature to determine the extent to which such changes should be made. Having reached these conclusions, it is clear that the plaintiffs' claim for recognition of their Canadian marriage must fail as must the challenge to the relevant provisions of the Tax Code.

IVANA BACIK: I think that there was a reticence. But you know there had been a lot of *obiter dicta* comments by judges in past cases where they had referred to marriage as between a man and a woman, so there was no doubt we were on an uphill battle, and we always knew that. But I do think the arguments and rationale and logic were on our side … We really felt that Judge Dunne didn't engage with many of the more logical arguments we put forward. And you know, the US case law was so compelling, particularly when the courts had referred to the US Supreme Court case ruling against miscegenation, marriages between black and white people. It's just such a clear line of authority, and I still think that's right.

GRÁINNE HEALY: When the court case happened and they weren't successful, Judge Dunne herself, her thing was: there isn't such a big demand out there for this, it's all very new, I understand these women are discriminated against, but really the State needs to do something about that. So even she didn't come straight out and say this is absolutely a constitutional issue and needs a referendum.

CONOR O'MAHONY: The beginning point was to say it is a living constitution. The next point was to say current consensus wasn't relevant to the definition of marriage. And what was set out at that point was questionable. And she then went on to look at current consensus anyway, and use current consensus to define marriage. So you've two passages going in one direction, one passage going in the other direction. At best the judgement is confusing; it's ambiguous.

KATHERINE ZAPPONE: Mary Wilson from *5-7 Live* rang and said, 'Will you go on?', and we went around to the hotel there on Stephen's Green and said, 'Can we do that? Can we actually pick ourselves up and get ready to go out? And what will we say?' I always tried, and I think Ann Louise did too, to be honest as we were communicating with the media. At the same time, to never let go of a sense of belief and a hope that we will get there some day, just now is not the day. And to kind of put that together with really how we were feeling. When we then took what felt like a really lonely journey out to RTÉ, I can still remember the cab, and getting in. Mary, at that stage, had moved from being the crime reporter into this show. We had really developed a lovely bond with her during that period and so she wanted us and really not too many people at that point wanted to talk to us. And so we went out there and we got on the radio and said, 'We lost. It's very hard and it's really upsetting. But we're gonna keep going, anyhow.' I just remember saying, 'If you're out there listening, and if you were a young person and you wanted to get married to somebody and you were just told you can't – what would that feel like? That's how we feel right now.' That was a big low point rather than a high point. But it was good to be able to say that.

BRIAN SHEEHAN: I suppose our analysis was either: one, they were going to win the case constitutionally; two, they were going to lose the case on constitutional grounds; or three, the court was going to say the legislature was the answer – 'We're not going to make a decision; it's up to the legislature to decide things.' In two of those cases, you needed political parties either if there was legislative possibility, so that was critical, and secondly if they lost on constitutional grounds, you still have to go the legislative route in order to get space for constitutional amendment. The experience was shown in every single progress, even when Norris was on this case through the courts, it still took a political process. That's the pattern here. I suppose our sense was if there was a constitutional win possible, then that was fantastic, and we strongly supported that case very publicly and had no problem doing that, but I suppose people legally were saying this won't work constitutionally. But also we weren't going to put all of our eggs in that basket either … But actually the position on children was very poor – 'We have to wait for evidence' – which was just fucking disgraceful.

DENISE CHARLTON: I think some of the moments where Katherine and Ann Louise coming from the court at different stages and not being successful and the dignity they had when they spoke to the media, they thanked their legal team, 'onwards and upwards' even though they might not have felt like that – that was significant. Their courage and how uncompromising they were about accessing the same rights as everyone else – that was really the message I got from them all the time.

DAVID NORRIS: I thought they were splendid. I think it's a very important case and they behaved with great dignity. I think the judgement was regrettable and in my opinion I would hope that the challenge will be successful in the Supreme Court.

GRÁINNE HEALY: Their case and how they comport themselves really lit the spark under the marriage equality movement. There may have been political things going on; Labour put their bill forward, David Norris had his bill. There had been moves towards same-sex relationship recognition, but the KAL case and those two women lit the fuse. I can still see it. I can hear their words. I can still see them.

KATHY SHERIDAN: Those women are icons to me. I think they're magnificent.

7

CIVIL
UNIONS

'That was the pivotal point in GLEN's strategy
where we said we were going to go for it.'

– Kieran Rose

In 2006, the same year Colley published its report, the Labour Party was planning a
legislative move.

BRIAN SHEEHAN: At some point, Eoin and Kieran went to a meeting with
Labour in 2006 with Brendan Howlin. We had been doing the rounds with
parties and this was another one in the rounds of parties. Basically what
Labour said was, 'Look, our legal advice is that marriage would be uncon-
stitutional, would require a constitutional referendum,' and Katherine
Zappone's case had either been heard or was in the middle of being heard.
So they said, 'We will bring in a Civil Unions Bill which is marriage in all legal
constructs, but it won't have constitutional protection. Will you support it?'

KIERAN ROSE: The meeting with Brendan Howlin ... I don't think we
knew exactly what they were going to put to us. So it came out of the
blue. And it was one of those situations where you have to make a very
strategic and rapid judgement and I thought that this was fantastic.
I thought that this is amazing, really. And I, as chairperson, said, 'Yes,
we would fully support that,' because that was our GLEN policy, for civil
marriage and supporting progress towards that goal.

EOIN COLLINS: We said we wanted marriage. And they said 'no', they
couldn't get marriage across, it would be unconstitutional; that was their

advice, but they were taking Colley, and they were at least going for full civil partnership, and they were calling it Civil Unions.

BRIAN SHEEHAN: In a sense GLEN had to turn on a sixpence because here was a real concrete offer that was serious in legislative intent, serious in consequential intent, and with the political reality of the party who were the nearest cheerleaders that we had saying there was a constitutional problem. What do we do? So in effect what we said is, 'We will support your Civil Unions Bill' … and [I am] happy with that decision, you know – it wasn't an easy one. But I suppose partly because we think it would be irresponsible and unconscionable to say we'll not take what's on offer here because it's marriage in all but name in a legal consequence. And when I say marriage in all but name, I'm not losing sight of the symbolic importance of it or the constitutional status of it. But in terms of practical consequence. Because there were absolutely urgent unmet needs that needed to be addressed. Critical.

KIERAN ROSE: That was the pivotal point in GLEN's strategy where we said we were going to go for it. We were going to go for civil unions as a lead-in to civil marriage. And in a sense that was the key that unlocked everything afterwards.

BRIAN SHEEHAN: In a remarkable event the morning on a day in December in 2006, Katherine and Ann Louise's judgement came from the High Court, which was terrible. And I remember leaving the Four Courts in a hurry at a quarter to twelve to get down to the Royal Hibernian Academy at twelve o'clock, where Labour under Pat Rabbitte were launching their Civil Unions Bill.

KIERAN ROSE: Up to then we had been saying, 'it has to be civil marriage', and we didn't accept the constitutional arguments because constitutional arguments are often used as a smokescreen and stuff like that. But that was the first time we had something on offer, a Civil Unions Bill, one of the leading political parties in the country going to put it before the Dáil, which would really bring it up the agenda.

IVANA BACIK: December '06, the same day as the High Court judgement in the KAL case, Brendan Howlin launched the bill. So you can see the confluence of things. So those were Private Members' Bills – obviously

Brendan Howlin was in opposition, but they were the catalysts that were spurring on the government to finally introduce Civil Partnership Bills. You often find, like with Mary Robinson's contraceptive bills in the Seanad in the '70s, the Private Members' Bills signify the change in thinking and then eventually are adopted by the government, or the principle is adopted by the government.

EOIN COLLINS: Interestingly at that time there was no division in the lesbian and gay community at that point because the galleries were packed. There was a real sense that getting the Labour Party policy over the line would have been a huge bit of progress.

BRIAN SHEEHAN: Pat Rabbitte was the leader of Labour and he brought it in, I think, in February. Michael McDowell got rid of it in – as we said at the time – a total failure of political nerve because he came up with an amendment to it, which would have postponed it for six months, which saw it beyond the general election. It was terrible – a cheap shot – because it didn't take the debate seriously. But really interestingly, in March we had had Christine Quinn over and a reception in Buswells Hotel. Christine Quinn was then deputy speaker of New York City Council, and because she wasn't marching on St Patrick's Day, she was coming to Ireland instead. She had read the debates that had been in the Dáil in February/March, that had been on Labour's Civil Unions Bill, and said it was quite extraordinary that somebody from every political party spoke in favour of legal protections at a comprehensive level for lesbian and gay couples, including Ciarán Cuffe in the Greens talking about marriage, and Labour talking about marriage.

The next year, Labour reintroduced the same Civil Unions Bill.

EOIN COLLINS: The Labour Party then were already doing it anyway, I think, but we pushed them to do it, to reintroduce the Civil Unions Bill. It was the same bill.

SANDRA IRWIN-GOWRAN: The Labour Civil Unions Bill in the Dáil was a hugely emotional night as well because you had a packed gallery. There wasn't a seat to be had. There were a few spontaneous [bursts of] applause from the gallery as people spoke in favour. Do you remember

Fianna Fáil TD Charlie O'Connor? Charlie, I don't know how, but I think it would be fair enough to say he took a shine to me, in a platonic way! He wouldn't have been who you would have expected to speak in favour and he did in the Dáil that night around the Civil Unions Bill and he talked about children and all of that. Those kind of things. I remember Shatter being really positive. He was obviously in opposition at the time, but really positive around the children's stuff, and [I remember] being very heartened by that because Fine Gael were quite conservative.

CIARÁN CUFFE: The government voted it down, as it does – that was Howlin's bill in November 2007, and that's the nature of parliamentary politics. Every week the opposition brings forward motions that are then voted down and that's frustrating, but it's part of how the political system works.

STEPHEN COLLINS: I don't recall the bill being shot down on the basis of 'we don't want civil partnership'. More that 'we can do this bill the right way', that it wasn't a government bill.

EOIN COLLINS: And this time the government didn't go for it either, but in some ways there was a positive shift.

JOHN LYONS: I think the Civil Unions Bill that Brendan Howlin put forward had a very profound impact upon setting out the platform for future LGBT rights. Obviously the Civil Unions Bill got slightly diluted. It had to, apparently, in order to get it past. But I mean, people bringing forward things like that. I might sound party-biased there, maybe I am. How can you not be biased when you're in something?

EOIN COLLINS: One thing we couldn't shift and never shifted thereafter was the view that marriage would require constitutional change.

8

MARRIAGE IN
THE CONSTITUTION

'The State pledges itself to guard with special care
the institution of Marriage, on which the Family
is founded, and to protect it against attack.'

– Irish Constitution, Article 41.3.1

One of the main bones of contention throughout the debate on marriage equality is whether or not a referendum would be necessary due to how marriage is defined in the constitution. Then the Civil Registration Act in 2004 included, for the first time, a ban on same-sex marriage in legislation.

DERMOT AHERN: I don't think I even knew about that – 2004? It may have, but I don't recall it coming into consideration. But, I mean, I don't think it would have even come across my desk – that it was already accepted that there couldn't be same-sex marriage as such because the constitution didn't allow it.

The constitutionality of same-sex marriage has been the subject of much debate. There are broadly three schools of thought:
(1) That same-sex marriage is unconstitutional on the basis that the authors of the 1937 constitution would not have considered the idea of marriage equality, and therefore the definition of the institution of marriage as one solely between a man and a woman is implicit. Plus, in previous case law, the courts have assumed and defined marriage as an opposite-sex one.
(2) That although marriage is not defined as a gendered institution, the vagueness around this, along with the explicit same-sex marriage ban in the Civil Registration Act, 2004, and the assumed inevitable constitutional challenge that would arise

*without the constitution being changed, means that a constitutional change via a refer-
endum would offer more solid clarity on the issue.*

*(3) As marriage is not defined between a man and a woman, there is no need to
have a referendum, no need for a constitutional change, and therefore the government should remove the ban in the Civil Registration Act and introduce marriage
equality legislation. If a challenge did arise, let it be challenged in the Supreme
Court, and if a referendum is required, so be it, because the leap to marriage equality has already been made, and therefore, a positive referendum result would almost
be a foregone conclusion.*

FIONA DE LONDRAS: It's an untested claim. You can talk to ten lawyers
and they'll all say different things, but the constitution doesn't define
marriage. Courts have defined marriage, but if you went to the Supreme
Court and said, 'Dear Justices of the Supreme Court, is it constitutionally permissive for a man to marry a man?' We haven't had that case; it's
untested, and therefore very questionable.

CIARÁN CUFFE: There was the issue of Paul Gallagher, who was the
Attorney General. I never felt any great sense of enthusiasm from him
about the issue as well, but he's an impartial advisor to government.
At the time of the Labour Party Bill in November 2007 he advised government that their bill might be unconstitutional and, if proceeded with,
marriages might be pulled down by the Supreme Court, that that perhaps was his view. Not being a member of cabinet, I didn't have access to
that advice. So I found that quite frustrating at the time.

CONOR O'MAHONY: I think one of the things about the Irish constitution
is that an awful lot of people don't engage with it an awful lot. That's not
just the general public. Even people who you'd expect to engage with
the constitution frequently don't. So that would include politicians in
particular who have to make decisions on a regular basis that have implications in respect of the constitution, but don't necessarily take the time
to go and read the relevant provisions or the surrounding judgements.
They just simply refer to legal advice, and that's the end of it. And so
I think there's a perception out there that the Irish constitution defines
marriage and particularly marriage equality, which is based on nothing
more than people repeating something that they heard somebody else
say. After the Zappone and Gilligan judgement, this became absolutely

accepted wisdom, that the High Court had now ruled against Katherine Zappone and Ann Louise Gilligan and it was accepted that by definition almost that because they lost their case, it must be the case that the constitution precludes marriage equality. The reality was that most of the people who were saying this probably hadn't read the judgement. The judgement, if you do read it carefully, didn't actually say that at all. In fact, it seemed to suggest that what was more important than the definition of marriage was the most recent piece of legislation [the Civil Registration Act, 2004], and not necessarily what it says in the constitution. This disconnect between what people were saying and what the judgement said was something that wasn't really questioned by anyone. It was simply the case that because the Attorney General's office had read the judgement in one particular way, nobody in the political establishment was in any way minded to question that. They simply accepted that, as they generally do with Attorney General's advice. Also, I think it probably suited them to accept that, because it meant that all the major parties could stand on a pro-marriage equality platform without actually having to take the political risk involved of actually pursuing that.

ANNA MCCARTHY: It's this vicious cycle of the courts saying that it's up to the legislature, and the legislature saying it's up to the constitution, and the courts not interpreting the constitution because they feel that they would be legislating from the bench and all this. So it was catch 22 for marriage equality, and it still kind of is.

DAVID NORRIS: I also read all kinds of things like Declan Costello's 1967 review of the constitution, and he pointed out – and I latched on to this quite early – that in fact as the constitution was written, it did not specify that it had to be between a man and a woman. And he said it clearly leaves open a challenge to permit marriage between persons of the same sex and this loophole should be stopped. So that actually undercuts the government's argument that a referendum is necessary. It is not, because it doesn't specify a man and a woman. There may be some subsequent court cases dealing with that, which could be some kind of impediment, but the constitution itself is not clear and in fact according to Declan Costello in 1967, which was before we even started off, before there was a gay rights movement in Ireland, he recognised that the constitution did not prevent same-sex marriage.

ANNA McCARTHY: An ongoing frustration is that after the KAL case, the line from government was, 'it's a constitutional issue, it's a constitutional issue', and it's just so frustrating because the Supreme Court have never ruled on that fact, you know? The ban exists in legislation that was brought in in 2004. At that, it was a very last-minute amendment to the legislation.

By putting same-sex marriage before the Constitutional Convention in 2013, and by the Convention recommending a referendum on marriage equality, and even offering prospective wording on that referendum, the idea that a referendum was necessary and legislative change without one no longer the most viable idea, became almost enshrined in public and political discourse.

CONOR O'MAHONY: As strongly as I feel about it, I have really put up the white flag. The key moment was the moment it was before the Constitutional Convention. It set in motion a pretty unstoppable chain of events at that point because once it goes to the Constitutional Convention, that sends out a message very clearly that this is obviously something that requires an amendment. Then once you get a recommendation from the Convention saying that there should be a referendum and you get the government accepting that recommendation, it's more or less impossible to turn around after all of that and say, 'Well actually, we were wrong all the time. And that whole process that we went through was completely unnecessary.' There's a political and public expectation now that this needs a referendum and that there will be a referendum. And so trying to actually explain to people that wasn't the case, it would be very hard to get the public to swallow that. So I think, yeah, it is a *fait accompli*. The referendum will go ahead and I think in the event that the referendum would fail, I think realistically a second referendum is a far more likely course of action than trying to redirect it through the legislative process. It's very hard to see the public accepting a piece of legislation off the back of having voted against the constitutional amendment to that effect. It's very difficult to see any government proposing it for the very same reason.

CONOR O'MAHONY, UCC MARRIAGE EQUALITY LECTURE, 28 MARCH 2014: The idea of information cascades is a fancy term for something you probably all experience and instinctively understand, which is a situation where something gets said enough by people, particularly high-profile

people or people who are in a position to know, and then others begin
to believe as well, even though those others might not ever have gone
to any effort to find out for themselves or to verify that information.
They just hear other people say it and think, 'Oh, well, that person is in
a position to know, now I think that too, I believe that. Who am I to say
that all those other people are wrong?' And if enough people say that,
then something just becomes accepted as accepted wisdom and nobody
dissents from that view, even though perhaps the person who started
the ball rolling might not have actually been 100 per cent accurate to
start with. A core of my argument is that this is what has happened with
respect to whether or not the Irish constitution permits marriage equality. And I think it all really started after the Zappone-Gilligan judgement,
which I'll come back to. With this press conference where Brian Lenihan,
who is no longer with us, who was the Minister for Justice at that time,
said, 'My strong belief is the sound legal advice that gay marriage requires
a constitutional change. My view is a referendum on this issue would be
divisive and unsuccessful and would jeopardise the progress that we've
made.' So right from the beginning after that judgement, it was put out
there by a Minister for Justice, who himself was a trained barrister, that he
believed that he had strong legal advice that the effect of the Zappone-
Gilligan judgement was to clearly establish the Irish constitution did not
permit marriage equality and a referendum would be required. I don't
know whether Brian Lenihan read the judgement or not. I suspect what
he's saying there is that his view was based on legal advice rather than
his own interpretation, so I suspect not. I certainly suspect all the people
who followed didn't. This is just a sample of different parties. Martin
Mansergh from Fianna Fáil in 2010 said there was 'common ground in
this understanding that a referendum would be needed'. Fine Gael – we
see Brian Hayes saying the exact same thing, and this one really illus-
trates what has happened with this issue whereby this suits everybody in
the Irish political establishment to believe this, because on the one hand
what Brian Hayes is saying is, 'I'm pro-marriage equality; I would legislate
for marriage equality if it wasn't for that pesky constitution.' At the same
time he says here absolutely clear protection [should be] given to marriage between persons of the opposite sex. So it suits them all. Nobody
questions it. They all think, 'I heard somebody say once that we need
a referendum and it suits me to say I'm pro-marriage equality but my
hands are tied because that way I get to play both sides of the audience.'

It's striking that every political party was in favour of marriage equality in Ireland and they couldn't even bring themselves to legislate to hold the referendum. They had to refer it to the Constitutional Convention to put one further step between the decision and the politicians so that they can say, 'Well, we're in favour of it, we didn't even decide to hold the referendum; it was the Constitutional Convention that decided to hold the referendum. It was the people who decided to introduce change; it wasn't us who did it.'

9

MARRIAGE EQUALITY:
A NEW ORGANISATION, A NEW MOVEMENT

The establishment of the KAL Advocacy Group as a fundraising mechanism and organisation surrounding Katherine Zappone and Ann Louise Gilligan's High Court case was the beginning of a new single-issue group. Initially set up to focus on the case itself, it became clear that its remit should be broadened.

GRÁINNE HEALY: I was working as a consultant developing European-funded projects, mostly to do with social inclusion, employment ... So that's really what I was doing for maybe twenty years. As a result of that, I did an awful lot of travelling, particularly in Europe. I was in the early days chair of the National Women's Council, so that was my voluntary stuff. From that I got involved in the European Women's Lobby and I was the vice-president of that for ten years in a voluntary capacity. I chaired the observatory on violence against women, so again, that took me to a lot of UN things: here, New York, Geneva, wherever ... So my background has been really in the women's sector and in the social inclusion sector, and it's really only through my work in Marriage Equality that I have specifically become active in recent years in the whole lesbian and gay rights. I would have been involved on the outskirts, but I was never really central to any of the previous campaigns that were around.

ANDREW HYLAND: My first memory [of talking about marriage equality] was in a pub with a boyfriend on Camden Street, and us talking about marriage and we got into this big debate. It was the first time I really thought about it – of course I want to get married some day. That's where my involvement in that side of things started. I became very passionate from that conversation about the need for us to get married, but also I realised there was huge reticence amongst the community.

ROSS GOLDEN BANNON: I've been involved in gay politics since I first came out when I was 16 or 17. I was involved in setting up Cairde, which was the first support group for gay men who were HIV positive or with AIDS in Ireland. So from a very young age I was involved in gay politics and my coming out was intricately linked to that … What really struck me about the campaign for marriage equality is how enormously different my life would be now if when I was growing up and when I was a teenager I shared a positive vista of my life like all my straight friends did. They knew what they were going to do: they knew that they were going to get married and have kids and settle down. And when I looked ahead I never saw that. I never had that vista. I never had this idea that I would be living next door to great neighbours like I grew up with, like my mum and dad grew up with. I never had that long-term vista of stability to look forward to. And as time went on, that's damaging, that's psychologically damaging for a kid and a young teenager not to have that vista. And I believe that has damaged me in the very long run. Campaigning around marriage equality, the achievement around marriage equality in Ireland means that other kids won't grow up with that. That'll be gone. It's over.

AILBHE SMYTH: I do remember the early days of our meetings around the Gilligan and Zappone case, where it was called the KAL case, so we were the KAL organisation or the KAL group. And I remember those meetings where we began to thrash out a strategy. I remember in particular up in Ann Louise and Katherine's home, a very early meeting, where – and I think they had several of these meetings – where a number of people gathered together to talk about strategy, whether it was legal, political, financial, social and so forth. And that was really interesting because it certainly led to greater understanding of how the issue had been put on the agenda and advanced.

LINDA CULLEN: I am a lesbian feminist [and] didn't necessarily want to get involved with the institution that is marriage. So that for me was the most interesting thing about this whole journey to marriage equality for all. That thing of kind of understanding myself that actually I do want to have this, not necessarily that I'm going to do it, but oh dear God, of course we should have it. That it was an issue of equality, and access. That actually took quite a while for myself even to come around to thinking. Well, it didn't – it took one really good conversation actually!

With Denise Charlton. We were talking about the KAL case, so presumably it was around 2004 – the KAL case was a huge motivator around those conversations. And it was that thing of, 'Oh God, would you want to get married?' I presume it was Denise who said, 'But it is just an issue of equality, isn't it?' And I said, 'Well, of course it is. I'm not saying I would want it, but I have the right to have it.'

DENISE CHARLTON: They were looking to set up some sort of working group, you know, to support the KAL case or to support the concept of marriage, the extension of marriage. She [Gráinne Healy] asked me would I chair it with her and I said I would.

GRÁINNE HEALY: A number of us who had maybe talked about doing fundraising stuff privately met subsequently – five or six of us – and that group formed the KAL initiative … A number of us met to do a fundraiser. I can't remember was it a pub quiz or something like that. Ellen O'Malley-Dunlop from the Rape Crisis Centre who was also there – they're coming back to me now; Monica O'Connor, Denise [Charlton], myself, Maureen Lynott must have been there as well. So five or six of us met in a pub in Harold's Cross just to have a conversation about what we might try to do to raise some funds. Some people there were just interested in the fundraising. Denise and myself started to talk about how a court case was one thing, but actually we felt that I suppose because we'd been involved in campaigns over the years, that it was going to need more than that. Just even the court case was going to need a lot of popular support around it. So this was something that was going to need a campaign. So it was really Denise and myself who thought we're going to have to form this campaign thing. We didn't even form it and say, 'Let's form a campaign.' We thought, 'Let's put a support group around the KAL case.' They had already begun to call it the KAL case themselves, so we became the KAL Initiative. And there were a couple of other women; Deirdre Hannigan who had done some work out in the Shanty and she had fundraising experience.

AILBHE SMYTH: Well, when they rang me and told me, I felt this is something which one way or another I'm going to find myself involved in. There is this notion that when you're involved in political things that you make a decision to do things, but I'm not sure you do so much. It's very often things find you.

MARC SOLOMON: I remember knowing about the couple [Zappone and Gilligan] early on in Massachusetts when I was running the marriage campaign there, and I believe they came to Massachusetts to visit at some point in 2005 – maybe earlier, 2004. I didn't meet with them then, but I remember they had come to the US.

GRÁINNE HEALY: We got some money then from Atlantic, to kind of seed fund some thinking around what kind of advocacy support this case would require. We started thinking about that and invited other people in to talk with us and think about that, including Ailbhe Smyth. We began to think actually this needs something much wider, and we also need to be doing things other than the court case in case the court case didn't actually win.

ANN LOUISE GILLIGAN: This is not about us. And when the KAL case was to move to Marriage Equality – and yes, we did influence that naming – that was a delight for us. We had no need to be the two women keeping this whole show on the road as we've already described. But I think again, for a social movement to really have the educational change of consciousness in a society to really happen, it has to grow beyond two people or one person.

MARC SOLOMON: I came out to Ireland for four days to help them, to help the couple and Moninne [Griffith] and this guy named Ronan who was working as part of it. And we spent like a day and I did a PowerPoint presentation about the sort of ideas for creating a marriage campaign based on our work in Massachusetts and elsewhere. Moninne took me and showed me to some of the creative [work] they were considering using. It was soon after then that they came out with their Marriage Equality Ireland campaign.

DENISE CHARLTON: He was very influential in kind of affirming what we were doing but then also I suppose he was kind of the catalyst for Marriage Equality, and being very clear then on the different strands we wanted to do, which were legal, mobilisation, communication.

MARC SOLOMON: I would have talked about first and foremost getting people to sit down with their lawmakers, same-sex couples, parents, family members. I would have talked about the quality of contact with their lawmakers. So getting couples, but also important people in their communities – clergy, business leaders, labour leaders, others who can have an impact on the lawmakers. I would have talked about quantity of contact too, lots and lots of postcards and emails to lawmakers and outnumbering our opponents with respect to the number of contacts – that would have been at the heart of it. And then just finding [people] in order to get the high number of contacts, finding festivals and events that people can go to to collect postcards and getting people to sign up and really go about building and organising a grass-roots movement in order to show how powerful our movement is – and not just gay people too.

DENISE CHARLTON: We were kind of up against it at that point. Really, marriage equality was a long way away. And I think there were two things I remember about it. He was as uncompromising in his position as Katherine and Ann Louise were, which was 'this is equality, anything less isn't', and they always held that position. And I think that was very important. He was the same, and they had had a lot more successes in the States. The other was then the communications aspect of it. That was so core to it: the telling of the stories, the making individuals visible, making families visible, making partnerships visible.

DENISE CHARLTON: What Moninne did is that she kind of brought it to a different level – much younger, mobilisation. Really she was a huge catalyst with Andrew [Hyland] in terms of the community. Gráinne and I would have had a lot of experience in terms of communication and advocacy and lobbying, but we wouldn't have had that. Moninne really brought the mobilisation and she also had a legal understanding, a really good legal competency.

MONINNE GRIFFITH: They were looking for somebody to take the organisation to the next step. They were applying for a bit of money from Atlantic Philanthropies to expand it from just being around the case to being more about general media and mobilisation of people and all that kind of thing. So I applied for the job and got it, and I started then. It was a kind of baptism of fire … That's where we came on, the five strategies: continuing to support the legal route, having a robust communications strategy about increasing visibility and changing hearts and minds, a mobilisation strategy to get people involved and broaden it out much further beyond just LGBT communities, to get other human rights and equality organisations, family organisations, children's rights organisations, trade unions, everybody involved, and also mobilise the base supporters to get involved, and then the political strategy which informed that was around lobbying and briefing politicians and people working in Leinster House who were power-brokers and could advise and help and give us access to the people we needed to convince. And then the fundraising strategy to sustain all of that. That's when it was born and I came on board. I started in November 2007.

ROSS GOLDEN BANNON: I would have been instinctively supportive, but I was asked to join the board – I think it must have been 2008 – quite early on, maybe about a year after they started. As soon as I joined I discovered that the voluntary sector had changed radically from when I was involved in campaigning many years earlier! Much more professional, much more focused, not so many egos around and people very aware of recruiting on to the board particular skill sets that we were missing, reaching out to the business sector, reaching out to community knowledge with advertising knowledge. So I suddenly found myself part of a board who really seemed to know what they were doing. That immediately put my mind at rest. The very first board meeting I was like, 'Ok, this is good, we're going to be ok.'

Initially, GLEN and Marriage Equality were occasionally working together and sharing an office space. Marriage Equality began to poll public opinion on same-sex marriage rights.

GRÁINNE HEALY: So we've been able to track that. Our communications strategy was very much targeted on that – changing public opinion, getting people to see that this was about justice, it was about family, it was about children's security. It was about equality, and honing some of those messages. So we would have spent quite a lot of time talking to communications people, getting communications advice, honing our messages, deciding where to place them. Social media has been hugely important for the campaign, hugely successful … So we would have done work with the NLGF. The NLGF have been really strong partners for Marriage Equality, both with people in the board, so Ailbhe Smyth would have been on the board from NLGF, with two other people from NLGF. And subsequently the current chair is also on Marriage Equality. Those organisations – we've been really working closely together.

Marriage Equality began to do research and publish reports. In February 2008, they published a paper titled 'Making the Case for Marriage Equality' by Dr Jane Pillinger.

JUDY WALSH, FOREWORD, 'MAKING THE CASE FOR MARRIAGE EQUALITY', 2008: Any civil partnership scheme creates a separate and unequal institution. In short, to legislate for civil partnership is to ascribe second-class citizenship to gay and lesbian people.

In July 2008, they published a document on the flaws within the proposed civil partnership scheme in terms of immigration, as problems with immigration and civil partnership were emerging, technically meaning that an Irish person could only enter into a civil partnership with another person who had residency in the State. The Missing Pieces report launched by Marriage Equality in October 2011 identified over 169 differences between civil partnership and civil marriage across seven areas: the family home, finance, legal procedures, administration, parent and child, immigration, and equality. That number of differences became a key part of Marriage Equality's messaging. At the heart of Marriage Equality's methodology was a focus on winning the hearts and minds of the Irish public through telling personal stories. Their personal and positive communications strategy opened channels with the media and the community in a new way.

DENISE CHARLTON: Tell the stories, tell the stories why this will make a difference, and also why 90 per cent should care about 10 per cent, why would that make a difference.

MONINNE GRIFFITH: It was always about raising visibility. We knew that talking about the issue of marriage equality in the abstract academic human rights equality sense – nobody connects with that except other activists and other people working in the sector. So it was always about the human stories.

Marriage Equality attended the Electric Picnic festival and gathered thousands of signatures. They held concerts and lunches and teamed up with Ben & Jerry's to launch a new Marriage Equality-themed flavour, told stories of happy gay and lesbian couples and same-sex-headed households. While GLEN worked behind the scenes and didn't particularly foster a grass-roots connection with the contemporary LGBT community, Marriage Equality, along with LGBT Noise, emerged as the popular and recognisable face of a burgeoning movement amongst the community.

ANDREW HYLAND: I became the [PR/communications] consultant for Marriage Equality in 2008. I would have set up the communications strategies, the messages.

DENISE CHARLTON: Jesus, we did a piece in *The Times*, and I think we did the *Daily Mail* on the same day and the guy came, took a photograph and off he went. I was going to Brussels on a flight with some civil servants, and the next thing I saw a little photograph on the front page, and I opened up the health section and there was a front page photo of me and Paula [Charlton's partner] sitting on a beanbag. The civil servant who was with me just closed the paper and put it away. Ha! So he didn't mention it, I didn't mention it, none of us talked about it. Mortifying! And I remember Pat Montague [Montague Communications] saying to me, 'Jesus, you've come out anyway!' I was like, 'Eh, I think I was out already!' But that was it. That was one very significant one. Another one we did was *Women's Way* actually. It was a young journalist, Donna, and she came and I was like 'Jesus, *Woman's Way*, seriously?' But she did an amazing article. It was absolutely brilliant – one of the best, actually. And that was significant. And then we did a piece with Fiona from RTÉ that was kind of families, different types of families, and she came and interviewed people. They were the ones where we got a lot of feedback from. And then 'Modern Families' recently did with Áine Lawlor. I got masses of feedback from that … Who wants to put their story out there, really? But I felt very strongly that it was important for the campaign. That was our bit, you know? Paula, who would do a lot less media than me generally, saw Mary Robinson on the TV and she was saying something like, 'If you want to effect change, you have to give personally.' And she was like, 'Ok, we'll do some more.' Actually *The Irish Times* was the last one. I rang her from the airport – you know that red-eye flight – saying, 'Get out of bed, you're on the front page of *The Irish Times*! You better tell your mother!' It is a bit of a cringer and not something anybody wants to do, but at the same time we thought it very important. We had a story to tell. And we were available. But then loads of young couples came and it wasn't a big deal for them at all. They were saying, 'God, people keep saying to us "you're brilliant". We're just telling our story, it's not a big deal.' Even the change within that period of time – seven or eight years – was great. I suppose I think the visibility is so important because even as a family, I remember the first day going into school saying to Paula, 'Fuck, I forgot I was a lesbian.' You know, you just get on with your life and suddenly you see all these straight couples going in the door, you know? I remember one guy saying to me, 'I actually didn't think you should have children; I didn't mind you being gay and I thought you should definitely have the rights, but I did think it was harmful for children', and he said, 'I can't even remember that lens now, you're such an ordinary family.' I think that's what it does and that's what we try to do in the media. That's the aim of it.

GRÁINNE HEALY: If we hadn't had the media, I don't know how we would have gotten the message out. The fact of the matter is, the appearance of couples and their lives and the picture of them and their children and happy faces and the notion that here are individuals and families who have been traditionally invisible and by their invisibility othered – here they are. And people are opening their papers and thinking, 'God, isn't it terrible those people are being treated like that?' That's the basis of the 60 per cent, 70 per cent of attitudes changing.

DENISE CHARLTON: I remember Mark Garret [Eamon Gilmore's advisor] saying to me, 'Just keep telling the story the way you are, it's very compelling.' And I think also at the time there were probably a fair amount of advisors who were gay and not out and certainly they were saying, 'We're not interested in marriage.' I would know one or two, but you know, and that's fine … even Bertie with his sister-in-law, Sarah, I think at the time wouldn't have been an advocate, and subsequently has got civil-partnered.

BRIAN FINNEGAN: What happened with marriage equality is that it became a popular movement, really.

CIARÁN CUFFE: I think Marriage Equality is a great organisation that is working on the same agenda. It takes time to effect change, and God knows, I'd been in the Green Party for twenty-five years before we went into government. And a lot of people said, 'No, no, no, don't go into government yet.' If you keep waiting around you'll be dead, so you have to take opportunities for modest achievement when they present themselves.

MONINNE GRIFFITH: I'm extremely proud of what we've achieved as an organisation and as a movement, because there were so many players in the movement and we've kind of been one of the leaders in the movement, but there's been so many other people. We've exceeded expectations. When I look back at our short-term and medium-terms goals [which] were around increasing visibility, making the case for marriage equality, I think we've done all that, you know?

ANDREW HYLAND: One thing Marriage Equality has shown is that from a community point of view and from a societal point of view anything's possible. When we started, people were really going, 'Who the hell are these people?' and 'Within their lifetime do they really think marriage equality is possible?' When we started, people thought it was so far off. To turn this around from 2008 in that sense, from when Marriage Equality has been around and really from when coming out of the KAL case, nobody thought it was possible. Anything's possible. We were a community that were very much second class, that's not just a language we use to motivate people.

ROSS GOLDEN BANON: Here's when people power worked, here's when a group of people voluntarily came together and brought real change. I think it will be used as an example of how ordinary citizens can bring about change – I hope.

KIERAN ROSE: Marriage Equality had a desk in our office up the road in Fumbally Court. We never had an issue with Marriage Equality or LGBT Noise. We had no problem with people campaigning with civil marriage and saying civil partnership wasn't enough. And that goes back to your point that there can be a role for two voices, or two emphases or something like that, but what we thought was irresponsible and unconscionable and all of those adjectives was to effectively primarily campaign against civil partnership and that's where the relationship broke down.

10

THE FIRST DIVISIONS

'It was very divided, and it's still very divided.'

– Brian Finnegan

KIERAN ROSE: I could never figure out in my head how saying no to progress was going to achieve progress.

GRÁINNE HEALY: I think the fundamental belief that I had, and that the organisation had that I was leading, was that this was about equality, so anything that was less than equality was unacceptable. So that meant that when civil partnership was put forward and we were pushing for more than that, we had to keep saying, 'This isn't equal, it's not enough, it's not the same.' We did our Missing Pieces research where [we discovered there were] 169 actual differences in statute law between what you get. And some people think, 'Oh, you know, that's all rubbish.' That is the lived reality of being a lesbian or gay person in Ireland if you have a civil partnership and you can't be married and you want to be married. If that's what you want, if you just want to be civilly partnered, and I know there are lots of people – if civil marriage does come in and everybody gets upgraded – there are a lot of my friends who are saying, 'I don't want to be married, I want to be civilly partnered', so I think that'll be another issue. I suppose when we got the support from within the community that it was the equality package that most people seemed to want and that fitted with what we viewed we should be advocating for – once we felt we had that, we then started to look at wider advocacy, getting champions, non-lesbian and gay champions, public speakers. Fergus Finley, for example was very supportive. People who were publicly known to be heterosexual and maybe sitting on children's rights who would speak about this from that perspective to try to move others so that they weren't thinking, 'Well, that's the usual suspects, that's what they'd say.' So we started work on that wider communications piece of work. And I suppose when we were doing that and we were going in and talking to politicians, meanwhile GLEN were going in and they were saying, 'It's ok, we're going to think civil partnership and if we can get this', and that has always been GLEN's MO, even back as far as '93 in terms of decriminalisation. GLEN always had that thing, 'We'll get this, we'll get that package and then we'll move on to the next thing', so that is their *modus operandi*. It has worked for them and that's great. For us we just couldn't say, 'This is acceptable and this is enough.'

COLM O'GORMAN: At times it was a reasonably heated debate from my recollection about civil partnership versus marriage equality, about ownership of these demands and what demands were being made – were these demands the demands of middle-class, middle-aged gay men, as opposed to the demands of a community that was much more diverse than that? You know, that really pulled people into a conversation and a discussion that in a way started to politicise people more and when the thing started to take off, suddenly options and possibilities opened up for people and then, of course, opposition to even civil partnership galvanised people too.

KIERAN ROSE: I suppose I have a very, very strong interest in strategy, just as an intellectual thing. How do we achieve change? And learning from what you've done in the past, learning from other organisations – and I think in that sense, that's what's very interesting about what you're doing; is that it's looking at two different strategies, that's what I would see it as, to achieve change. GLEN going civil partnership, as close to marriage as possible, children's legislation that we knew would follow and children's legislation that is based on equality, taxation legislation because it had to be separate because a money bill has to be a Finance Bill, and that was equal to marriage, citizenship equality and so on. And then other people who were saying, the other strategy was saying, 'No to civil partnership, withdraw it, we don't want it, it's civil marriage or nothing.' And that is a totally – and has proven to be a totally – failed strategy. We would now – lesbians and gay men, couples – would now have no rights if their strategy, if they had won what they had been demanding. I mean, the organisations who were effectively saying civil marriage or nothing. The people who tore up the bill at Gay Pride. Yeah, and Marriage Equality.

GRÁINNE HEALY: We had the lovely Chris Robson come on to Marriage Equality at the very beginning and Chris is a personal friend of mine and when it became clear that GLEN were holding the line, that they were going to go for civil partnership and not push for marriage, I rang Chris and we had a really good conversation, and he said, 'Look, I think it would be best if I just stood down from Marriage Equality, and when this is over and we're working back together again, I'll come back on.' So Chris got it. We didn't fall out, you know? That was the way it was better for him not to be in an organisation where he was beginning to feel, 'You're doing this and my own organisation are doing that.' So rather than having this kind of fighting on the board, he said, 'Look, grand, we're going off and doing this and good luck to you and I think we will all come back together again.' That certainly was my view and Chris' view at that stage – that one way or another, we were going to have to come back together, which is where we are now.

KIERAN ROSE: I remember saying to somebody, a friend of mine who is a political person in the Labour Party, that I found the marriage/civil partnership debate bizarre because there was no sense of rationality about it. Facts didn't effect people's opinion. You could say that 99 per cent of legal and political opinion says it requires a referendum and people just ignore that. That's a fact. The overwhelming 99 per cent of legal, constitutional lawyers believe rightly or wrongly, whether it was fair or not – that's what they believe. And the political establishment, all the political parties believe that it would require a referendum. Now I would prefer if that wasn't the case, but those are two huge facts. And whether they were right or they were wrong, that's what they believed. So that was a barrier to introducing civil marriage by legislation. It had to be by referendum and people just didn't accept that. They just kept on saying, 'No, no, no, you can introduce a Civil Registration Act', which wasn't on offer. At times I thought it was a form of zealotry involved; you know, like a religious conviction, where you believe something very, very strongly but it's impermeable to rational discussion or facts. It's something you just believe and that's it. And the weird thing is that people now more or less accept that a referendum is required. Katherine Zappone is a legislator. She could introduce an amendment to a Civil Registration Act if the belief is that civil marriage doesn't require a referendum. But nobody's doing that. That was what we were told when the Civil Partnership Bill was going through: 'Civil Partnership is not necessary, all you have to do is amend the Civil Registration Act.' But that's forgotten now.

LISA CONNELL: For the time that I was involved with Noise, we had a very strong relationship with Marriage Equality all the way along. Marriage Equality were very good with skill-sharing and, for example, when they did media training, they'd always try to include one or more of us … I mean GLEN, that's, you know, that's – I don't know how honest you want me to be. GLEN, I mean – ok, well to be frank there was always a disconnect between GLEN and the other groups. GLEN were very much working on their own agenda. They were very much doing their own thing in their own way, and that was very much about lobbying, very, very specific lobbying. So there was no real sense of connection really to GLEN. I mean, I have personal connections with GLEN in that I've known or would have known Brian, and through working in *GCN* would have connections to GLEN. Brian is an activist in a way, but it's his job. It's a corporate version of it. Whereas Noise was always very grass-roots. So we didn't really have a huge amount of intersection with them. Certainly not when I was still involved. And when I moved on? I don't really know. I don't think there was ever a big change in that. But, you know, GLEN were always I think really on their own track, whereas Marriage Equality and Noise were sort of in terms of ideology … like, I had a conversation with Brian Sheehan and I don't think he would be sad about me saying this, but his opinion always was we were being idealistic and having a great ideology, but that he felt in terms of legislation, pragmatism is the sort of route of the day. My rebuttal to him would always be pragmatism without ideology leaves you with shitty legislation. So it kind of comes down to, I suppose, how people think it's best to *achieve* their goals. My only disappointment around that is that I think you should always aim higher than what you even think you're going to achieve.

KIERAN ROSE: We were always saying we were for civil marriage. That was our policy from day one and it still is. But their campaign – many's a time Marriage Equality and Noise became less for marriage but more about stopping civil partnership.

BRIAN FINNEGAN: Oh God, I mean it got very heated, it did. It was very divided, and it's still very divided. At one stage, Gráinne came in and she was doing a piece of work about what she thought the next steps were beyond civil partnership, because it was without a doubt what was going to happen, and I was saying to her I think it's a clear opportunity to align, you know? Because you've got the same goal. But they haven't aligned, which is very interesting. And it's a gender divide as well. To me it's a gender divide. I don't know if they see it as a gender divide. But downstairs [GLEN's offices] it's mostly men. And, you know, Marriage Equality is mostly women.

GRÁINNE HEALY: I mean, you do know that when Atlantic went to give GLEN their big grant, they raised that question with them about the fact that at the time they had almost — I think they had one woman, maybe two women on their board. And GLEN did a whole process, recruited women on, and all of those bar one has left. So there is an issue for the organisation. I'm not in there. I don't know. I think possibly there may be clashes of personalities. I think there are clashes of politics. Does it just come down to gender? No, I don't know. Does it play a bigger part for them than it does for us? Again, Marriage Equality is probably seen as more woman-y — although we actually have men on our board and we have a lot of male activists and volunteers, you know?

KIERAN ROSE: I mean, there is that perception. And I'm the chair, and Gráinne was the chair of Marriage Equality. And there would have been more women on the board of Marriage Equality than there was on GLEN. Yeah. That's a fact.

SUZY BYRNE: I think it's interesting to watch GLEN emerge from an organisation which was not interested in civil partnership to one that became interested in civil partnership 'but let's not talk about marriage', to then going, 'Woohoo! Marriage! And children!' That was actually really interesting. GLEN didn't want to talk about kids at the time when they were starting the civil partnership issues. And that's where a lot of women were very critical. At the KAL lunch, GLEN put little notices out. They were trying to find lesbians to go on the board because there weren't any lesbians on the board. We called it 'Rent-a-Dyke' at the time.

KIERAN ROSE: I think even Arthur [Leahy], who's on our board, who's from Cork, says there's a kind of effective executive part of the board, because myself, Chris, Eoin, Brian, latterly Tiernan – we're involved with GLEN since 1988, so there's a kind of a tightly knit group. And I think it's very achievement-focused, and maybe not enough process-focused. Do you know what I mean? As chair, I would take the blame if that is it, or the responsibility for that, that we should have had more women and a better gender thing on the board, but you're in the midst of a very, very, very intensive campaign and a lot of work, and getting people on to a board – you shouldn't do it lightly. You should go about it very seriously, as you would do a job interview.

MARIE MULHOLLAND: GLEN was seen as a bunch of nice, white, middle-class boys who had friends in high places and behaved with what came across as quite a degree of arrogance in that 'we know better' and 'we know what's good for you' way and also had lacked any transparency, lacked any accountability to the community, didn't have any kind of openness about the activities. There were no AGMs or anything like that. And you know, they really blotted their copybook, I think, in the mid-noughties when under pressure [about the fact] that there were no lesbians involved in GLEN at decision-making level or anywhere else. They decided to recruit lesbians to their board. And you had to fill out a four-page form and one of the questions on the form was 'your lesbian experience'. This was only 2004, 2005. I mean it was appalling stuff. They got a consultant and everything in to recruit lesbians, you know. Instead of just having a public meeting and saying, 'We're looking for some lesbians; we want to have your input, nominate somebody, or let's have a working group around how we can better represent lesbians and how you want to be represented within the organisation.' God, no, that would be much too democratic. So GLEN were a problem, right? And within that as well you also had Atlantic Philanthropies, who were really keen to put money into LGBT initiatives in Ireland. They were already giving GLEN money. They knew that GLEN weren't popular, that was feeding back to them. But Atlantic also operated on their own agenda. Atlantic operated very much on the agenda of 'we need professional organisations rather than people organisations' ... So they were funding GLEN and the criticisms of GLEN, which were valid, were that GLEN wasn't representative. So you've got a gap in the market there, right? And the other thing, and this is where I come at it differently, is that of the original people who set up Marriage Equality, 70 per cent of them were friends of the men in GLEN – not just friends, very close to the men in GLEN. Some had actually been on the board or tried to be on the board at some stage. So it was almost like the same gene pool, except the gender had changed. And it was white, middle-class women initially who set up Marriage Equality. Another thing I will say to you on this as well that the vast majority of them had not been involved in any kind of lesbian or gay activism previously. These were women who to a large extent were pretty privileged in society; you know, they had good jobs, they had good incomes, they came from the best parts of town and the only thing that was missing to make them 'just like everybody else' was the fact that they were gay. And so it felt to me that this was about making gay the same as everything else, you know?

KIERAN ROSE: We didn't do enough, obviously. We expanded our board and we said we were looking for additional women on the board. We did that. Unfortunately there were resignations from women on the board.

SANDRA IRWIN-GOWRAN: It was difficult. I mean, certainly there was the implication that at times maybe that GLEN wasn't interested in [children], that civil partnership would give financial and other securities, so the perception that would suit lots of gay men. Certainly as a lesbian working in GLEN with a child and trying for a second at the time, that was difficult.

ANN LOUISE GILLIGAN: I mean if you engage in a gender analysis of the strategy for civil partnership, it was absolutely male-led. And it was absolutely male-led within the official political Oireachtas, because unfortunately we have a very small percentage of women in governance in our Irish institutions, but those men were lobbied by and large by men, who moved along with this strategy on behalf of the gay and lesbian population. None of whom, or very few of whom, were really engaged in any kind of referendum democratic input: do you really want us to do this? … I think GLEN, very much as a very male-led organisation, decided in their own wisdom to absolutely go for or push through that rather incremental position related to civil partnership. In talking with some members of GLEN at different points, the point was often made to me that they were pragmatists. Now, philosophically, 'pragmatist' is quite an interesting self-description. But what you have to be very, very careful about when you're a pragmatist in a patriarchal society and a patriarch oneself is that actually your pragmatism is an interpretation of what you believe is needed at this time. I think one of the safety nets of pragmatism is: if you believe these are the actual steps to be now taken, it's not just about your belief and your drive that can go with this, because you will leave in your wake a lot of people whose voice you haven't listened to, and whose lives have actually been left diminished because your pragmatism drove you to make certain choices on behalf of the rest and I think that is quite dangerous actually. And I think when this history is written, I think there will be eruptions of clarity in relation to what I just said. I think at present it is a moment of history that is to be profoundly regretted. That the male organisation called GLEN, with some female members of course, who do very good work, do a lot of excellent work in education, offered as a network a lot of support to many gay, lesbian, bisexual, transgendered people – none of that is under dispute. They now, as they are moving forward in this point in history, are very well funded from some philanthropies in their ongoing work. Whereas Marriage Equality – and we've already engaged in the gender analysis of this, with marriage being now the emerging issue, with Marriage Equality being the organisation against all the odds and they have punched so high above their weight with a tiny group of people, they have done magnificent work, and this will be mentioned ultimately in the real history of this period – are now severed from core funding from philanthropy. And that is just in my opinion. It's more than regrettable. It makes me feel very angry, of course, but I don't know that the real gender analysis of what's going on here has really been done. It will be done in history. And this tale will be told as it should be told. But there are all sorts of attempts at this time to slightly already – what would you say? – place emphases in this narrative that are not accurate.

MONINNE GRIFFITH: I came fresh to be honest to the battlegrounds, if you like. I had no prior knowledge of who they were or their history or their legacy or how other people in the LGBT communities felt about them. I came fresh to that, which was probably a good thing, because then I had no preconceived notions or biases. We had some of them on our board. I always thought the strategy was kind of to be a good cop, bad cop. So they would go for civil partnership, and we would keep pushing for marriage equality. And that would work very well. So they would push for civil partnership, we would keep saying, 'No, we need more, we need more,' and then it would pave the way for better, stronger civil partnership, which wasn't our goal but it would help them. Somewhere along the way I think they got pissed off with us and I think we certainly – there were meetings; we were summoned to meetings and asked to shut up, asked to tone things down. And [they] said that we were threatening to derail civil partnership and all this kind of stuff. And it was really, really annoying. It was hard to listen to that, you know? Some things that were said around our messaging even – 'Don't put gay dads on the TV, people don't like seeing that. Blah blah blah.' Like, no. That's the reality. We have to. We have to get people used to seeing two daddies or two mammies. It's not the whole thing – marriage isn't just about being a gay parent, and the reality is, it's a small minority of same-sex couples who have kids – but it's to push out those norms and get people used to it. It was a very frustrating time. So what we did was we decided to try and keep that frustration contained and not let people know about it. And I think we did to a certain degree. But other people were very annoyed about the way it was messaged around civil partnership and called 'marriage-like' and it was called 'marriage in all but name', and all this kind of stuff. So people felt they were being lied to, I think, and being sold something. So things were hard, but they achieved what they set out to achieve, and I think with, for example, the help of our research, Missing Pieces, we were able to push for some improvements in the civil partnership legislation, and subsequent improvements. So stuff around citizenship and naturalisation, our research directly informed. Senator Katherine Zappone was able to go into the Senate when that was being debated and propose amendments. Likewise, around the taxation stuff, a lot of our research helped inform that. But that hurts a little bit I suppose, when GLEN tells that story, they leave out the fact that it was our research and Senator Katherine Zappone that pushed for that. I don't know, maybe [there was] a sense of ownership over civil partnership and worrying that if we don't all sing and dance about how great it is, that they are getting the kudos for something. That's kind of what happens with social movements. People move on.

Despite occasional rumblings of discontent, these divisions were very much kept inside the activist community. If anything, they were played down.

MONINNE GRIFFITH: I think we had no choice, because otherwise things could implode. And we would have been seen then as in-fighting. I thought it was very important for that not to leak out, and I think it worked, because I know now that our allies within government and politicians now see us as a respectable organisation because we didn't implode, and we didn't go bitching – we just bit our lips and kept on going with our strategy, which we were confident that would deliver. Otherwise you get sucked into it, and all your energy goes into it, and we didn't want to do that … We chose to just continue the work and not get sucked into that.

TIERNAN BRADY: It's very difficult to be the person outside the Dáil with a poster saying, 'The minister is a git', and wondering why you don't get a meeting with that same minister who is a git the following Wednesday. That's hard actually, because you have to sacrifice whichever decision you make, you have to sacrifice some level of either effectiveness or popularity. And we made a call to go the incremental route. And the flip side of that as well is that it's not to say one is wrong and one is right – you need both. It's about understanding you can't *do* both. You can't – you need two sets of people, you need two organisations pulling and in a way that's a tension that is creative. It's obviously not nice to be in the middle of it, but I can see – if I could stand 10 miles above it and look down – I can see how that works. But when you're in the middle of it, it's hard. It was very emotionally hard for people to see a very loud public rejection of it [civil partnership] by some people when we were convinced and remain convinced that it has been a key step to getting there.

BRIAN SHEEHAN: Every group is a group of self-appointed activists and that's fine. I don't have any problem with that. But nobody has a mandate… So nobody can claim to speak for lesbian and gay people.

THE LOBBYING GAME

'Our sexual orientation is not an incidental attribute. It is an essential part of who and what we are. Sexual orientation cannot, and must not, be the basis of a second-class citizenship. Our laws have changed, and will continue to change, to reflect this principle.'

– Bertie Ahern, GLEN's office launch, April 2006

KIERAN ROSE: Our strategy was to consolidate our supporters, win over the doubtful, pacify those opposed, and isolate the irreconcilables.

CIARÁN CUFFE: I think our marriage policy probably was round about 2006 in the run-in to the 2007 election. We would have produced a policy on marriage. And we said very simply marriage should be available to all consenting adults, and we also said we wanted to see civil partnership introduced for all consenting adults as well, and greater recognition of cohabiting couples. So in a sense there would be several options available to adults who wished to have stronger ties with their loved one. There was a group working on it within the Greens. My colleague Roderic O'Gorman was very involved.

GERARD HOWLIN: You had a very cautious group – in social terms – of politicians whose conservatism is much more to do with caution than anything ideological. The projection of liberalism or conservatism is largely wrong. There's a little of both, but my memory is the overwhelming absence of either. It was just a very practical [question]: is this for real? How many people are affected? Is this something that seriously affects people? That a community for these people growing up was invisible. So these were largely middle-aged men; so their life experience growing up was not of other gay men or women or whatever because all of that was largely invisible to them. So here they are now in government, they're middle-aged and they're asking themselves: is this a tiny number? What's going on here? So I suppose they felt their way through all of that and because of the much criticised sort of clientelistic system of Irish politics, they're very in touch with what's going on on the ground and all the rest. And I think the fact that lots of significant people were being visited very quietly by people in their constituencies: this is who we are, this is our situation. That very effectively communicated that this is real Ireland and it really has to be dealt with, and was highly persuasive.

AVERIL POWER: For a long time it wasn't necessarily being pushed politically. It wasn't a hot political issue per se. I remember when it must have been the 2007 manifesto, Fianna Fáil had a commitment to Civil Partnership and I actually worked on that manifesto at the time. I worked with people to draft that language of how we would push for CP and we put it in that manifesto … I'm trying to remember why we would have done it. I can't get the chronology right in my head, but I know Bertie Ahern went over and opened the GLEN office.

BRIAN SHEEHAN: We built a programme called Building Sustainable Change. And Atlantic funded it, €2.3 million – I'll check the figure – over five years from 2006 to 2010. So all this was going on at the same time as this enormous amount of work with Atlantic. So we thought, 'Ok, we have a programme, we have to engage politically.' Again, it's GLEN's MO, we knew an incrementalist approach isn't a bad approach necessarily. We knew we had built over time both political and Irish public support by presenting every win as a win for the Irish people, not a victory for 'the gays', if you like. We had our offices up in Blackpitts; this was real Celtic Tiger land. We wanted to engage at the highest possible level we could. I think it was Kieran made contact with Una what's-her-face [Claffey, Bertie Ahern's advisor]. We must have issued a letter I suppose saying, 'Would ya?' … Gerry was his advisor at the time.

GERARD HOWLIN: As far as I remember, they got Bertie Ahern to do one or two public events, which was important. If you go to open something, you make a speech. And that speech then gave another opportunity to expand on the whole issue. And my memory is that that speech was very well appreciated at that time and was very positive.

BRIAN SHEEHAN: If I remember correctly, I think it was one of first times ever that a serving prime minister head of state, well, prime minister in our context – in other countries it would be a head of state – would turn up at a gay event in an office. I think it was before even Tony Blair had done it. Really interesting, you know? But he made a brilliant speech [in which he said] sexual orientation isn't an incidental attribute it shouldn't be the basis of second-class citizenship, the law has changed and will continue to change to reflect that principal. That was phenomenal. That appeared in everything we did from then on.

Around the same time, political parties were compiling their manifestos ahead of the forthcoming 2007 general election.

AVERIL POWER: The manifesto was drafted as a staff thing. I'm not sure, but generally they wouldn't be cleared by the parliamentary party or anything like that. I can't remember that anybody had an issue with it being in the manifesto.

CIARÁN Ó CUINN: I remember there was a kerfuffle at the time about putting civil partnership into the manifesto and it was put in, but there was no big deal about it either way, it was like, 'Oh yeah'. There were four or five issues that people raised – whether they'd be put into the manifesto – and there was no big deal about it.

AVERIL POWER: I suppose throughout FF's history, because it's a very big party, it's had different groups. So when people say to me, 'Is the party centre left or centre right?', for me it's absolutely centre left but you ask somebody else? Like, for me on economics it's definitely centre left, but you ask somebody else and they might say it's centre right, because traditionally we had so many TDs, it was such a big party and there was a place for people with totally different points of view. So I don't know if the party as a whole was as socially conservative as people might think. I think a lot of our ordinary members aren't that conservative. I remember doing *Vincent Browne* and Vincent asking, 'What would Dev think of this?' I was like, 'I've no idea!' That's slightly before my time, know what I mean? I didn't join the party because of Dev's vision of comely maidens dancing at crossroads – or any of his economic visions either. So all of that is kind of irrelevant to me. What I would say is the difference with Fianna Fáil is that the party represents Middle Ireland, right? So when FF leads people on social issues – and I think we've a responsibility to do so on marriage equality – people listen. And I think it's our job to be ahead of where people are at and challenge them a bit and get them to move on things and persuade them. And I think we're in a stronger position to do that than maybe some of the more traditionally socially left parties because people look at that and say, 'Well, they would say that, wouldn't they?'

EOIN COLLINS: One of the issues that really came up for us was we were getting just so many people with immigration issues, Irish people with a partner from America or anywhere and they just were facing deportation, facing loads of problems. McDowell was so concerned when he heard that. And to any people with problems he kept saying, 'Just contact the department and I'll make sure I'll help in any way I can.' And he did. He sorted out a lot of the issues. So I think McDowell might have been intellectually arrogant at times, but he was, I think, on this issue fundamentally decent around it and really did want to do things, but he just got into a fix around 'gay people don't want marriage' ... McDowell took those cases very seriously. He was really very good and you know he said, 'Send any of those over to me.' And we did. And he sorted them. I think it's important to put that on the record.

12

MARGARET
GILL

'David Quinn said to me, "I'm very uncomfortable coming out on this issue." And I said, "Well David, go home."'

– Gráinne Healy

While lobbying was happening in the background, the human stories were beginning to emerge. Marriage Equality and the community recognised the need to win the hearts and minds of politicians and public alike. If there was going to be a sea change in public opinion, real people had to come forward. One of those people was Margaret Gill.

SANDRA IRWIN-GOWRAN: We did a 'Share Your Story' piece where we tried to get lesbian and gay couples to talk about the impact legal recognition would have on their lives. And one of them was, if you remember, a woman called Margaret Gill. Her daughter [Barbara] was an ex-work colleague of mine from my previous job before I worked with GLEN. And Barbara actually was one of the first people who responded to me when I sent out an email around the 'Share Your Story'. She was in a long-term relationship, herself and her partner – did they have the baby at that stage? They were on the verge of having the baby, they were expecting. She had agreed [to take part in the campaign]. I was quite surprised because I hadn't seen her in years, and she wasn't very out when I knew her. So I was really pleasantly surprised. She had agreed to do a piece for *The Irish Times* to write about, because she would have been the non-biological mother, so that role and the importance then of being recognised as a family and impending motherhood and all of that.

MARGARET GILL: Barbara was very much aware of all this, absolutely aware of it all, and she was just beginning to do a campaign on the local radio as far as I know. She knew the situation that they were in … Barbara had left everything to her dad and I in her first will. And when Barbara and Ruth realised they were going to have a baby between them, they very sensibly went to the solicitor and brought up a will and organised between themselves what they wanted. Then the solicitor said, 'Just don't sign them until the baby is born, and when he or she is here, come back to me and we'll finish off everything.' Unfortunately, that never happened because Barbara was killed. She lived in Kilkenny in Castlecomer with Ruth and she got up on her bicycle – she used to take her bicycle with her on the train – and at Heuston Station, a skip lorry should have been going straight. It turned left unexpectedly, never saw Barbara. She was down behind it. She was brought to James' Hospital. Wonderful, wonderful nurses and staff there. The surgeon did everything he could but it just wasn't to be… We were away; it was our twenty-fifth wedding anniversary. My son rang and said, 'Mum, you've got to come home.' I said, 'We're only here twenty-four hours!' He said, 'Mum, there's been an accident. Bar is very ill. There's only a 50/50 chance she'll survive. I've booked a plane for you from Verona. You have to get to Verona. I've booked the taxi for you.' He did that from London, our youngest boy. Everything was organised. We jumped on the train, and we got to London. I didn't know whether she had gone or not, but my daughter-in-law was a little lone figure standing at the airport arrivals entrance as we came off the plane. I said, 'What is it, Val?' She said, 'Andrew will ring you.' I knew when I heard that that it wasn't good. We stayed the night in London, the two of us, and then we came home. The airline people were superb. They sat with us, they knew the circumstances. When we came in, it was all over. She died at six o'clock. They thought they had her at three, but it was inward bleeding so she went. Ruth was up, and her dad, Sandra, my daughter who's a nurse got there, and my son and his wife. Thank God they were all there to be together. We weren't there.

SANDRA IRWIN-GOWRAN: We wanted to, I suppose, help them in terms of trying to sort out the legal mess, because Barbara was the main breadwinner and they had two properties and all of that kind of stuff. And obviously, then, her partner was going to be left with a big tax bill in terms of inheritance. We were working with Margaret and her husband Bill to try and support them in making a case with Revenue for them to waive the inheritance because the parents were very clear: they wanted to respect Barbara's wishes and have her estate go to her partner and child.

Barbara died on Thursday, 19 April 2007. The lack of provision for legal relationship recognition for Barbara and Ruth meant both families were in a legal quagmire. Ruth had been left with nothing, while Barbara's parents were left property they wanted to transfer to Ruth but were financially prohibited from doing so.

MARGARET GILL: We tried everything. We went locally. We lived in Offaly, so of course Mr Cowen was our TD at the time. We put everything before him, everything we could think of, every case, we explained the situation. We went to the other man in Fine Gael in Mountmellick, Charlie Flanagan, same thing, 'We'll do what we can.' But you keep getting letters back, 'Sorry, nothing we can do.' There was no law. Nobody did anything for us really – that's it in a nutshell. I spoke in Leinster House and our case was put forward by David Norris in the Seanad. You just got so far, but no further.

DAVID NORRIS: This woman who loved her daughter, her daughter's lover had the baby, the partner died and the child was left in limbo. That is child abuse by the State.

CHARLIE FLANAGAN: I would have known Billy and Margaret Gill. I would have dealt with them as constituents. Upright, decent people in County Offaly, and it was some time before I became aware of what their circumstances were and Barbara, which was a striking case in point as to how our laws were discriminating. I was very happy to highlight that case on the floor of Dáil Éireann. This was a case of blatant and unacceptable discrimination in my constituency where the tragic death of Barbara had resulted in a situation where her son didn't have any legal connection – in terms of succession, inheritance, was written out of the equation, resulting in a legal quagmire. I felt it was unacceptable that this hadn't really been raised before in any meaningful way. I'm sure it wasn't unique. I'm sure it wasn't the first of such cases, but it was the first I was aware of in my constituency. And as a public representative, representing all the people of Laois and Offaly, I couldn't stand over that. And I felt that it required change.

Margaret embarked on years of legal wrangling.

MARGARET GILL: It wasn't easy; it was very difficult. And you didn't get a lot of help. We kind of had to go through it ourselves. Then there was no compensation, because the skip lorry man had no tax, no insurance on the lorry. The lorry was wrong, the indicator [on the lorry] that killed her wasn't working. But we didn't get anything, absolutely anything … I couldn't believe it. I simply couldn't believe it. The twists and turns and the way everything was. It was just unbelievable. We went up to the courts and it was the first time we had the case. It was thrown out because the address was wrong. The police – after reams and reams of stuff they had, he was able to get out of it. A solicitor got up and said the wrong thing was on it. He changed the address the day we buried Barbara. So the police hadn't a leg to stand on. They told us there was absolutely nothing they could do, that it was the wrong address. A technical hitch they call it – a great, great term. It was the end of the world for us, because it meant absolutely nothing for Ruth. The State solicitor asked me when I was coming out was I happy with the outcome. I said, 'Happy?', I said, 'Do you understand my daughter was killed?' I said, 'Nobody seems to realise that or accept that. Everyone's talking about the lorry, talking about this, talking about that. Nobody says to me, "Your daughter was killed by that lorry."' So she said, 'Oh, well, we'll have to look into it.' So the next court case we had was the driver was being accused at this stage. The first stage was the lorry man. By the way, I went to him and I said, 'You are forgiven totally.' Because he was given a lorry he shouldn't have been given. Everything was wrong with it and he shouldn't have been given it, but unfortunately he was. And I know he shouldn't have turned left, but he was probably under pressure. I imagine that he was under pressure and he thought that if he turned left he'd get quicker up the side streets. He was from Lithuania. He had no English. Even the judge said to him something about the blind spot, 'I do not understand, I do not understand.' He didn't understand. The solicitor did pursue everything, but it all came to nothing.

Coupled with the legal action, Gill appeared on high-profile current affairs programmes, outlining the situation, including The Late Late Show *and* Prime Time.

MARGARET GILL: Pat Kenny came to me as they do just before you go on air and he said, 'What are we going to talk about? Are we talking about tax? Are we talking about access?' I said, 'No. I have a story to tell.

You've asked me here to tell that story about my daughter and her partner and her baby, and that's it.' He said, 'Oh, that's grand, that's grand.' He was relieved, I think! … With Miriam O'Callaghan. I did that at home. Basically two people came and interviewed me through RTÉ, in my own kitchen, which was lovely. That was interesting. It was easier, I suppose. She wrote me a gorgeous letter, which I treasure. She said I was just like her mum and that I spoke very, very well and put my case over very well. Pat Kenny said, 'Are you bitter? Are you angry?' I said no. There's no point in being bitter and angry in these situations. As my darling daughter Barbara would say to me, 'Wasting time, mummy, you could be using it for something more useful. You're wasting time getting angry.' So I think of her. She said a lot of things that I still think about today.

GRÁINNE HEALY: I did a *Prime Time* piece with David Quinn and Miriam O'Callaghan. They had the mother on screen from her home – she was from the Midlands. So I'm there, and David Quinn is there, and I mean it was such a powerful piece, because the mother – this is her beloved daughter who has died and is the mother of her grandchild, and her partner is now going to have to sell the little cottage they had in order to pay their debt duties so that she can continue to provide a roof over the child's head. So it was a tragic case, but a wonderful case in terms of bringing home to people the reality of what it means not to have relationship recognition in Ireland. And I remember that particular interview, reminding myself that I didn't need to be doing the heavy stuff with David Quinn, that this was something that he was going to have to speak against if he was going to make his case … We were up in the room beforehand and on the way down the stairs, David Quinn said to me, 'I'm very uncomfortable coming out on this issue.' And I said, 'Well David, go home.'

EXTRACT FROM AN ACKNOWLEDGEMENT NOTICE PUBLISHED AFTER BARBARA'S DEATH: We have been greatly comforted by what has been written and said about Barbara. She was very special to us but we hadn't previously understood how special she was to so many others in Ireland and across the world. Her dream was to help build a school in Eritrea, Africa and the many donations offered will enable us to fulfil this dream soon through the Self-Help Foundation. Thank you.

MARGARET GILL: People have arguments and they say a, b, or c. The fact remains that you don't go out to be a lesbian or a gay person – you *are*. It's a natural thing. I can't understand people – I know it's hard, but we're a conservative Church of Ireland family, the most conservative in the parish! And still, we have come to terms with it. I find absolutely nothing wrong … I don't think they look into it. They haven't lived it through … She's up there looking after me, and she just says, 'Get on with it, mother! If you're going to do something, do it right!' I believe that. I have great faith. I'm thrilled to be able to do it. I want this recorded. I really believe that everyone has to know about it. I think we've come a good long way, I have to say. When I spoke on *The Late Late*, a lot of people wrote to me. A lot of people phoned me and said, 'Look, I'm in the same position, and I was so unhappy, but since I heard you I have come to terms with it. Our son or our daughter is so much happier.' So, my goodness, isn't that a wonderful legacy to leave behind? When people say to me, 'you're inspirational', I don't think I'm inspirational! But I still would love if people would just listen and take it on board. You love your daughter or your son; it doesn't change because they are what they are. You have to accept they're different; there's no use in thinking they're not. But that's life. We all have ups and downs. I would say Bar was unhappy in school a bit, in boarding school, but then she got happier and then she went away, had a friendship with a boy, but she knew it wasn't right. But nobody fully understood that. She really became happy when she met Ruth and had a partner. Life was beginning. And she was taken from us … She rang me the night before, and she said, 'Mum, have a lovely holiday. When you come home, I'll come and talk to you, I want to hear all about your holiday.' She said, 'Mum, I'm the happiest person in the world. I've just bathed Stephen, and I've given him his feed. I'm the happiest person in the world.' I never heard another word from her after that.

13

MAKE SOME
NOISE

'Why the fuck are you watching your *Sex and the City*
box set when you should be rioting in the streets?'

– Panti [Rory O'Neill]

RORY O'NEILL: Older gays – for want of a better description – they were used to going on marches. They still don't think the Pride parade is a parade, they think of it as a march. They're used to being politically engaged and fighting for things. They remember Declan Flynn getting murdered. They remember decriminalisation. It's just part of their DNA. Obviously as you get older, most people, gay and straight, find it hard to keep up the energy for those kinds of things except for the ones who are very dedicated; the GLENs and the Marriage Equalitys and the Ailbhe Smyths and so on. The younger gays, that wasn't part of their DNA. Going out on a march was something they never did. … They've never been out on the streets. To them, going out on the streets was a big party on Pride where they wore wigs and skipped along, which is great, and I love that and it's fabulous. But it's not a protest. They had no connection to that. And so I think [LGBT] Noise gave them not only an opportunity, but also an excuse to get involved in something like that. I think it made younger people feel they were useful. Suddenly they felt they had a power. You went to those marches, of course you did. The Marriage Equality marches, the Noise marches, there was a real energy about that, wasn't there? A sense of all these young people out with their placards. I'm quite sure a lot of them had never walked down the street with a placard in their lives.

On 31 October 2007, when the Labour Party's Civil Unions Bill was failing in the Oireachtas, the evening began with a protest outside government buildings and ended with a new LGBT rights group.

ANNIE HANLON: It was a very spontaneous creation.

LISA CONNELL: Labour LGBT organised a candlelit vigil outside the Dáil. I was kind of standing there going, 'Why are we having candlelit vigils? Why is it so sober?' It seemed very sombre for something that was becoming, or seemed to me to be becoming, a really important issue... So we were in the pub afterwards, and I was really mad. I was like, 'Why did it even look like that? Why was that the kind of protest we had?' And then sort of famously said, 'We should be making some noise.' And Annie went, 'Ooh, I like that!'

ANNIE HANLON: I realised that night there was a real sense of people wanting to do something. A lot of people felt there was no outlet for normal people who weren't involved in politics ... There was a real need for a non-affiliated independent protest group, especially at that particular moment, when the government was making such huge decisions about our future. We wanted out voices to be heard en masse, rather than the odd letter to a TD ... I was talking to Lisa at the time when I said to her I really think this group should be started up. I just got the motivation that night to start asking people in the Front Lounge. I just started walking around and talking to random people I didn't know, asking if they'd be interested in joining such a group if I was to create one. A hundred people that night gave me their email addresses, and that was how Noise started.

ELOISE MCINERNEY: I moved to Spain in 2005 and there marriage had already been brought in, so when I was living there I already felt like, 'Here I'm fully equal, here I have these rights.' When I moved back to Ireland then in 2007, just a couple of months after I moved back I attended the Labour LGBT demo outside the Dáil after the Labour Civil Union Bill had been defeated. So that was the first time I got actively involved in anything. So we were there at that and then with some friends thinking and talking about it and thinking about ways we could expand this kind of demonstration, get more people involved, and the need for a large-scale grass-roots movement that would really push this issue to the fore in Ireland.

ANNIE HANLON: I asked a lot of people if they would be interested in organising, and that night I met Eloise in the pub. Lisa was of course with me and she said she'd love to get involved. And I think Mark [McCarron] and Paul [Kenny] were there as well. It was purely from the excitement of the protest we'd just come from that kind of inspired the creation of an independent group.

LISA CONNELL: So we had really intense conversations all of that week, and basically sort of started forming Noise. We started saying, 'Ok, what kind of group? Who would we be? Who do we need to talk to?' And immediately we made connections with Zappone and Gilligan and talked to them. But I was very adamant, as was Annie at the beginning, that it needed to not look like the candlelit vigil-style thing. So the whole idea, and us taking cues from the word 'noise', would be that we would specifically be a protest group ... We started talking to people we knew who were fairly kind of interested or active. So people like Eloise McInerney, and Mark and his partner Paul, and then along the line people like Una McKevitt and Edward Matthews, and for a time Emily Scanlan. And Noise has always been – since its inception, it's always been about not about who's doing the work, but about the collective idea.

ANNIE HANLON: At the time I was studying in Trinity. I was studying music there, so we went into a practice room and had our first meeting beside a grand piano in the music department in Trinity.

ELOISE MCINERNEY: We all went to her [Annie's] house and started discussing our first ideas for a movement. She was out in Drumcondra, I remember, tea and Viscounts ... We organised 'Sing For Civil Marriage', our first demo then only about three weeks after we were founded. So we had a really short timeline, very intense. None of us had really been that involved. Annie was the only person really who had been involved in political activism before. The rest of us were newbies, so we had to learn a lot very quickly.

ANNIE HANLON: It was more word of mouth and friends of friends. We did a bit of a campaign where we got in contact with all the LGBT societies around Ireland and members. I went to Cork and I spoke in Trinity, UCD. We just went around. First we got the students involved through the LGBT societies, telling them about us and our aims. It took off quite quick then through that. We became known as 'the young ones' by older gay rights activists.

ELOISE McINERNEY: I ended up in charge of media.

UNA McKEVITT: We only had one official position, apparently, which I remember was the press officer because somebody had to do the press. And that was Eloise. So it's like, 'Is Eloise the boss then, because she's the only one with a title?' I mean, we literally had meetings to try – at one point we were meeting in the Irish Midwives and Nurses Organisation – and we were having meetings to manage how we could talk to each other without fighting. So that's when I left. That became exhausting.

ANNA McCARTHY: I just moved to Dublin in – was it the end of 2007? I'd been following in the newspapers about the KAL case … Noise had an afternoon protest, 'Sing for Civil Marriage', outside the Gaiety in December of 2007 and Gloria sang, and I think KAL were there. I went along to that, I heard about it on the radio, and that was kind of that.

ANNIE HANLON: Lots of little old ladies were around doing their shopping, [and they] would come over to listen to the music. There were lots of volunteers all around and we'd all talk to anyone who came along if they were interested in speaking about marriage equality. I think we were just really taken aback by the positive conversations we were having with people on the street. Prior to that we had only really been talking to each other. Once we went out, it was the first time we got a gauge of the general population's opinions and attitudes and we were really heartened by how much support we got that day. I just remember that day feeling that our work had the consensus of people outside the gay community too. It wasn't just the gay community that wanted equality themselves, it was Irish people.

MAX KRZYZANOWSKI: I came out in 1993, the year that homosexuality was decriminalised, and that wasn't an accident. It certainly, I think, helped. It was a tipping point thing for me. I was hating leading a double life and feeling very shamed about it. But it gave me a little bit of added courage to come out … I grew up during the AIDS epidemic as a teenager, so there were two things that I knew about being gay. One was that the world hated me, and the second was that I was probably going to die. So I was terrified of intimacy as well as terrified of what the world might say and do about me if they knew. So on the idea of equal rights like civil partnership or marriage and stuff like that, I'd sort of emotionally put that to bed. I thought that would never happen.

WILL ST LEGER: The first Noise protest I went to was outside O'Callaghan's Hotel. I think it was January 2008.

ANNIE HANLON: That was an impromptu one.

WILL ST LEGER: Whatever time it was, it was freezing. We were outside with one banner. There was about eight of us if I can remember … The Iona Institute were having a meeting in there. So it was directed at them and the participants. It was really nice because the cops came along just to kind of see what was going on. I don't know who called them – knowing Noise they probably let them know beforehand because they're very considerate like that. A very handsome Garda on a motorbike was there and he was saying to us, 'What's the story inside?' We said, 'Oh, it's the Iona Institute; they think that marriage is just for heterosexuals to procreate and we're not allowed access to marriage.' And he was like, 'That's terrible!' So I had this feeling either he was a really liberal person or a card-carrying homosexual guard – maybe hope for the latter, you know, he was quite cute.

ANNA MCCARTHY: Early January [2008] I went to a debate in the Front Lounge. I'm not really sure if it was a debate, but I kind of just arrived into this scene where there was Paul and Mark and Lisa from Noise and Eddie and Una. It seemed to be more community feedback than a debate, trying to have a discussion, like a forum or something. And it just struck me there was a real mixed bag of opinions from the audience, and people sort of saying, 'Why are you bothering with this? Why are you doing it this way? Why are you expressing these views?' And then there was support as well. I just thought to myself, 'This is something that I would really like to get involved in', because I felt I hadn't been involved in LGBT student politics since college, so I had a bit of a break. And it just seemed like a group that appealed to me – that they were going to be getting out on to the streets. A protest group … I remember I walked up to Eddie Matthews, who was one of the organisers at the time and I said to him, 'To be honest with you, I kind of felt that some of the language being used by some of the organisers I thought could have been more inclusive.' So I just went up and I mentioned this to Eddie. We had a conversation, and he said, 'Well, you should be up there talking about this,' and I was like, 'Well, how can I join?'

ELOISE MCINERNEY: I know there was another one [protest] we did outside the civil registry office, which was like breaking the chains! Haha! We actually got a giant lock cutters and were symbolically trying to break the chains of the civil registry office. We didn't actually try to break them.

ANNA MCCARTHY: It was quite tense at times, you know? We all had equality as our goal but I think there was a kind of a split down the middle on people's views on marriage in particular … There were people who had maybe more of a traditional kind of view of marriage, just adjusting it to a same-sex relationship and sort of they felt like they wanted to hold up marriage using language like 'a treasured institution', to 'cherish' it, and all of this, and 'we want access to such a positive thing for society and for people'. Whereas then there would have been the other side to that where I would have fallen, and I would have said that well, it's a human rights issue, a civil rights issue, an equality issue. And marriage to some people isn't necessarily a good thing, but regardless of that, they should be able to choose not to have it either. I was sort of trying to bring more of a feminist perspective to the language we were using, more equality language, and there were a lot of clashes for a good couple of years actually in the early days of Noise, up until really 2010, we were still having that kind of clash.

UNA MCKEVITT: We did a photo shoot, Emma and I in our apartment in Elsmere Avenue for *GCN*, which is actually a nice photo. There's the six of us all standing up. I can't remember who took the pictures. I remember that, because that was a social evening. Mostly I just remember the tyranny of structurelessness. I think it's quite often [the case] in disenfranchised groups; nobody wants to have a leader. So I remember those dynamics more than anything else. The clashing. The clashes. The meetings of clashing of personalities.

ELOISE MCINERNEY: The plan was then to continue always with this idea of getting colour and fun into the movement as well because we thought this would be a good way of getting media attention. So we always kept it a little bit tongue in cheek, something that people wouldn't feel we were just being angry gays. The next one that we did [was] on Valentine's Day in February; then was a giant Valentine's Day card to Bertie Ahern, which was filled with messages and poems that we'd asked people to send into us or we'd gone around to the bars, various bars and clubs asking people.

LISA CONNELL: One of our biggest jobs in, I would say, the first year of Noise was to convince our own community that this was something worth fighting for. Our main way of trying to get people involved was to go out and basically canvas the bars, bring flyers in, do information pamphlets, all that kind of stuff – what civil partnership was going to be possibly, and what we should be asking for. But to be honest, at that stage, we realised the literature was too far ahead. We actually needed to talk about equality in really simple terms because by and large we were going into bars and people were saying, 'No, we're not the same, we don't deserve to be treated [as such].' It's really, really interesting to me to see the sea change that happened and how quickly it happened, because honestly when we first went out, there were even at times hostile reactions from people in bars. They were just like, 'What are you even trying to do? We're not the same.'

ANNIE HANLON: At the very beginning, what we did find – and I was actually really shocked and saddened – was that an awful lot of gay people actually believed that civil partnership was enough. As in, they felt like they didn't deserve to be equal. I felt very sad about that. So many Irish people had it ingrained in them that they didn't deserve equality. I was really surprised that the first year of Noise was actually more about changing the hearts and minds of the gay community than the people outside the gay community. So we actually spent a lot of nights going around different bars and clubs with flyers and talking to people.

ANNA MCCARTHY: It was really difficult to get a groundswell of support in 2008. There was just no appetite for it. People are in the middle of the Celtic Tiger, people are pretty comfortable, people have great social lives. There was very little discussion in the community or in wider society about

LGBT rights, apart from the work that GLEN was doing at a government level. You'd have the odd press release from them, but there was no kind of community engagement, or a community social realisation of you know, 'Here's the plethora of areas where we're discriminated in.' There was none of that. So like when we would go out and talk to people in the bars and clubs we were really trying to go out to find people to talk to them about this issue because there was no other outlet or facility to find them.

LISA CONNELL: A lot of people didn't care, to be very frank. A lot of people were like 'whatever'. Interestingly, older people – some were assholes. I think people believed in their psyche that they weren't good enough, so then they believed that civil partnership was probably even more than they deserved. So there was a sort of a feeling or a sense that 'we don't deserve marriage because we're not worthy citizens'. And now, I don't mean to misrepresent it, that wasn't, I don't think, the overriding feeling. I think a lot of people were on the fence about it, they didn't know … We'd be in the Front Lounge, PantiBar, The George, The Dragon – we'd go anywhere we knew we could get a concentration of gay people … You'd see maybe one or two people that you did talk to in a bar at the next protest. And that was kind of heartening because it's like, 'Ok, it's working.' And certainly that was a slow burner.

ELOISE MCINERNEY: Myself, Mark, Paul, Lisa and Annie – we used to do it in shifts, and people would take different bars on different nights of a weekend, and we did this every weekend, especially for all the protests up to the first March for Marriage … Just saying, 'Do you know what the differences are between civil partnership and civil marriage?' … And I think definitely over the course of that first year was a huge time, even the first two years, for education.

WILL ST LEGER: For anyone to have joined the movement for marriage equality, I'm going to guess and say about 80 per cent of the people had to make a shift in their head of thinking outside civil partnership as an idea.

UNA MCKEVITT: The fact that I was an activist is hilarious to me now. So weird. But I went down to Limerick University, which really freaked me out because it was so religious. The university just had God shit everywhere. And I was always keen to have this gay bus that would go into town and like all these gay people would just spill out, and we'd all just be gay everywhere! Which is why I went to the Lisdoonvarna thing [The Outing]; I knew I wouldn't enjoy it, but that really interests me, the rural/urban divide which is big in any social movement that there's ever been in the country … Soon after we went back – I don't know *why*! – and we were sitting outside this café and we were holding hands and this guy started quoting all this weird stuff from the Bible, like about man, bestiality and weird shit, and then these people called us dykes and stuff. So I remember that moment, being in Limerick and going, 'Alright so, eh, my sense of freedom and un-self-consciousness that I have as a gay woman in Dublin wouldn't be the same down here. We're an anomaly. We really stand out. And this is meant to be a city?!' So I do remember thinking at the time that the work we were doing was important for those reasons, as a reach-out.

ANNA MCCARTHY: At that stage, social media was really kind of starting to get off the ground, so we utilised social media as well. I'm pretty sure it was our first gathering, outside the Central Bank. I remember Max, who had just won Mr Gay World, spoke.

MAX KRZYZANOWSKI: My parents got divorced when I was 12 and my mother joined Divorce Action Group and she was a campaigner on the topic of marriage back when I was 14 or 15. Myself and my sister got a little bit involved as well. My mother actually chained herself to the Dáil railings, quite a vocal advocate for equal rights for women, and that Church-dominated rules shouldn't be what mandate what everybody else can do. And so that's kind of a bit of I suppose where I have the cultural impulse to be involved in activism and social issues. I had a very strange year at the end of 2009 when I won the Mr PantiBar competition, went on to participate in the Mr Gay Ireland competition and then I won that, and the prize was to enter the Mr Gay World competition in Vancouver in 2010. I ended up winning Mr Gay World, and when I came back, there was a little event in PantiBar, and I was approached by two guys who were members of Noise who asked me if I'd speak at a rally at the Central Bank on Dame Street. I think it was a few days later, a Tuesday or something like that. I wrote out a little speech and it was a little bit about me and my feelings and when I went down to give this, the speakers at this blew my mind: Tonie Walsh, Rory O'Neill, Anna McCarthy, Gráinne Healy, there was a letter read out from a young man that had been sent in as well, somebody I think who might have been as young as 13 or 14. And the whole event I found incredibly emotional. I hadn't, I don't think, been at a political gay public event rally sort of thing like that before. There had only been 250, 300 people there. But the words had a very powerful effect, as did a conversation with Anna McCarthy, who was in Noise at the time … I perceived them as smart, radical, fired up, passionate, engaged, wanting to change the script. There was a certain amount of impatience about it as well.

TONIE WALSH: Noise got me to make a speech on Central Bank on Valentine's Day. It was 'Love is Blind', I think, was the theme, a few years ago. One hundred and fifty turned up. It's that famous rally where they had me and Max speaking and I took as I do, potshots at the Church, my *bête noire*, and Rory – Panti – reported it on her blog afterwards and was really indignant about the lack of concern, the lack of focus and the lack of anger.

LISA CONNELL: Then of course, with the blog from Panti, that really kind of kicked it up another notch.

ELOISE MCINERNEY: Panti had done her righteous anger blog, which really finally I think galvanised people. I think it was a snowball moment really where everything changed.

MAX KRZYZANOWSKI: It was a seminal moment in the marriage equality movement.

TONIE WALSH: Maybe simply Rory and Panti were just stoking the zeitgeist, but there was a noticeable shift, and of course you can see it.

WILL ST LEGER: There were fuck all people there, and then that kind of transformed an awful lot because then the infamous letter, 'Dear lazy-arsed gays' or something like that. That was incredible, you wouldn't believe. It's such a simple thing, but it shows you that you know in a tacit way, the greatest advocate in terms of moving people on was somebody who is a very popular entertainer and a very well-liked person. And it's funny; no one seemed to mind being called a 'lazy-arsed gay' for not going, because they all thought 'shame on me'. Even Rory's fans were going, 'Fuck it, I should have been there, that was stupid.'

ANNA MCCARTHY: I think Rory just seemed to get annoyed, and, you know, I think my own perspective would be that people were, I suppose, very comfortable, in that to a large extent for most people, their lives weren't interfered with that they realised, that they weren't touched by discrimination. They weren't touched by inequality. They were probably earning, they were probably in a job. Their social life was fulfilled. And then the older generation had kind of come to accept the discrimination, so there was no kind of motivation there either. So there was just this *apathy*. I guess that just sparked him to write the blog post.

BRENDAN COURTNEY: Rory would have been my educator. I would have been caught up in the mundanity of things, whereas Rory is someone who's political and is reading the newspaper every day, and knows an awful lot about the politics of things. So if I was asked to talk about something, I'd ring Rory up and ask, 'Where are we on …' or 'How do we feel about …' and we'd chat about it. Rory is all of our educators in a way.

BUZZ O'NEILL: More or less it was a rally call: where the fuck are yiz?

PANTI, 15 FEBRUARY 2009, BLOG POST, 'NO MORE MR NICE GAY': Lazy-arsed queers.

On Saturday afternoon, Penny and I went to the 'LGBT Noise' demonstration on Dame St[reet] to support their campaign for gay marriage (and *against* the weak, second-class, civil partnership bill that is due to come before the Dáil – though I wouldn't hold your breath). There were about 150 people there, mostly the usual suspects, and we had a pleasant, social afternoon. Long-time activist Tonie Walsh made a rousing speech (delightfully, he couldn't resist aiming a few kicks at the Catholic Church. I howled when he referred to the Pope as 'that German eunuch in Rome'!) and Penny got lots of attention and met a few other gay dogs… It was nice to see some politically engaged young gays, and those of us who were there had our batteries recharged somewhat. And I think Noise were happy with the turn-out as it was a lot more than their last demonstration at the Dáil.

But 150 people? That's pathetic. There were a couple of thousand gays drinking and dancing and hitting on Brazilians within a 500 yard radius of Dame St[reet] twelve hours earlier. Where the fuck were they? Where the fuck is the righteous anger?

When some bouncer in the George is mean to a drunk gay, the forums light up with horrified nellies, protests are mooted, and Facebook groups are set up. But when a fundamental human right, available to everyone in every civilisation since the formation of human societies is denied them, they can't be arsed getting out of bed. Where is the righteous anger?

When Sunday clubbing hours are curtailed, angry gays join angry protests outside the Dáil, petitions clog up our inboxes, and outraged gays shout about the nanny state. But when the government that taxes them the same as everyone else, tells them that in return they'll only have *some* of the same rights afforded to everyone else, they can't be arsed having brunch an hour later than usual. Where the *fuck* is the anger?

When Alexandra and a bunch of other people you'd never heard of a few weeks earlier, make it to the *X Factor* final, you won't leave the house and no one can get through to you because you're furiously text voting, but when you're told you're a second-class citizen and your relationships aren't *real* relationships, you can't be arsed walking over to Dame St[reet] from H&M because the cute assistant has just gone to check if they have that cute jacket in your size. Where the *FUCK* is your righteous anger?

And don't bother telling me that you're not interested in marriage. That you think it's an outmoded institution, a hangover from a patriarchal society that was only about the protection of property. I don't give a crap. Plenty of other gays *do* want to get married, and you should be *furious* on their behalf. Furious that something as basic and fundamental as marriage, something that is taken for granted by everyone else, something that society expects, encourages and cherishes for everyone else, is closed off to them, and them only. *Anyone* else can get married. Any race, any creed, any gender... Hell! Any idiot, murderer, rapist, child molester. Any asshole, racist, queer-basher. Any dumb-fuck soccer hooligan. Any mentally disturbed lunatic. But not the gays! The sky will fall down!

And where were those gays who *do* want to get married? The ones who'll be rushing to the registry office if and when the weak-brewed, watered-down, domestic partnership version of marriage is thrown at us to shut us up, and the government slaps itself on the back for being modern and progressive.

Why the fuck are you watching your *Sex and the City* box set when you should be rioting in the streets?

What is it going to take to make you angry? What is the spark that will finally light a fire under you? Are you waiting for a gay Rosa Parks?

Well, you have one. In fact you have two. Katherine Zappone and Ann Louise Gilligan have already refused to sit at the back of the bus. Do you need a gay Emmeline Pankhurst to throw herself under the king's horse? Will that finally wake you up? If you think the fact that you can hold hands with your boyfriend in Top Shop is progress enough, then that's all you're going to get. If you act like a second-class citizen, you'll be treated like one.

And it's not just the gays I'm pissed off with.

I'm pissed off with the pensioners. When their medical cards were threatened, the streets were in tumult with anger. And rightly so. But the sleight against the pensioners was much less than the one against us. The government wanted wealthy pensioners, who could afford it, to pay for their medical expenses, not deny them all a fundamental right given to everyone else. Can you imagine the reaction if the government had decided that pensioners marriages were no longer valid? Or even if their marriages were to be downgraded to a weaker version of marriage, a *faux* marriage, because after all, old people's relationships aren't *real,* they're just *pretend* relationships so a *pretend* marriage should be good enough for them. They would have torched the Dáil. And the pensioners didn't protest alone. Gay people were out on the streets. Gay people wrote to newspapers. Gay people lobbied their TDs, called radio shows, threatened to oust the government at the earliest opportunity. But where are the old folk when we need them? Why isn't your granny calling Joe Duffy to express her outrage that you are expected to take on all the responsibilities of citizenship, but only some of the rights? And don't tell me she has a religious objection! I don't give a toss if she has a religious objection. She's welcome to it! We're not asking to get married in her church. We're asking – *demanding* – the right to civil marriage, under the same law, in the same state, that we too are supposedly equal citizens of. It's payback time Granny. *Quid pro quo.*

And where are the bloody students? When college fees were muted, gay people rallied too. We scratched their back, and now they can bloody well scratch ours. *Quid pro quo.* And the farmers? *Quid pro quo.* And the unions! Where are the bloody unions? Gay people pay union fees too. And the nurses, and the teachers, and the rest. In the '80s, the Dunnes Stores workers went on strike rather than handle oranges that came from apartheid South Africa, a country and a people half a world away. And yet they couldn't give a toss that the guy working on the checkout beside them is segregated.

But it's hard to see why they should care when you don't seem to.

Perhaps the problem is that we gays have wanted to be left alone for so long, that we're used to keeping our heads down. We don't like to draw attention to ourselves by rocking the boat. Well I'm fed up not rocking the boat. It's my bloody boat too! I want to scream and shout and kick and throw things. I want to riot! I want to take to the streets and hurl abuse. I want people to know how pissed off I am. I want to break things and tell the people who campaign to keep us in our place to fuck off. I want to scream, 'How *DARE* you! How *fucking* dare you stick your nose into my business! How *dare* you try to tell me who I can and cannot marry?! How *dare* you tell me that my relationships aren't real?! How fucking *dare* you! Fuck off and mind your own bloody business, you interfering, mean-spirited, petty, backward, ignorant, patronising asshole!'

I have a lot of respect for 'NOISE' and their campaign. At least they're doing something. But I think the time for protests that are about making pretty pictures that will hopefully make it into the *Evening Herald* are over. What we need, is righteous anger. What we need is a Stonewall riot. Oh I'm not suggesting we rip up the pavement slabs and loot Arnotts. But what we need is a 1,000 gays to get angry on the street. What we need is 2,000 gays with eggs to turn up at the Leinster House railings at Merrion Square and have them hail down on the cars of country TDs, to chain the gates shut, to refuse to move, to pour paint on the pavements. What we need is for fifty gays to get arrested. So what if we get arrested? A day in court and a fine? We'll have a whip-round! But we need to get angry. We need to be our *own* spark.

No more Mister Nice Gay.

MARIE MULHOLLAND: I remember one night watching I think it might have been the old *Questions and Answers*, and there was a discussion, one of the questions was about gay families, same-sex marriage and adoption and children and stuff. And LGBT Noise was in the audience, and one guy who was known as an LGBT Noise activist said, you know, 'Every child needs two parents.' And I thought, 'Fuck you.' You know? 'Fuck you.' That is twenty-five years of my community activism and you just fucking totalled that, you know? We've been trying to stand up for lone parents for years, and you just decided that every child needs two parents in order to promote your agenda which is about gay parenting. It felt to me like lots of really important stuff was getting rolled back.

MAX KRZYZANOWSKI: There've been many people and many public spokespeople and that's where I think we have made the most visible and obvious impact. But there's a lot of writing legal submissions to the law reform commission, to the constitutional convention, to hearings on gender recognition legislation, asylum and immigration policy – all of this hard work that requires an ethical compass that points to what you genuinely believe to be true north, and honest and practical appreciation of the processes that can get things done. And so it's been a learning curve over the course of Noise's time as well.

LISA CONNELL: I'm really, really proud of Noise, and when I take a moment and think I have a hand in setting that up, it makes me really happy. We had, always, really passionate people involved. And that was part of its success and part of the reason it got to the stage that it's now at. So with passion there's always going to be, you know, it wasn't always the easiest thing to work with – six or seven people at a time who all have very specific ideas of how they want things to go. But mostly it was really good. I mean, you go, 'Oh God, I'd like to throttle so and so', at certain meetings, but then thankfully people were mostly able to put their own egos aside and think of the bigger picture. But yeah, I mean, it was challenging at times, but overall I would say a really positive experience.

Lisa Connell entered Alternative Miss Ireland representing LGBT Noise and bringing the issue of marriage equality to the stage of the Olympia Theatre. She subsequently ran in the local council elections on a single-issue marriage equality ticket.

TONIE WALSH: I'm attracted to LGBT Noise; they're angry, they're vocal, they have some extraordinarily savagely bright, articulate people. And I also think they get it in a way that other LGBT NGOs – I think they get it, the sensibility around marriage equality that I find very appealing is obviously quite distinctive to Marriage Equality, the organisation, and GLEN and the NLGF or whatever. I think LGBT Noise get the equality part of the equation more than the marriage part of the equation.

UNA MCKEVITT: I think it's brilliant that it's still there. I don't feel associated with it in anyway, bizarrely. I totally forgot I was in it! Ha! So that will tell you that. I think what appealed to me was the demonstrations. I've always wondered why people are so timid. So what attracted to me about Noise was the idea that we were going to do physical demonstrations, actually you know, do things in an extroverted, proud, out, kind of way. And I think that's their strength, the reason it was called Noise. Those are the good things about it.

ANNIE HANLON: I think the biggest impact has been changing the hearts and minds of gay people. Education. A lot of people weren't even aware, especially younger people who wouldn't have thought about marriage or anything yet – they weren't aware of a lot of the issues, and it was just great to get everybody informed about these things … I don't think GLEN walk around the streets and talk to people. That's a big difference. Also, in a way, certain groups, I feel sorry for them, because they have great ideals and do great work, but they're often held back because of the people who fund them, in that they have to waste a lot of time with administration, writing reports to the philanthropic organisations who are helping them out. But Noise was very free. We didn't have to answer to anybody at any point. That freed us up in a lot of ways to sometimes have a slightly more radical stance or be much stronger about things. We didn't rely on government funding, so we never had to please anybody in politics.

BUZZ O'NEILL: I personally have always had a problem – and myself and my friends in Noise have debated this back and forth many times – with us doing that on a Sunday afternoon in August when not only is there no one in the office, the Dáil isn't even sitting. I've wanted a proper political protest outside the Dáil on a Thursday night at five o'clock. That we're on the same political platform that everybody else is, when they want to get something done or changed.

SUZY BYRNE: Politically naive? Probably. And I would have said that publicly at one stage, or written it as well. However, they did build a space for people's non-gay friends to be involved in things: the marches in August and things like that that have taken place. I've criticised [that]. You don't go marching in August on a Sunday for anything, but it did give a space for people to support each other. As much as I criticise GLEN for being too politically organised, savvy, clandestine, I think you do need an element of that when you're organising a campaign. That lacked in Noise sometimes in what was said and how it was done. However, it was very visual.

ANNA MCCARTHY: Thinking back to outside the Central Bank where there was thirty people it was like, 'Oh my god, why are we bothering? Is this actually going to go anywhere?'

14

ELECTION

'We were of the expectation that if we could get a commitment for civil partnership at least that would be a large step along the way.'

– Dan Boyle

In 2007, Fianna Fáil again did exceptionally well in the general election. This time, however, they sought a new coalition partner in the Green Party. As the Programme for Government negotiations began, the Greens pushed for a commitment to relationship recognition for gay and lesbian couples.

EAMON RYAN: The process leading up to the Programme for Government was one where we took a lot of soundings with the German Greens because they had been in government. And in about 2005, 2006, we realised that there was a chance of us being in government. So we really took a long-term two-year lead-up to the election in 2007; we knew when the date was going to be, in terms of what our manifesto commitments would be, or what were the things we would do if we actually got into government. There was a guy called Reinhard Bütikofer who was German, in the Bundestag then and a member of the European Parliament now who very strongly advocated: you need a list of ten things, you need certain things you go for, particular projects. From fairly early on or right through that process, gay marriage or advancing civil partnership as a first step towards it would have been seen as one of those doable, distinct, clear [things]. I can't remember the exact list of ten things, but my recollection is civil partnership would have been central to it.

EOIN COLLINS: We published the positions of all political parties and that was right through from the most supportive, which was the Green

Party were supportive of marriage, Fianna Fáil civil partnership, right through to the worst actually, which was the PDs. They continued to hold this domestic partnership thing. And it's funny when you see Colm O'Gorman talking about it, because we've had debates on the radio about this, but that's the platform he stood on as a PD candidate in the 2007 election. So that was the worst model. And you know, I think it reminds me that we can all change our opinion as we move forward, and I think a lot of people have.

CIARÁN CUFFE: In Fianna Fáil's 2007 manifesto, out of the 153 pages, they have four lines which essentially say they would legislate for same-sex civil partnerships and it's got to be remembered that not all of a manifesto gets delivered on. And I don't think civil partnership would have occurred without the Greens' presence in government.

BRIAN SHEEHAN: We lobbied very heavily at the formation of the Programme for Government to ensure we could get marriage or as much as we could get of relationship recognition in. And that was an intensive couple of days here where we engaged with both parties, Fianna Fáil and the Greens, where it got in as the very last item in the Programme for Government. I think that tells you something about the political gain – sorry, the political appetite rather than gain. There wasn't much. We just kept at it. We were writing formally to both parties and the negotiators, but also making calls and speaking with any contacts that we had from official level to TD level in both parties, to highlight the issues, to highlight Bertie Ahern's language, to say that this was something that was urgent, to keep a key focus on including this in the Programme for Government.

EAMON RYAN: We set up a negotiation team, which would have been Dan Boyle, John Gormley, Donal Geoghegan, to negotiate with Fianna Fáil. We would have had a team based here [Green Party offices] in terms of adding up was it worthwhile, did we have enough to go into government, did we have enough wins as it were, enough things we could see that we were going to be able to deliver. And there was a big board posted over there. I wasn't directly involved in the negotiations, but I think there was a conservative tendency in FF which made it difficult. I think in some ways – I think Bertie Ahern – that they would have seen us as a way of getting stuff through their own party that mightn't otherwise have taken place, so in other words, 'Oh, the Greens were insisting on it!', was in some way an easier way of them getting over what might have been objections from their own backbenchers.

EOIN COLLINS: We actually gave a suggested wording, which is almost identical to the wording that went into the Programme for Government, but in the end what went into the Programme for Government was a commitment to civil partnership, civil partnership taking account of Colley. So that was it. Civil partnership got in. We were disappointed in one sense that there wasn't still the kind of freedom maybe to move with marriage, but there it was and that's all the Greens could get. It was so at the end, it was the last item in the Programme for Government. They really pushed it to the end, and they got it in at the end. I remember a board member of GLEN was in touch with Dan Boyle all the time and he knew what was going on, and they really pushed it in.

PROGRAMME FOR GOVERNMENT, 2007: Civil Partnerships: This Government is committed to full equality for all in our society. Taking account of the options paper prepared by the Colley Group and the pending Supreme Court case, we will legislate for Civil Partnerships at the earliest possible date in the lifetime of the Government.

DAN BOYLE: What happened was that the talks weren't progressing very well. We felt that we weren't getting anything from Fianna Fáil in the talks. John Gormley was very unhappy with the type of progress that was there. It was a three-person negotiation team: myself Donal Geoghegan and John Gormley. John wanted to fold the talks, basically before we actually did walk out. This was about the Tuesday or the Wednesday of the talks, walked out on the Friday. And he chose to make marriage equality the issue in which we'd face down Fianna Fáil. We didn't have a standard position on that. The other two negotiators and I think he was basically calling Fianna Fáil's bluff. Technically we may not have gone into government and the talks might have collapsed on the issue of marriage equality itself, which probably isn't commonly known. I'm not too sure to the extent to which John was just choosing an issue that he knew Fianna Fáil were going to go on. That was the issue he chose to go on. Eventually we got negotiating again over a weekend after we walked out. We felt we got a strong enough commitment on civil partnership.

15

BUILDING CIVIL PARTNERSHIP

'The job was to meet everybody. We had to.'

– Tiernan Brady

With Fianna Fáil and the Greens in power, GLEN set about lobbying for the civil partnership commitment in the Programme for Government to be seen through. But in the LGBT community, the conversation was already moving on to marriage equality.

EOIN COLLINS: This is slightly technical, but it came up in Colley as well. [Brian] Lenihan's [the then Minister for Justice] view around civil unions was a belief that civil unions would be unconstitutional, not because of the way it was written. And we had talked about this in Colley, the subtraction method or what they call the enumeration method. In Denmark they had what they called the subtraction method. It was civil partnership – I know they have marriage now, but before that – civil partnership where marriage read civil partners also. In Britain, however, what they did was they enumerated all of the things from scratch, delivered the same thing, but it was in order to get it over the line in their terms constitutionally. So what you had in Britain was like a 280-page bill, and in Denmark you had three pages. Equally with Labour at this time; Labour's bill was the subtraction method where marriage read also civil union. And so this gave us a little bit of hope, which was that we could then push Lenihan around doing the kind of British method, which was to enumerate everything. And to get as much as we possibly could. And this turned out to be possible. At the end of the year we had Lenihan launch our annual report and I had talked to him. I had been at a meeting with Katherine and Ann Louise actually down in Galway just after the election, and he had said there at that, which I thought was difficult, that they would wait for the outcome of the Zappone-Gilligan case to legislate. And as we know, that could mean kicking it into touch forever.

STEPHEN COLLINS: Even though Bertie in one way was 'the great Catholic' – and would always have the ashes on his forehead during Holy Week and was a regular mass-goer and all the rest of it – he was kind of, I'd say, fairly liberal on the issues. Bertie Ahern was pragmatic going into government when this was what the Greens wanted.

BRIAN SHEEHAN: We met with Brian Lenihan and asked Brian to launch our annual report. We asked him to remove the block of not waiting for the outcome of the Zappone-Gilligan case because if you waited for that – as it turned out, by the time CP had passed, it hadn't even been heard at Supreme Court. So he said at our report launch that we didn't have the time to wait for the outcome of that case in the Supreme Court, we had to go legislate now – there were urgent needs that needed to be addressed – and legislate on the basis of equality and do the in effect the enumerative method of CP and that was December of 2007.

TIERNAN BRADY: There was an advisor to a senior minister at the time and he was a gay man and he had coffee with me – I'm a good friend of his – and I remember sitting down and he said, 'I'm not sure of this job,' and I said, 'What do you mean?' and he said 'There is no chance in hell civil partnership will pass.' And that was a gay senior advisor who was in favour of it. He had seen the mountains were too high and in the world of political pressure and political priorities, it wouldn't get through the net. And that people on the back benches would be watching people on the back benches across the aisle, terrified of what would happen. At the time, most members of the house hadn't really any engagement on gay issues. They didn't know what to expect. They didn't know who was going to come in to lobby them. They didn't know what the impact of the bill would be on the electorate because there was nothing to measure it with. So there was a real – I'm not going to say terror – there was fear. Fear is almost strong. People were circumspect. They weren't sure was this the third rail of Irish politics. One TD, an opposition TD at the time, said to me, 'You guys have to stop this being the third rail. Politicians fear that if they touch it they die.' And that was a real sense of it.

Even if they could vote for it in Dublin, 'This isn't something that's going to play well at home and it's something that my opposition is going to use against me.' Especially then when you factored into the fact that this wasn't a priority really for at the time you had Fine Gael – Fianna Fáil took up 80 per cent of the Dáil – it wasn't a priority in terms of electoral return. Because people know there isn't votes in it really.

CIARÁN CUFFE: I remember Brian Lenihan saying very bluntly that he would need to be lobbied on the issue. At that stage, we were in the middle of the LGBT Noise and Marriage Equality campaigns and he said, 'I have had one couple come into me'. One couple doesn't register on the lobbying scale. And I was very frustrated by that, because I said it very directly to Gráinne Healy in Marriage Equality and I just felt even the other groups – the Noise group were big into having great demonstrations outside the Dáil gates. That's not how lobbying works. Lobbying works in face-to-face conversations with your local TD in your office or in Buswells or somewhere else. And I was very frustrated by the public manifestations that weren't grounded on the same amount of back-room activity. And I think GLEN felt the same. I mean I can't speak for GLEN, but GLEN had their head down trying to pursue what we had in the Programme for Government, as well as wanting to see full marriage. And I said at the time – and I remember you had an article that was highly critical of me in the *Tribune* – I said change happens incrementally in government. And that is the reality of government.

STEPHEN COLLINS: The Greens were pressing it. But I didn't get an impression of huge resistance in Fianna Fáil, or serious resistance in Fianna Fáil. In fact, I got the opposite. It was just a question of when it would happen.

DERMOT AHERN: Those people in the parliamentary party who found fault with this I would always say, 'But lads, you agreed to this. There it is in black and white – you agreed to it. You didn't get up at the parliamentary party and say, "I disagree with this"!' I was doing it sort of factiously in a way to, you know, 'You can't have it both way, lads. You can't.' I used to be happy to say that, 'It's not the Greens that are necessarily pushing this lads', saying this to the Fianna Fáil people, 'We put this into our manifesto before we had even any idea of going into coalition with the Greens or the PDs.'

GERARD HOWLIN: Brian Cowen, by the way, going way back was very pro this. Maybe there are stereotypes about him and all the rest, but I know in private discussions at cabinet and in the corridors and so forth, he was always very positive. So it's not just something he was lumbered with as Taoiseach. It's something that he had been very positive about for quite some time previously.

DAN BOYLE: It was progressing quite well with Brian Lenihan as Minister for Justice.

BRIAN SHEEHAN: To be fair to Brian Lenihan and his departmental officials, they began drafting the Heads of Bill then and the principle was clear that they were going to draft on the basis of equality across as many grounds as they felt was constitutionally possible. So at that point until the Heads of Bill came, our involvement was lesser than it was subsequently, because the political decision had been made to do it on the basis of equality across all the various grounds. And it was in a sense a 'wait and see' what the Heads of Bill would come out as. And the Heads of Bill came out quite strongly on a few things actually. We had a couple of meetings with advisors over that period while the Heads of Bill were being drafted. Both with the advisors to the Department of Justice, the minister, and the advisors to the Taoiseach. And would have pushed for the principle for equality and the inclusion of families. It's an interesting thing that at the same time there was a huge – my timing mightn't be right about this – there was a huge fuss at the time about Cathal Ó Searcaigh, and I suppose that was one of those things that complicated an issue around inclusion of families and children.

TIERNAN BRADY: One step at a time. It was slow, slow process of work. Building up mass engagement on a one-on-one basis and on a party basis. So we would have done presentations to parties first of all. Also we had to start going in and meeting individuals, talking them through it, investing that time because that time is the bit where you build trust with politicians. Politicians get lobbied by hundreds and hundreds of people on a monthly basis so they have to decide, 'Who can I engage with that isn't selling me a pup?' The biggest part of that was literally that slow process of sitting down, going through stuff, cup of coffee, meeting for half an hour, coming back three months later.

Every backbencher possible. Everyone who would take a meeting ... There were a few very strong advisors – Ciarán Ó Cuinn in Dermot Ahern's office.

CIARÁN Ó CUINN: I've a strange political background. I was doing a PhD in Trinity, I was Conor Cruise O'Brien's research assistant and I was a member of the Labour Party, and I ran out of money. I looked in the paper and I saw a job for a researcher. It looked great, speech-writing and everything. The only problem was it was for Fianna Fáil ... So I ended up at the age of 25 or 26, working in the Fianna Fáil research office in Leinster House. Six months later my boss left – he just got a better-paying job – and I ended up as Head of Research in Fianna Fáil from 2000 to the 2002 general election. My interest was policy and policy advice so I became special advisor at the Department of Communications and Natural Resources working on broadband policy and north/south issues. I worked on the north/south energy link up. The Head of Research in Fianna Fáil traditionally does a lot of the Northern Ireland stuff so Dermot [Ahern] asked me to go with him to Foreign Affairs. I went to Foreign Affairs and worked on the Peace Process, some development issues as well, but basically the Peace Process for give or take five years, from just before the Northern Bank robbery up to when the final deal was done, the Westminster Agreement and all that. I then went off with Dermot to the Department of Justice. I told him I didn't want to go. I had no interest in law and justice and these sorts of issues but he told me at that stage he was coming to the end, and would I just do one more ministry with him. So I said fine, and went off to Justice and spent two and a half years there working primarily on Northern Ireland dissidents, gangland, and on civil partnership.

TIERNAN BRADY: Averil Power would have been an advisor with Mary Hanafin at the time.

AVERIL POWER: When I was a student union officer in Trinity – I was education officer and then I was president – I remember getting asked to do a debate, a joint debate, the LGBT Soc and maybe Pol Soc on marriage, and whether people agreed with marriage equality. So I suppose that was the first time I had the question – should gay couples be able to get married? And I spoke at that debate and I said, 'Yeah, why not?' Why wouldn't people – if they're happy and committed to each other, why wouldn't they be allowed to get married? To be honest, it was probably the first time I even kind of thought about it, but my instinctive reaction was: yeah, obviously they should.

CIARÁN Ó CUINN: I went in on the third day Dermot was in – second or third day – I was wavering whether I'd go or not and he rang me. So I went into the department and said, 'Ok, I'll look around.' I scouted around, looked at the Programme for Government, talked to the officials, went into the minister and said, 'Right, what are you going to do for the next year? Pick your two or three things.' And for him it was clear. He said, 'The gangland stuff we need to change. What's going on in Limerick is really serious. I'm not sure the State has the mechanism to deal with it so we need to deal with that.' One of them was to continue the work in Northern Ireland which he had, the security bit was very important to that. The third thing was he said, 'Look, civil partnership, we need to do that as well; it's in the Programme for Government. It's in the manifesto.' I said, 'Fine.' So they were the three things he wanted done from the start. It was pretty blasé. We didn't feel particularly revolutionary about it. His advice to me was on the civil partnership thing, he said, 'We need to do this properly; we need to get support for it, so you know, we're not going to set up straw men to knock down. We're not going to be too loud about it. We're just going to make sure it gets right, and we get it done properly. There's a lot of misconceptions there, so just talk to people.' So I was sent to go off and talk to people; talk to members of the parliamentary party, members of the opposition, civil society, whatever. Shortly after that Brian Sheehan got in contact with me and I went down to their office and said, 'Look, this is one of our things, we want to do this.' They said from GLEN's point of view, marriage is the first thing, and they had advice, a member of the Board, Fergus [Ryan] who works in DIT, had a paper put together and said you don't need a referendum. I said, 'Lads, that may be so, but the Attorney General's advice' – and if the Attorney General gives you constitutional advice, that's what you go by, you can't legally go against that for a cabinet – 'is saying you do. So there's the perimeters; we are where we are. We want to do this, we want to do it right, so it's an opportunity to do it.' They said, 'Fine.' I said, 'Ok, we're going to have to work together on this to make sure it happens.'

CONOR O'MAHONY: Attorney General's advice is kind of treated by politicians as being the last word, but one of the things about constitutional law is because the constitution is so vague, it's invariably open to competing interpretations and that's why when these cases go to the Supreme Court, you often get split decisions and so on. So there seems to be a disproportionate amount of emphasis placed on an opinion that comes from the Attorney General or perhaps from just one member of staff from the Attorney General's office, which is then seen as sacrosanct and not open to question, when in reality, interpretations of the constitution are always open to a lot more debate than that.

TIERNAN BRADY: The job was to meet everybody. We had to. Out of 166 TDs, I'd say we sat down with probably 130, 140 of them.

EOIN COLLINS: When it went through the Dáil. We were there all the time, just battling away different amendments and really just constantly meeting up with TDs. On one day I think Tiernan and I met seventy TDs and senators walking from office to office. We worked with the ICCL as well, doing kind of information sessions in the Dáil, which were really good as well. We were pretty much entrenched there.

TIERNAN BRADY: I remember meeting Geraldine Feeney. She was a senator at the time and there were two senators in the office. I walked in and I knew the other senator – he's dead now and I would have known him, we would have always got on well. I walked in and he stormed out, walked out past me and wouldn't say hello, first of all. This is an example of there was genuine – I won't say anger – suspicion, and 'this isn't my thing'. He stood outside the door. Geraldine said to him, 'Tiernan's in to talk about the bill. Do you want to sit in?' He says, 'Nothing to do with me, nothing to do with me.' And out he walked and stood outside the hall for about ten minutes, then stuck his head in and went, 'Is he finished yet?' Now this is somebody I knew and Geraldine was mortified, absolutely mortified. The rest of the meeting consisted of Geraldine apologising on behalf of the other senator … And it wasn't nice to experience. It was people who knew you suddenly seeing you as a cultural enemy. And their antipathy and animosity towards the subject was stark. It's the one example, but it's not the only example. There were lots of meetings that were very cold.

BRIAN SHEEHAN: Marriage Equality were setting up as an organisation, and we housed them for the first year or more. We did a joint 'Share Your Story' campaign with them, they ran with the 'Out to Your TD' piece. We also did audio-visual room briefings, and actually Enda Kenny came to that. We were trying to prepare the ground for an equality-based problem resolving fully inclusive civil partnership model. We did an awful lot of engaging with TDs, dozens and dozens from all sides around that period.

GRÁINNE HEALY: We had spent some time trying to, I suppose, get articles into the press. Moninne would have spent quite [some time doing that]. I went around speaking wherever – student bodies, whatever the places might be – talking to the community and asking the community's views on this, so this was going on the same time when GLEN were very heavily pushing for civil partnership. And I've always had a sense that there was support within the community for that, but once the KAL case happened, and we started pushing for marriage equality, it was almost like the community then went, 'Why are we settling for this?' So in a sense, a wave of support for marriage equality washed up behind GLEN and their push for civil partnership.

TIERNAN BRADY: I always think the key thing about political lobbying is to understand the world of politics for people who are in it is not what people perceive it to be. It's a hugely pressurised place. And it's like being a deer in the jungle. You're under pressure from everywhere. You're under pressure from the opposition. You're under pressure from the media. You're under pressure from TDs in your own party who you're jostling for position with. You're under pressure from your constituency. And you're under pressure from people who are underneath you in your own party, your local councillors who want to be you after the next general election. So understanding that this is an incredibly pressurised job for people that is 24/7 was critical.

GRÁINNE HEALY: Our third strand, the political work, the political lobbying, talking to the political parties, trying to get them, going to their conferences, taking stands and stalls, talking to their leaders, going in at a local level. All of us going in talking to our local politicians. I have Paschal [Donohoe] in my constituency, and Joe Costello, so people that were in our own local constituencies going in, talking to them on a personal basis and asking them what their positions were and trying to push them. Labour people didn't have to be pushed; it was an open door. They had passed their policy; they had it as policy. The Shinners took it on as policy. Fianna Fáil once they were out of government took it on as policy – couldn't get a meeting with them for two years before that, but that's life!

CIARÁN Ó CUINN: No other organisation in the whole LGBT area ever made contact. Never picked up the phone. Never emailed. Never called the whole way through it. It's strange but it's true. It is strange, it is weird. Now, there would have been sort of postal campaigns, there would have been letters, but actually GLEN worked out the nodes in the network, picked up the phone and said come down and talk. From then we worked with them hand in hand. There were a couple of really good civil servants in the department who were working on it. GLEN would have worked with them. We were very hand in glove the whole way on the minutiae of the bill. And, you know, it wasn't always pretty. GLEN would have been pushing a lot, especially the whole family area. And for example on marriage, the AG [Attorny General] had said, 'Look, here are the perimeters of the bill, we need to keep a certain amount of separateness from marriage on the scene if we don't want to have a constitutional referendum.'

GRÁINNE HEALY: The Greens took it on politically, and again we had very good connections with them, so, you know, and the Greens, like us, always realised that the aim was marriage equality, but once they got in they realised, 'All we're going to get here [is civil partnership], so we're going to go for that.' And we would have had private conversations with them where we said we accept that, but publicly we're going to keep pushing for this. So we didn't fall out with any of those political people even though we had rows with them on radio or television saying, 'It's not equality, you're not going so far, blah blah blah.' Because you know, this is politics.

EOIN COLLINS: We met up with Dermot Ahern when he became Minister for Justice and again we'd a whole new relationship to build. He wasn't terribly supportive at the start at all. We had a first meeting with him and it was very frosty. And we felt that the momentum for civil partnership had gone with Lenihan. So that was difficult. Also the economy was starting to collapse as well.

DAN BOYLE: We found we were stonewalled quite a lot with Dermot Ahern as Minister for Justice.

TIERNAN BRADY: He's [Dermot] a real story of success, a man who spoke in the most cautious, to put it politely, terms in 1993 about decriminalisation – to move from there to being the driver of the bill. That's what success looks like. You do hear the argument about a younger generation replacing the older, but a big part of it is: you have to persuade an older generation as well, our parents of the world. When they say it, they address a whole pile of the fear and concern people have about any kind of change. Everybody fears change at some level. When those guys come on board they become almost reassuring voices for a big chunk of the middle who are saying, 'Yeah, I get the point and I understand the argument but …' I started work here [GLEN], the Heads of Bill were just about to come out about civil partnership but I knew from the house, even in Leinster House, Dermot Ahern, being the minister responsible, had an incredible calming influence on a lot of backbenchers. Because he was Mr Tough. He certainly wasn't seen as Mr Woolly Fluffy. So for him to take the leadership on this role, a lot of people were going, 'Ok, that's ok, Dermo's doing it.' Mr Gangbuster is doing this, he's not one of the softies … His kudos and street cred with backbenchers was phenomenal. Him being appointed to Justice was definitely a moment where you went, 'Actually if we can pursue this bill through him, he is the man who can deliver it for the Fianna Fáil backbenchers.' That was definitely one of the key moments.

DERMOT AHERN: Ciarán Ó Cuinn, in fairness to him, would have been very close to people like Tiernan Brady and Kieran Rose. And Ciarán would have pushed me in relation to it.

CIARÁN Ó CUINN: Well, yeah, it was part of my job. I was also enthusiastic about the all-Ireland energy market. To an extent I was just a technocrat just doing what I thought was implementing the Programme. So I was just doing the job.

EAMON RYAN: You have to remember the minister is running around. The Minister for Justice probably has twenty pieces of legislation on the go – or ten, whatever number – at the one time, at various stages. He's not up there late at night with a pen out writing the text. The text is written by public servants. I mean, they can take sometimes from international [sources], so it's not all drafted from new. Some sections are standard *pro forma* if you're setting up an agency, various provisions for the agency, but it's first and foremost written by the public servants. Ministers have a chance to amend it; cabinet and government have a chance to amend it. And often, when I said that we'd be going in to have a row with the Attorney General, that would be at a stage where we have a draft wording we don't like; we got to resolve the differences. So you'd need to get it to a certain level so that cabinet can agree with it. And even then, ok, the ministers then have a certain flexibility when it comes to Dáil committee, Seanad stage report and other stages, but even in that process, the civil servants are there with you all the way. Your big briefing folder is prepared and presented by the civil servants, so you shouldn't underestimate the influence civil servants have right through the legislative process. It's not final, it's not absolute. It is the ministers' prerogative to accept amendments or to suggest amendments, and a good minister will do that. Others are slightly more cautious, maybe rely on their civil servants more. Or busy. And that's not an insignificant factor. The volume of work is amazing. You tend to maybe really concentrate on certain sections of the legislation where it tends to be contentious. So you do ration your time a wee bit, but the civil service have a significant role.

CIARÁN Ó CUINN: So for two years we worked. There was very little work done in the department when we came in. It took a lot of time to get the Heads of Bill together. We got the Heads of Bill and it was going out at say three o'clock. We showed it to GLEN around one o'clock, but they had been talked through the whole way. It would be disrespectful to show it to someone who wasn't in cabinet before you go to cabinet, so it would have gone to cabinet, cabinet would have finished at half twelve, we would have shown it to GLEN at one. So TDs wouldn't have seen it. There were no surprises. We worked with them the whole way through it. But the relationship wasn't as if they were embedded or we were embedded. There was conflict. There would be kickback. They would work very well; it's actually a lesson in lobbying. They work very well at low and high levels in the department with people on the minutiae of text, on the minutiae of legislation.

DERMOT AHERN: Literally every 't' had to be crossed and 'i' dotted to make sure it would pass constitutional muster. And the last thing we wanted was a challenge to it. So I do recall the Attorney General saying to me, 'Look, this is as far as we can go,' he said. 'I'm stretching it as far as we can go.'

EOIN COLLINS: I remember one thing I was kind of horrified by, considering I had all these people with immigration difficulties at my desk, was that there was nothing in it about immigration in the bill. Then I rang an official in Justice and they said, 'Well, you know, there's no legislative hooks in a way for this because there's so little family reunification in immigration law,' so he said, 'What we'll do is we'll put out a statement.' This was all done in such a hurry and a panic. So the minister put out a statement saying that he would ensure that there was full equality between civil partners and married couples in immigration regulation. So we got that through. I was personally delighted about that because it meant so much to people.

CIARÁN CUFFE: There was four or five crises happening offstage at the same time, so we were kind of consumed by the many other issues that were happening around that time. I remember when the bill was published, we brought a copy down to GLEN and had a chat with them about it. And I remember continuous to-ing and fro-ing with the Department of Justice to make sure that the legislation was published. My feeling was that we had to continuously engage with the Department of Justice to make sure that the proposals were progressing.

EOIN COLLINS: He produced the Heads of Bill – I think it was June 2008 – and we thought it was good because it was very close to marriage. Fergus Ryan, who's on the Board of GLEN, did an analysis of it and the big glaring exception was children, which we really highlighted. But it was close to marriage, and to us that was an important step because it meant then that relief was being delivered for lesbian and gay people in issues but also in the context of a legal model that was firmly based on marriage. So we supported the Heads of Bill and again kept trying thereafter to push, have the bill then reflect as much equivalence to marriage as possibly was the case. That's when a lot of division came in.

CIARÁN CUFFE: I think GLEN are the unsung heroes of that discussion, because I guess we're of a similar mindset: that we both wanted full civil marriage, we both realised that due to the innate conservatism of Irish politics – particularly Fianna Fáil and Fine Gael – that would not happen today or tomorrow, despite opinion polls saying that the majority of the population wanted it to happen. So we worked on the nuts and bolts of getting civil partnership across the line … I thought they were very professional in their understanding of the political process, in working to very clear agendas when we met. So in terms of the hundreds of groups and individuals that you meet in the lobbying process in Leinster House, I would put GLEN head and shoulders above many others. They were very sharp and very precise in what they were trying to do.

ANNA McCARTHY: A lot of the time I suppose the line from government was, 'You're lucky to be getting even these, this amount of rights. What are you complaining about?' And I suppose there was still that attitude in the community as well, people saying, 'Well, sure isn't it great that we're getting something? We've had nothing for so long.' Just because you're getting something doesn't mean you should not criticise it, that you shouldn't seek more, and seek equality. That was really frustrating, that people were kind of, I suppose, I guess – I don't want to say that they were internally homophobic, but that they were so ready and willing to accept their second-class citizenship. And that changed, that did change over time. And recently people are less willing to accept it, but I think that attitude in the community kind of frustrated me. And the line from government that we should be happy with this really frustrates me.

16

TAKING TO
THE STREETS

'I said to the lads, "How do you feel if I was to rip up the bill?"'

– Anna McCarthy

KIERAN ROSE: There's no point in just saying, 'We want it, we want it, we want it'; you have to listen to people's things they're saying to you. If they say to you they've a problem, they agree with you but they've a problem – they want to get it over the line – you have to take a level of responsibility for that if you want to. You can't just say, 'No! We're just going to criticise you come hell or high water if you don't deliver like 110 per cent of what we want.' And some NGOs do that. But we took part of the responsibility of getting it over the line. So we didn't say that it was marriage-like, because it made it easier for the minister to get it over the line, and we got criticised for that. If you're serious politically, you have to take that hit. And if you're not prepared to take that hit you shouldn't be involved. You shouldn't be taking Atlantic Philanthropies' money or you shouldn't be putting yourself in a leadership position.

DENISE CHARLTON: I'm not a natural protestor on the street, and Noise and Marriage Equality getting together and getting that amount of people out on the street, it was really emotional and significant.

While civil partnership legislation was progressing, a protest movement within the LGBT community was building to a level never seen before. The annual March for Marriage was bringing thousands of people out on to the streets who were dissatisfied with the proposed Civil Partnership legislation and were calling for full equality. For the first time, generations of LGBT people, their children, their families, friends and straight allies were gathering en masse in protests co-ordinated by LGBT Noise with support from Marriage Equality. Internationally, too, the conversation was getting louder. Protests in the US, pro-marriage equality videos on YouTube, social media-friendly campaigns, and increasing coverage in the mainstream press meant that a domino effect of marriage being extended to lesbians and gays was inevitable. This was a movement growing in confidence and numbers and gay people and their straight allies everywhere were ready to take up, and pass, the torch.

BRIAN FINNEGAN: Rory's blog coincided with LGBT Noise's March for Marriage. And there was a sudden kind of idea that we could effect change, or people suddenly thought, 'Well, I'm going out there to get what I want.'

KIERAN ROSE: A lot of people went on those LGBT Noise marches, and I think they were fantastic in one way. As a mobilisation, I think they were brilliant.

ANNIE HANLON: I left the country for two years so I was very removed from it, but Anna would send me emails the odd time, letting me know about different things going on. I know when the first huge march for marriage happened, I was in France and she sent me an email to let me know about it.

ANNA MCCARTHY: We tried to create more of a social space as well. We felt it's hard for people to engage with the boring kind of legal arguments, the boring political stuff. So when we had the march we said we're going to try to have a barbecue afterwards, we're going to have a night after. I think regardless of what people thought, it was still the place to be, a bit like Pride. So I think from there it brought in people who then became involved and aware of the issues and that just kind of hurtled.

In 2009, LGBT Noise publicised the first March for Marriage, a street protest that would become an annual event. For many gay people, it was the first time they had ventured out on the streets to protest against inequality.

BRIAN FINNEGAN: There was a real sense of fun on that March for Marriage, that particular one was almost like we had two Prides that summer. And people, yes, they've got their banners, but they come out and they're doing that for Pride in a way too … It's very hard to get people really interested in the minutiae of politics. And also to get people to believe that they can effect change politically.

ELOISE McINERNEY: I remember being woken up to take interviews already at 8 a.m. and I hadn't even got out of bed yet so it was pretty insane, but very, very exciting. We'd had the most media coverage ever leading up to a march, so from a week earlier we had already been on the radio, we had already got some pieces in the various national and local newspapers, so we knew that there was a big buzz in the air. We were very excited about what was going to happen. We didn't expect to get as many as we did, which was close to 5,000.

ANNA McCARTHY: There's always this terrible anxiety for the few months beforehand and then there's actually still anxiety up until about five to three, or whatever time it is, and then suddenly people come out of everywhere, and you're just like, 'Thank Jesus!' You're just standing there and it's usually just you and a couple of volunteers and maybe the samba band and you're like, 'Is anybody actually going to come to this? Please!' Then thousands of people show up and it's just when usually like you get up on the stage at the Department of Justice, and you just look down the street, and there's just a sea of people with placards. And every year it kind of increases that there's more children and more families coming and more parents and relatives and all that. Seeing that diversity and the age profile – it's obviously a young crowd, like, but you see an older generation coming as well, increasingly so. It's amazing.

BRENDAN COURTNEY: I became immensely aware of the rights issue. And so that led to the day I spoke at the march … It pricked my conscience to recognise how important it is and what it comes down to it – it's a human right … Speaking at [one of the marches] really made me think. And hearing people like Max speak as well; he's an amazing orator. The real issue for me that day was seeing gay families, gay parents with kids, and how they were expressing their concern about protecting their families. I feel that's a really important thing, and I didn't know the ins and outs of it where the legalities stood, and all the rest, so I went off and found out and so I could talk about it and campaign. It's a no-brainer, isn't it? It's absolutely a just cause. You'd have to be crazy not to be involved in it. The overriding arch for me was I was young, ambitions and a bit of a lazy gay. And all of a sudden I wasn't.

BRIAN FINNEGAN: To go on that march and see so many people from Ailbhe to my contemporaries to the next generation down to kids in their early twenties all marching for that one goal and fully believing that it was their right. And I don't think really there's been many political movements in Ireland that have been so all-encompassing of the generations.

BRIAN SHEEHAN: I remember on the first March for Marriage that a comment from the Department of Justice on the Monday morning was, 'Well, where are the 30,000 people?' The media reported 5,000 people marched for marriage, and the comment was, 'Well, where are the other 30?' 30,000 had marched on Pride. And they were saying there isn't obviously an appetite for marriage in that sense, do you know what I mean?

BUZZ O'NEILL: We marched on the street. And for me that was a hugely important thing; that it wasn't Pride, which is very organised and sanctioned as an event. This was still an impromptu, political march to the Department of Justice. I thought it was really important that we were marching on the street and that in some way we were having an effect or just getting noticed.

The community was also becoming more informed about the legislation and the differences between it and full civil marriage.

RORY O'NEILL: They organised an explanation panel thing in PantiBar. They had Ivana Bacik and Fergus, the barrister. And anybody could come. And that was one of those moments where I thought, 'This is sort of exciting, this feels like something in bloody *Milk*!' I just remember it was absolutely packed with young people who were really engaged and asking questions and wanted to know about things like partnership rights for their Brazilian boyfriends and all that kind of stuff. It was like, 'This feels like a real movement here.' They were super engaged. This was when the level of discussion had actually gone up a notch and it wasn't 'love is equal, let's all get married', it was the real nitty-gritty, where this panel were trying to explain the differences between civil partnership and marriage exactly. It was quite involved. And for whatever, two hours, there were hundreds of 22-year-olds hanging on Ivana Bacik's every word and asking, like, involved questions and I really sort of thought, 'God, this isn't just an excuse to go out on a march and get their picture in the paper. These kids are really actually involved in this now.'

At the Pride parade in Dublin in 2009, one of the most controversial movements within the LGBT community during the movement for marriage equality occurred, confirming a division within those who were advocating for civil partnership with marriage in their sights, and those who viewed civil partnership as a completely dissatisfactory step.

ANNA MCCARTHY: I said to the lads, 'How do you feel if I was to rip up the bill?' And they were like 'Oh. Yeah. Em.' I think one person said, 'Burn it!' Ha! No, no, we can't do that. Just tear it up like, and everyone was like, 'Yeah, let's just do that. Why not?'

TIERNAN BRADY: That felt hard. I sat in that crowd going, 'We worked so hard on this.' Genuinely, everyone in the office worked so hard on this. And we knew it wasn't everything. And we knew our goal was everything, that it would be civil marriage, but that we were utterly convinced that (a) this addressed the real need of people now, (b) this was what was politically achievable now.

KIERAN ROSE: I remember being at that Pride parade where the bill was torn up. I started going on gay pride events and public events down in Cork in early 1980s, and I have never felt more intimidated than I did at that Pride … Ripping up of a bill and the cheering, and GLEN are in the audience and people were so angry and so unreasonable. It was a very, very peculiar situation. It shows you a level of something – emotion – going on. That was the first time that an element of divisiveness was brought into a lesbian and gay Pride parade, because it was always the one time that we put our differences aside and said this is a celebration of being lesbian or gay. Not even at the height of the hunger strikes was that divisiveness brought in.

ANNA MCCARTHY: I didn't think much would kind of come from it. But in the energy of the moment there's 8,000 people around, trying to convey to them what this actually means for them, and that you are a second-class citizen, but now it's enshrined in law, and here's the law. And a couple of people were holding the banners on stage with me and I was like, 'Now we're going to rip up the bill. This is what we think of it. This is an insult to equality,' and all this. And the crowd went nuts. Absolutely nuts. I don't think Pride were too happy with us. They had to pick up all these pieces!

EOIN COLLINS: I remember when the bill was torn up at the famous Pride. That was the only time where I felt actually threatened at a lesbian and gay event. I thought that was terribly sad. And my sister and her kids were there and they left because they felt threatened. Also I felt really sad for a lot of the people with immigration problems who were really just terribly – so hard pressed. People who were literally crying over my desk and who knew this was going to deliver something for them. And then having people just tear up that in front of you.

KIERAN ROSE: I think it was ripping up people's aspirations. I thought it was an incredible thing to do. An incredible lack of human empathy … It mightn't be what you'd want but it was what – as we now see, what thousands of people wanted, needed and were looking forward to. And the kind of – I don't know, how you could just ignore that? And again, I think the arrogance, the arrogance of it, to do that. And again, like, the heat of the moment, was it? But these were savvy people. This isn't some 19-year-old, 18-year-old lesbian or gay man who is coming out and is full of anger and stuff. These are people who had responsible positions in other aspects of their lives. And that was the other thing that amazed me: people who had very high-level positions and responsible positions in society in employment terms. And I was thinking, 'Would you bring the same approach into your workplace or into your professional life? That you'd ignore facts? Ignore reality?'

ELOISE MCINERNEY: I could see why some people, supporters of civil partnership might have been offended and seen it as attacking rights that were very badly needed by certain couples, or that we were attacking the great work that had been done by previous campaigners, so I could see why some people might have taken that perspective. We would still stand by the fact that we believed that we needed a strong rhetoric to really show that this wasn't going to be enough for us. We never made a statement that nobody should have a civil partnership. All we said was this isn't enough, we deserve to have more. Obviously it worked as a radical statement, the fact that Anna ripped up the bill. It meant we did get the media coverage that we were looking for. It did get the debate really out there. So it made people stand up and take notice. If we hadn't done that then I don't think we would have gotten the same coverage that we wanted to get or the same attention.

JEFF DUDGEON: It's become a test amongst young people, young people and progressive people almost. If you're not for gay marriage there's something wrong with you. It's a useful test, but a lot of other people are adhering to it. I'm a wee bit – I don't want to sound like too stuck in the mud, but I'm a bit nervous about people becoming too zealous in their gay campaigning. I think it's what happens when minorities get emancipated; they move along the crest of the wave. And it's a bit like some of all these guesthouses that are being put through the courts for not allowing gay couples to stay and that sort of thing. I don't really think it's necessary to hound people like that, and they could ultimately bite back. But I remember when I was campaigning for the gay law reform, gay people at the time said, 'Why are you doing this? You're just creating trouble. You're just drawing attention to us.' And we laughed at them. Maybe now others would laugh at me.

GENEVIEVE CARBERY, *THE IRISH TIMES*, 29 JUNE 2009: There was dissatisfaction with the Civil Partnership Bill among a larger than expected crowd which marched in the Dublin Pride Parade at the weekend. The city centre was filled with colour, costumes, balloons, music, whistles and chants on Saturday as thousands of members of the lesbian, gay, bisexual and transgender (LGBT) community made their way from the Garden of Remembrance, down O'Connell Street and Dame Street to a rally at Dublin City civic offices. Organisers estimate that 12,000 people took part in the parade. The parade followed the publication of the Civil Partnership Bill by the Government on Friday that will give statutory partnership rights to gay and lesbian couples but stops short of allowing gay and lesbian couples to marry. The bill was compared to an 'apartheid system' by the parade grand marshall, UCD academic and feminist activist Ailbhe Smyth. 'We are not to be insulted and humiliated, we want marriage for lesbians and gays, our goal is equality,' she told the rally. A copy of the bill was ripped up to the cheers of the crowd by Anna McCarthy of protest organisation LGBT Noise. 'Civil partnership will officially make us second-class citizens in the eyes of the law and in the eyes of society,' she said. She urged the crowd to increase lobbying before the bill was debated by the Dáil in the autumn. Parade host Miss Panti (aka Rory O'Neill) spoke of the division in the LGBT community over the Civil Partnership Bill. 'Some think it is a stepping stone to full equality, some disagree and think full equality is the only thing that we can accept, all agree that the proposed bill does not go far enough,' Miss Panti said, urging the community not to become divided because they all had the same goal. 'Anyone can get married in this country except you, any soccer hooligan, any gay basher, any fascist, any murderer, any sex offender can get married, but you cannot,' said Miss Panti. 'Pride and Prejudice' was the theme of the parade with many wearing half a tuxedo or half a wedding dress to symbolise the 'half measures' offered in the bill. Katherine Zappone and Ann Louise Gilligan marched in the dresses they wore for their Canadian wedding in 2003. The couple is awaiting a date for their Supreme Court appeal to a High Court ruling against their claim to have their marriage recognised for the filing of joint tax returns. LGBT groups from Kerry, Waterford and Galway marched alongside members of the gay rugby team the Emerald Warriors, the gay football team the Dublin Devils FC, and LGBT sections of unions and political parties. The Civil Partnership Bill is due to be enacted by the end of the year, the government has said. The rights and obligations include the protection of a shared home, pension rights and the right to succession.

RORY O'NEILL: For some reason I always remember Will St Leger on top of the gates of Leinster House that time. Because there was a fun sort of ACT UP-style quality about that, and it's not the kind of thing Irish protestors get into all. We never had those Fathers for Justice dressed as Batman, we never had that, and there was Will St Leger on top of the pillar, you know? I just kind of thought that sort of stuff was fun and effective in a way.

WILL ST LEGER: Noise ended up being a demonstration organisation that moved people along, perfectly structured, I would never criticise Noise for what they did … The reason we set up Equals was we looked at a graph in a sense. You go to the right and you look at the organisations that were involved in the movement and you have GLEN on one side, who are working the corridors of power, have been there quite a while and are established and funded by the government, that kind of thing. A step over from that you have Marriage Equality who are very, very good advocates and media savvy. Then you have Noise, and Noise were like the people who got everybody out and they made noise and that was fantastic. But what was missing from that chain was a direct-action group. And it's a funny one because Ireland doesn't really have, in a modern sense, a history of non-violent direct action. You know, stuff that gets good media coverage or positive media coverage, it tends to be very negative. Look at Shell to Sea, or something like that – all the things you want to avoid, you know? I had been in

Greenpeace for about five years in the UK. I decided what me and Lisa would do is set up a specific organisation called Equals that would be a direct-action-based organisation. So we don't go out and march, we don't letter-write, we don't do all those things, we just do direct action: hands-on, locks, occupations, that kind of thing. Because it got to that point where we were completely frustrated … We had looked at various buildings that we were going to occupy. One had been the Department for Justice, which we had recced a couple of times. You could pass there during the day and take pictures and stuff like that. I shouldn't be saying this, but it's a bit late now. Anyway, we just felt that inside wouldn't have worked because once you're inside you're away from the media and message … Then we looked at the Dáil and that seemed like the most viable and prominent display.

LISA CONNELL: Basically myself and Will were having conversations and we were like, 'Ok, there's GLEN here, Marriage Equality, Noise. There could be space for something a little more full on.'

WILL ST LEGER: So on the day Lisa stayed over at my place because she's notoriously bad at getting up and I was afraid she'd sleep in. We got up really early, went into town, met up with Buzz O'Neill, who was helping us on the media side. Molly and her girlfriend at the time were our people on the ground. Myself and Lisa had practised down at my work. The plan was we would both go up on the plinth. But the night before, Lisa hurt her knee because she was doing leap-frog on Capel Street Bridge and fell over and hurt her knee. I was livid! How the fuck could you do that the night before? You're supposed to climb a ladder tomorrow! She was like, 'I can't do it!' That is why she did the gates, because originally she was going to go up on top as well; the two of us were going to occupy on top. So anyway, I don't know – stupidly, we had two locks that we brought. One was a bicycle lock, the other one was a really expensive one. It was €75. And we were fucking poor. We had no money to buy this stuff. That was the lock I took up on the plinth. Then we went to Buswells hotel. I was there having a cup of coffee, Buzz was there, Lisa was there, Caroline Kinsella was also helping out because it was her ladder that we borrowed. I had said to her, 'You know, you might not get this ladder back.'

St Leger and Connell made their way to government buildings, masquerading as builders. They distracted the Gardaí and actioned their protest.

WILL ST LEGER: I remember when I was up on the plinth – I remember getting the dirtiest look from Ciarán Cuffe as he wheeled his bike into Kildare Street looking up at me. I think he was really annoyed. I think he said something to media about that, 'It's all very well climbing up there, but this took years to come about' – all this kind of stuff. I was saying to Buzz afterwards, the fucking cheek of them. This is the same party who chained themselves to fucking trees on O'Connell Street because of sparrows when they were not a coalition partner. They had done the exact same thing five years beforehand for trees that had to be replaced. I was like, by the time they even say the words 'Green Party', that many number of trees in South America would disappear. Get the fuck over yourselves. Know what I mean? Green Party, what do they know? I was never in any political party so I had no trust in them, even though I knew them all from my days with Friends of the Earth.

Did Ciarán Cuffe have any memory of that?

CIARÁN CUFFE: No.

BUZZ O'NEILL: When the guards came and he [Will] was going to be arrested – while the two guards go to get Will, Lisa chains herself to the gates with a bicycle lock. They're coming back going, 'Ah Jaysus, lads, we'll have to get the big bolt cutters.' People have done it before; they're well used to it. All very nicely handled. And the arresting guard, as he's putting Will in, I'm with my PR hat running over to do a press release that says, 'He's being currently taken away to …', and I had to ask the guard, 'Where are you taking him? What station?' The guard is like, 'Don't worry about it. He'll be grand, he'll be grand.' I'm saying, 'Can you just tell me, are you Pearse Street? Are you Bridewell?' He goes, 'Are you the boyfriend?' I went 'No. I'm the one trying to do the PR on this thing! Just tell me.' He says, 'Pearse Street.' Grand! That was kind of funny from a sixty-something, almost retired guard from Pearse Street! 'Are you the boyfriend?' Fucking hilarious.

WILL ST LEGER: From being arrested before, the nicest part is after you get arrested, you've been up all day and you've a lot of nervous energy – I always go asleep in the cell. Like a guilty person! An innocent person would stay awake pacing around. A guilty person goes to sleep, like me. I'm fucked!

17

A GLOBAL MOVEMENT

1989

Denmark legalises same-sex unions.

1991

In Hawaii, the landmark case Baehr v. Lewin is initiated, where three same-sex couples argued that a ban on same-sex marriage in the State violated the State's constitution.

1993

Norway provides for registered partnerships.

1994

Sweden creates partnership rights for same-sex couples.

1996

Greenland and Iceland create partnership rights.

In the US the Defense of Marriage Act is enacted, allowing states to refuse to recognise same-sex marriages if they are granted in other states.

1997

The Netherlands brings in partnership rights.

1999

Belgium provides for partnership rights.

France brings in PACS, the civil solidarity pact, as a form of relationship recognition.

2000

The Netherlands becomes the first country to legalise same-sex marriage.

2001

Finland brings in registered partnerships.

2002

Belgium becomes the second country to legalise same-sex marriage.

Ontario, Canada, legalises same-sex marriage.

2004

New Jersey and Maine provide for registered partnerships.

Massachusetts becomes the first US state to legalise same-sex marriage.

Civil Partnership is brought in in the UK.

New Zealand brings in civil unions.

2005

Connecticut provides for civil unions.

Switzerland brings in registered partnership recognition.

Spain becomes the third country to legalise same-sex marriage.

Canada becomes the fourth country to legalise same-sex marriage.

2006

The Czech Republic brings in registered partnerships.

Mexico City provides for civil unions.

South Africa becomes the fifth country to legalise same-sex marriage.

2007

Washington DC, Oregon and New Hampshire provide for same-sex partnerships.

Uruguay brings in civil unions.

2008

California and Connecticut become the second and third US states to legalise same-sex marriage.

Norway becomes the sixth country to legalise same-sex marriage.

Ecuador brings in civil unions.

2009

Sweden becomes the seventh country to legalise same-sex marriage.

Iowa, Vermont, Washington DC and New Hampshire become the fourth, fifth, sixth and seventh US states to legalise same-sex marriage.

Mexico City legalises same-sex marriage.

Hungary provides for registered partnerships.

Nevada, Wisconsin and Washington provide partnership recognition.

Austria brings in registered partnerships.

2010

Portugal becomes the eighth country to legalise same-sex marriage.

Iceland becomes the ninth country to legalise same-sex marriage.

Argentina becomes the tenth country to legalise same-sex marriage.

Civil partnerships are brought into law in Ireland.

2011

The Isle of Man and Jersey bring in civil partnership.

Brazil legislates for civil unions.

Illinois, Hawaii, Rhode Island provide for partnership recognition.

2012

Denmark becomes the eleventh country to legalise same-sex marriage.

Maine, Maryland and Washington become the eighth, ninth and tenth US states to legalise same-sex marriage.

2013

Uruguay becomes the twelfth country to legalise same-sex marriage.

New Zealand becomes the thirteenth country to legalise same-sex marriage.

Rhode Island, Delaware, Minnesota, Hawaii and New Mexico, become the eleventh, twelfth, thirteenth, fourteenth and fifteenth US states to legalise same-sex marriage.

Brazil becomes the fourteenth country to legalise same-sex marriage.

France becomes the fifteenth country to legalise same-sex marriage.

England and Wales become the sixteenth and seventeenth countries to legalise same-sex marriage.

2014

Scotland becomes the eighteenth country to legalise same-sex marriage.

Gibraltar approves civil partnership.

18

POLITICS IN AND OUT OF LEINSTER HOUSE

'Some organisations weren't attuned to the actual realpolitik
of how the fuck were we going to deliver civil partnership.'

– Brian Sheehan

ANNIE HANLON: I remember one day we were called into the Dáil actually. It was the time the Green Party were in coalition with Fianna Fáil. I remember John Gormley had us into the Dáil. I can't remember who was with me. We went in and he basically called in representatives of all the different LGBT rights groups to tell us that they had dropped marriage off their agenda after the election. And that they had no choice; they had to do it because of their power-sharing agreement with Fianna Fáil. I just remember that day, us all feeling like banging our heads off a wall – that finally a party that was actually pro-marriage and had that in their manifesto was now just backtracking and forgetting it, dropping that particular promise as soon as they got into power. That really made us all realise how difficult a battle it was going to be in political terms.

BRIAN SHEEHAN: It was very interesting – [they] called in all the gay groups to the Italian Room in the Taoiseach's Department. You had John Gormley, Eamon Ryan, Ciarán Cuffe and others – Dan Boyle – and they outlined their progress in achieving that. It was a really interesting meeting, a lot of organisations there, and we had met with the Greens [in the] afternoon to talk through how they'd like to ensure they wouldn't sell what had been a very significant gain short and they didn't. But I do remember one person from another LGBT organisation kept asking John Gormley – John Gormley said, 'Look, we've got this, we can build on it, but it's going to take an awful lot of work to get this through our coalition partners, and we need to find the armaments, we need persuasion, we need to maximise this, the civil partnership process, and we have a challenge on our hands to even deliver this.'

JOHN GORMLEY: I honestly don't recall any meetings at that point.

BRIAN SHEEHAN: But somebody, another organisation board member was saying, 'What can we do?' – and they asked the question three times – 'What can we do to make the Greens deliver on their electoral promise?', and it was a really interesting one because I don't think other organisations got the point – that this actually was a huge achievement for the Greens and those in Fianna Fáil pushing for it to deliver civil partnership and that it was going to be a real challenge within the political structure to get civil partnership through cabinet, parliamentary parties, Dáil, and then on into the Seanad. I won't say [who it was]. It wouldn't be fair. I don't think they'd have that position anymore. But it was illustrative of the point that people in some organisations weren't attuned to the actual realpolitik of how the fuck were we going to deliver civil partnership. Even that was still a massive challenge in May/June 2007.

EOIN COLLINS: I think at this stage the division had opened up where I remember one person at the meeting just saying to John Gormley – actually this guy was a senior public servant, but he was saying – a gay guy, saying to John Gormley, 'Tell me, minister, what can we do to embarrass you sufficiently to get marriage into the Programme for Government?' And Gormley just explained everything around the issue of six seats that they had pushed as hard as they could and so there was just not a meeting of minds on that.

JOHN GORMLEY: This was the hardest thing to take. We were actually accused of institutionalising discrimination by some in the LGBT community. They turned it on its head. A real example of 'swift-boating'. Some of them met with me in my clinic in Ringsend and told me that if I introduced this legislation they would never vote for me again. I tried to explain to them that no change comes overnight. Look at the ending of slavery or giving the vote to women. It has always been incremental. I also felt that the Labour Party were manipulating these groups for political purposes.

EAMON RYAN: The Labour Party would have been seen as similarly interested, in fairness, in relation to the gay rights issue. To a certain extent, you're often looking at how it's perceived politically. From a Labour Party perspective, they wanted to be saying we were selling out, we're yellow, not green. It was part of a wider narrative in government. It's used politically to say to certain constituencies, 'Don't vote for those people, vote for us.' So I think there was a political element as well. That's just the way things are.

GRÁINNE HEALY: I think Ciarán Cuffe, because he had an equality brief, he was the one who felt our criticisms most painfully I think. He really wanted us to do as GLEN had done and say, 'Ok, grand, and we're all 100 per cent and this is hunky dory and we're all for it.' We said, 'No Ciarán, we can't do that. We're holding the line that it's equality.' And that means sometimes when we go to things and we speak as has happened at an event – I remember in the Hilton hotel where I said I was really disappointed that the Greens weren't holding the equality line and that they were settling. And he was furious, really furious, lost his temper.

CIARÁN CUFFE: It was frustrating. It was frustrating to take part in Pride and realise – I can't remember what year it was – there was a lot of Pride participants that were against civil partnership. But then again a lot of the gay and lesbian community did recognise it. And the facts speak for themselves that hundreds of couples have opted for civil partnership, so you have to wield your way through the different voices that are there.

GRÁINNE HEALY: I think he felt that once they were in power – and John Gormley would have had a touch of that as well – they found it very difficult to accept any criticism. Anybody who would have been a supporter – and I would have been a supporter of the Greens, never a member of the party, but I would have supported them and I would have done work with the party over the years – I think they just [thought], 'Now that we're in and we're doing our best, everybody just has to accept that and go with it.' I'm a huge supporter of the good things Labour have done over the years, I'm not a member of the party, but I'll say good things about Gilmore when he says it, but I'll also have to be able to say, 'I don't think you're doing the right thing.' So he [Cuffe] almost took it as a personal criticism in some ways, which the criticism was never meant as.

It was meant as: you're in power, we understand that you say that's as much as you can get, but that doesn't mean that we have to stop saying it's not enough.

During the progress of the legislation, a division appeared to occur between the Green Party and Fianna Fáil. From the outside, it seemed as though a Minister for Justice, Dermot Ahern, was perceived to be dragging his heels on the bill, while the Greens were exerting pressure to push it through.

CIARÁN CUFFE: I took it upon myself to meet on several occasions with the Ministers for Justice to progress various issues, and probably the most substantial one was to progress civil partnership. The nature of government is that the squeaky wheel gets the oil. In other words, things progress when there's political pressure for them to be progressed. You've a Programme for Government that might have fifty pages of issues, but the stuff that the partners in government decide to progress moves faster than other things. And I was aware from the earliest stage, our view was that the government would not last the full term and that we needed to progress certain legislation early on if we were to be successful.

DERMOT AHERN: He [Ciarán Cuffe] used to contact us and try to allege that we were dragging our heels on it, and that he was pushing us all the time. It wasn't that simple to be honest. They wanted it that simple, but it wasn't that simple. At the end of the day, particularly in Justice, every piece of legislation you pass, the Attorney General has to completely vet it and be happy. The Attorney General is at cabinet, so if I bring a piece of legislation to cabinet, I don't want the Attorney General coming up and saying, 'Excuse me, that's a load of horse shit, I didn't approve this.' So I had to be sure the Attorney General and anyone that he had advising him was happy.

CIARÁN CUFFE: I always felt I had to convince Brian [Lenihan] of the importance of this issue. Dermot Ahern was much more businesslike, probably less enthusiastic than Brian Lenihan – if that were possible – of the concept. So they were – I wouldn't say fraught, but they were tense meetings to seek progress on these issues. Sometimes with officials present, sometimes not. But I think Fianna Fáil would have been quite happy for the issue to have dragged on until 2011 or 2012, had they had their way.

DERMOT AHERN: They used to make out it was their baby and they had the complete monopoly on it. They would have said that was their big thing, big ticket item. I didn't want in any way to disabuse them of that or take any limelight away. I just did my job and I passed the legislation. In fairness it was sometimes made out our party were dragged kicking and screaming to do it. We weren't.

CIARÁN Ó CUINN: Well, look, number one, it was in the Fianna Fáil manifesto. So before the Programme for Government, before the Greens and Fianna Fáil ever dreamt about going into government together, it was in the Fianna Fáil manifesto. It was in the Programme for Government, that's fine. Ciarán Cuffe as a backbencher TD wouldn't have known anything about the AG's advice. Well, Gormley would have briefed him, I suppose. From my perspective, very early in Dermot's time in Justice, John Gormley gave a speech – I don't know what it was at, a GLEN annual report or something, but the text was sort of patronising, very much, 'Fianna Fáil don't want to do this, but we will make it happen.' Now an early draft of the text came over that was very badly drafted, just wasn't great, wasn't diplomatic at all. And what was actually happening was this was a very serious piece of law. It was taking time. And there was a lot of time being taken up in the parliamentary draftsman's office and the AG's office. That's what it was. That's all it was. But I remember seeing that speech and remember thinking my job was to make this happen and make sure it got through the Dáil and make sure it got through in the period of government. The Greens, I think, wanted to use this piece of legislation as a badge of honour to show 'The Greens in Government' and 'The Greens' Social Agenda'. And that's fine. Fair play to them. But you know, wanting to show how great you are and having a fight at Fianna Fáil's expense isn't always the best way to get something in through the Dáil. It's not always the best way of getting things done. So my whole attitude when that happened, and I'd been through this before in Northern Ireland communications and energy affairs, you just go, 'Look, I'm not going to play that game.' So I basically said we're not playing that game, and we just did it at our own pace, told them whatever we had to do whenever we had to, but just didn't let people play those sort of games with it. Like, Ciarán Cuffe and Co. are good people, but what did they expect Fianna Fáil to do? To say, 'We don't want to do this'? Or 'We're doing this because the Greens are making us do it'? I never saw the problem. Some of them are very bitter.

EAMON RYAN: The two gates of government buildings: one is the Attorney General's looking over, and the other is Finance. They're the two powers in government. And Paul Gallagher, he's not a soft touch, legally, when you're engaged in legal argument with him. Even at that time with Brian Lenihan, where we felt with Brian we had a similar-thinking person who was pushing it through reasonably quickly in a kind of creative enough sort of way, it's still not easy. It became slower with Dermot and maybe that's because it takes a certain time to draft complex legislation, but our relationship wouldn't have been as good, without disparaging the guy. It just would have been a slightly different perspective.

CIARÁN Ó CUINN: They liked the idea of having Dermot as they saw a very conservative sort of fella, or a socially conservative fella, who they could 'force' civil partnership on. But that didn't happen. If they have a narrative or had a narrative in their head of making that happen, that's fair enough, but at the end of the day, that's political and it's not actually what happened.

DERMOT AHERN: Anyone who painted me as being conservative was wrong. I've particular views in relation to things. I have a view in relation to abortion because I always used to say, 'It's very simple. I've adopted children. Need I say anymore?' That's my attitude. Here's me, here's my wife; we would take any amount of children as adoptive parents. So to say that I'm ultra-conservative is wrong. It's wrong to paint anyone, but there's nothing I can do about that.

EAMON RYAN: Just different outlook. Different philosophy. I got on with the guy. I wouldn't be critical of him since. But just by nature different. By nature he'd have a more conservative outlook, I think. And that's fine. That's his right. But it would be slightly different to our own – very different. The interesting question [was] in terms of would it have gone through or not? There is a tendency in FF not to divide. But, I mean, for us it was important. Particularly because the further on we went into government, we were under huge pressure and huge difficulty. We *needed* wins. And civil partnership we would have seen as one of the bigger wins that we could get. So it was important for us and it was a frustrating experience for us in terms of what we saw as a slowing-down of the process. And that would have created a fair bit of tension … Ach, just, there are various mechanisms. You have the mechanism of cabinet, and you've back-up teams. You've got teams who are there to smooth the process of dealing with civil service, dealing with agendas of the Programme for Government implementation. That back-up team would have been fighting fairly continuously in terms of, 'Where is it? Where are the provisions? Where's the next stage?' And the Department of Justice are not an easy one to fight with. They tend to be more secretive than other departments, more conservative than other departments. And they've got so much legislation in play. If you look at who has got what on the legislative bill, it's a huge amount. So they can slightly play, 'Oh, well, we've got this one. Criminals are running through the country with handguns, we have to put a handgun piece of billing.' Whatever. So the ordering of legislation and the delivery of it, unless you're controlling that department yourself, you don't have control over the process. You're relying on the minister and you have to trust the minister if he's saying, 'I'm going as fast as I can.' You can't reasonably go directly into the department and instruct the officials to go faster or do things differently. So with Justice it would have been one of our greatest points of tension, or ongoing negotiations – and more at that support-team level because that's where a lot of the work is done. If it gets to around cabinet, and then you've a real problem, again it would have been largely John [Gormley] driving that because as party leader in cabinet, his job is to negotiate if there are differences that he has to negotiate with the Taoiseach: 'Ok, where is it?' Whereas I would've tended to be a line minister, you know, there are certain areas I would have taken responsibility for, but other areas it would be heads of government, the Taoiseach with the head of our party. So I think John would have had fairly protracted negotiations with Brian Cowen to get Dermot Ahern to move quicker.

JOHN GORMLEY: We never got the impression that Justice was enthusiastic for this legislation. Lenihan seemed amenable. He shared a constituency with Roderic [O'Gorman]. Roderic felt he was a good listener.

CIARÁN CUFFE: We didn't control the Department of Justice, but my strong view would be that legislation wouldn't have happened but for the Green Party's presence in government. Now I would say that, wouldn't I? But my exposure to two Justice Ministers who had responsibility for it, I didn't detect any great enthusiasm for it from either of them.

SUZY BYRNE: It wasn't the Greens that got any of the credit for what happened. Dermot Ahern came out glowing, because he had been set up by GLEN even to be so.

JOHN HANAFIN: If the Greens hadn't looked for it, it just wouldn't have happened.

DERMOT AHERN: I mean, in fairness, Kieran Rose and those gave credit where credit was due. It's not a matter of claiming credit anyway. I did a job. I was asked to do a job. I saw it through. I didn't rush it, but equally so I didn't play politics with it. Basically Kieran Rose and his organisation came out and thanked me. When I announced I wasn't going forward in 2011, the first people who came out and issued a statement wishing me well and thanking me was Kieran Rose. And I do appreciate that. And they've been extremely complimentary to me ever since.

DAN BOYLE: We felt very badly about it because we did all the pushing. The work with the officials, with Ahern, would have been done by Ciarán Cuffe with the parliamentary party and Roderick O'Gorman as a party official who had a personal interest in the subject. They would have done far more work than anyone in Fianna Fáil on the issue. A lot of it was overcoming obstruction on the part of the Department of Justice officials and Dermot Ahern himself. It was a Green Party initiative having it secured in the Programme for Government and making sure it was delivered upon in a way that Fianna Fáil were not giving any energy towards.

SUZY BYRNE: But where you might have in other coalition governments the smaller party coming out victorious in something, the Greens didn't. They tried, saying, 'Without us this wouldn't have happened', but it was definitely 'This legislation was on Fianna Fáil's terms'. The Greens suffered a lot. They didn't have the spin or the ability to market the stuff as well. They got a lot of the pressure and none of the credit.

19

WON'T SOMEBODY THINK OF THE CHILDREN?

'It's idiotic that you can say, "Well, of course you can be nearly married, but we're just not going to do anything about the children.""

— Ailbhe Smyth

As the legislation was progressing, one of the most contentious issues was the absence of children from the Civil Partnership Bill.

CIARÁN Ó CUINN: It was very simple. There was Attorney General advice that said you couldn't include children. That was it. We didn't lobby, we didn't do anything. It was very early in Dermot's time that was received and there it was. That shaped the perimeters of the debate. We were open about that. That was said at every stage in the Dáil ... So I presume the AG was just being very careful on it just to make sure that didn't happen and you'd need a referendum. The AG was very clear. To avoid that happening you'd need to create very clear differences between it and marriage, between civil partnership and marriage. If at a stage in the future the people wanted to vote on marriage, that was fine, but you did need a referendum for that. That was the position. It's a very legalistic position, but that was the position.

SANDRA IRWIN-GOWRAN: We organised a joint seminar with the Children's Rights Alliance, under Jillian van Turnhout – she was the CEO at the time – and Fergus Ryan did a presentation at it and it was around the impacts of the Civil Partnership Bill, as it was then, in relation to children of same-sex couples. At the time we were kind of disappointed with the turnout at the event. Key children's organisations were there, but they weren't there really at a high official level. It kind of seemed like there wasn't – there certainly wasn't the groundswell of support now that there was back then.

JILLIAN VAN TURNOUT: The role for me, certainly when I was Chief Executive of the Children's Rights Alliance, was to always ensure that the children's voices are heard. When we looked at the Civil Partnership Bill, children were absent and notably absent from the bill, which I understood at the time was important because it allowed the Civil Partnership Bill to progress. But, you know, children are not absent from families and families come in all different types of forms in Ireland. So for us it was important to look at what the issues that faced children from a children's perspective. Most times when we look at these issues, we look at them from an adult's perspective. People talk about your right to adopt, which is not a right. You don't have a right to adopt. A child has a right to be adopted, but as an adult you don't have that right. For us we felt it was important that maybe we looked at and explored some of the issues without us coming down on one side or another or one perspective or another. So if your child is ill, parents being able to have access to medical attention, where the child will want the person who has cared for them to be by their bedside. To be told that you're not a family member and therefore you can't be by the bedside? You know those are some very real issues. Succession is an issue that comes up again and again. And then the day-to-day normality about signing forms for schools. So what we were trying to do was try and make it into a more normal everyday occurrences where the issues were being faced by children … well, in reality, and what we did say was that children were absent from the bill. So the bill was looking at the adults, which is understandable and we understood that certainly in our discussions with GLEN, that it was a step on the way to progress. I am a believer that change is incremental. We don't tend to go for the big wallop decision and take a big leap forward as a society when you're trying to bring legislative change about. So I understood, but it meant that there were issues that remained unanswered. And, I suppose, essentially at that time, I can understand why they were unanswered. If you look at how we're all hardwired, from going to school – all the books we would have read would have been 'mammy, daddy' and 'your average family', a 'typical family'. And the reality is from my work with the Children's Rights Alliance, there rarely is a typical family. You can add mammy and daddy, but one or either parent might not be as active in the family, may not be playing such a strong role. Every family is different. And certainly for me, I used to say my definition of a family was to ask a child to draw a picture and whoever they included – and children will sometimes include their grandparents, friends and neighbours – whoever they feel, is that family. And if they feel secure, educated, loved in a caring environment, I'm not going to challenge that definition of a family. That, I think for me personally, helped me to become comfortable with the issue of marriage equality.

MARIE MULHOLLAND: I thought it was a step in the right direction, but I thought the important parts were left out, which were around children's rights and the rights for gay families. In a sense civil partnership was very much about gay men with some assets. It was framed in that way. It had GLEN's imprints all over it, because that's what their priorities were.

TIERNAN BRADY: It was always the huge gap. I mean, it's the challenge to accept a certain level of change on the basis that we're going to build on it. At the time we said very clearly – every press statement we ever put out said, 'Our goal is marriage, the biggest gap in this bill is in relation to children and families, but this is a massive step forward, so we're going to bank it.' And we always knew that was going to be hard because the minute you start banking the incremental wins, you're going to get pummelled for what wasn't delivered in that step. And we did. We got pummelled.

AILBHE SMYTH: It's idiotic that you can say, 'Well, of course you can be nearly married, but we're just not going to do anything about the children basically.' And the reality is that lesbians and gay men have children, one way or another, in more diverse ways perhaps than straight people have children, but there still are children and they still need to come within the ambit of family law and our families still need to be recognised. It's deeply unjust and actually also crazy that they're not. Is it saying there are two kinds of children or is it saying there are two kinds of parent? If it's saying there are two kinds of parent, the law shouldn't say that. And if it's saying there are two kinds of children, it's against the constitution. And it definitely shouldn't be saying that!

COLM O'GORMAN: The major issue for me was that the State was going to legislate to create family insecurity for children for the first time – clearly, wilfully, consciously legislate to do that. Because the State sanctions and under its laws was open even at that stage to sanctioning the adoption of children by LGBT people but they could only adopt as single adoptive parents, not as couples because they weren't married. As I said repeatedly at the time, to ministers and others, you are now consciously developing a legislative model that writes in discrimination against the children whose adoption the State will sanction. You're going to write in a model that enshrines family insecurity for those children. So that was one of my major issues, that it didn't in any way seek to address the needs of children being parented in families that were headed by same-sex couples. And I just thought that was an appalling cowardice, actually, politically.

20

CIVIL PARTNERSHIP:
THE VOTE

'My concern was that I wasn't being authentic and
true to myself and to those around me who knew
my position and who knew who I was.'

– Jerry Buttimer

In the summer of 2010, with the Irish economy in free fall, the Civil Partnership Bill
was about to make its way through the houses of the Oireachtas.

DERMOT AHERN: I recall this. I had a decision to make coming up to
a summer break. Normally the Dáil rises on 6 July. I had two options.
Either I guillotine it and finish it before 6 July or the first week in July,
or else I put it back until September. The boys had organised meetings in the parliamentary party and I think about twenty people had
turned up in the parliamentary party meeting, like a subcommittee
of the parliamentary party, but basically it was organised by Labhráa
Ó Murchú, Jim Walsh, and whoever the other one was. And I used to
be told who was at the meetings and I'd think, 'Jaysus, I can't believe
so-and-so, or so-and-so is at the meeting, that they're part of an
opposition to this.'

SANDRA IRWIN-GOWRAN: There was the whole backwoodsman revolt in
Fianna Fáil at the time where people were running scared.

TIERNAN BRADY: A petition went around, which Jim Walsh was part of,
and I think it was twenty-eight people signed it. It was an innocuous
sentence about 'we believe in family values', but it was absolutely aimed

at civil partnership … We went in and engaged again on that. One of the things that happened as we engaged on it and people started saying, 'Hold on, this isn't as innocuous thing; this is about civil partnership, this is an attack on government policy.' TDs started to back away from it, openly back away from it. I had senators and TDs phone me up saying, 'I didn't know what I was signing. I thought this was apple pie! It's all lovely! Are you in favour of sunshine? Yes, of course I'm in favour of sunshine!' So when they realised it was about more, and the fact that they were phoning to say, 'We're jumping ship on this. I'm sorry we signed this. I didn't mean to sign this,' it was a sign to us that they know government is going to push this through because they don't want to be on the wrong side of their government. And they don't want to look like they've caused trouble for their own government.

EOIN COLLINS: Jim Walsh had got a number of senators to sign up to a letter saying they would oppose CP. So we got to meet them. It was funny. David Quinn and Iona were in before us making their pitch. So we were talking to them on the way out. I just laugh at that now when I hear that Iona say they were supportive of civil partnership … We just nodded at them going in and they nodded at us awkwardly. So we went in and made our pitch.

JOHN GORMLEY: I recall that letter. I have a clearer memory of a bishop intervening, telling elected reps how to vote. This annoyed me. I spoke on the radio at the time, and David Quinn attacked me. Breda O'Brien, for whom I have respect, was also critical of me. I've always believed in 'Render unto Caesar what is Caesar's and unto God what is God's.'

BRIAN SHEEHAN: Now we've never seen the letter, and I couldn't swear there was thirty, but that was what our information was and we knew this was an absolutely disaster if we're going to have problematic dissent into a division with Fianna Fáil. We knew the bill was going nowhere because it was a very sizeable number of TDs and senators in a rocky coalition government. And we went back on *Morning Ireland* and, in the way we always had, you appeal to the best of each party. So in Fianna Fáil it was the republican principles, and basically Kieran was on *Morning Ireland* saying, 'Look, in the true

Fianna Fáil tradition of republicanism, this is about equal citizenship for all citizens.'

KIERAN ROSE: We love-bombed them … and then out of that came GLEN being 'the Oscar Wilde Cumann' of Fianna Fáil.

BRIAN SHEEHAN: Apparently it was the winning broadcast because the letter went away then.

CIARÁN Ó CUINN: There was some letter going around that apparently forty TDs had signed in opposition to this. I went and spoke to loads of them and said, 'Look, it's not marriage; it's this, this and this. If it goes to marriage, that will need a referendum of the people and people would have to just agree or disagree.' And they were happy with that; that was fine. There was no problem.

DERMOT AHERN: I was a little bit worried that if I left it over to September, there would be a sort of snowballing effect of opposition to it. So my gut instinct – like, I was a former whip in the early '90s, so I sort of knew – what do you do? Do you go for it? Do you guillotine it? The Greens were sort of pushing us to finish it, but I didn't want to be accused by my own party of curtailing. Oh yeah, and Bertie had given an agreement that everyone would have their say and that there would be no *'uisce faoi thalamh'* stuff, that anyone who wanted their say would have their say. And I was worried that if it went over to September, those people who were against it, as always in politics – events, you can't control events, and maybe something would happen over the summer.

In July 2010, the Civil Partnership Bill finally faced a vote in both the Dáil and the Seanad. In the Dáil, the bill passed without a vote, given that it was a government bill supported by all parties.

GERARD HOWLIN: That's not a healthy thing by the way. That was not a healthy thing. Because the fact is that there are significant numbers of people in this country who do not agree and they're entitled to their opinion in a democracy and you can't have suffocating majoritarianism replacing another and claiming it's progress.

CIARÁN CUFFE: There are snakes in the long grass who know when to have a fight and when to retreat.

CHARLIE FLANAGAN: In my own speech on the bill, I specifically stated that this was a stepping stone or that it was a prelude towards marriage equality. Yeah, welcoming the bill, 'Change is incremental. And I hope that full equality is not far away.' Now you could say that a politician seeking full equality in 2010, you know, is probably not doing a great service to the State or the people. I mean, full equality should be a given, or certainly full equality of opportunity should be a given. But having regard to the country being characterised by oppression, patriarchy, dogmatism, and the rigid and domineering brand of Roman Catholicism, with an inflexible set of social rules that meant that one either had to conform or move aside, that this background is important.

While the bill was being debated, there were protests outside government buildings by members of the LGBT community who were dissatisfied with the bill.

SANDRA IRWAN-GOWRAN: I remember when the bill was being debated in the Dáil, there was a protest organised outside the Dáil. There was a couple there with their child holding it up, waving it at us with – not anger – with venom. I was probably white with rage because I just felt that people didn't understand that it wasn't a case of saying, 'Oh yeah, no, we're not going to have the children, thanks very much, we'll leave that for another day.' You know what I mean? This was the best possible, as far as I'm concerned anyway, the best possible – 'option' is the wrong word – the best possible scenario for that given time. When you're working in an organisation that is actively lobbying and engaging with the TDs and the Senators who are going to pass this bill, I think you're kind of more aware of the realities of the 'How is this going pass or not?'

EOIN COLLINS: I think it was December 2009. There was a huge protest that LGBT Noise had outside and there were people screaming at us going in. One woman I remember screaming saying that civil partnership was worse than the Nuremberg Laws.

MURIEL WALLS: I was in the Dáil the night it passed and it was just magical, absolutely magic to be there, and have lots of other gay and lesbian kids, 16- and 17-year-olds from BelongTo listening to the speeches. And of course there was all these things around the Dáil saying 'SILENCE' and when the thing passed, sure everybody just erupted in cheers, hugging.

JOHN GORMLEY: I sat beside Dermot Ahern. I praised the minister and said it was a proud moment for the Greens. I looked up into public gallery and saw the happy faces of activists and gay couples whom I knew. It was a brief good moment in what had become a very difficult time for us.

The bill moved on to the Seanad. Seventy-seven amendments were proposed, and a heated, emotional debate took place.

DERMOT AHERN: But the problem was it had already passed in the Dáil and there wasn't any opposition amongst the parliamentary party in the Dáil from Fianna Fáil. It was in the Senate. That's where the opposition was. And the Attorney General was sort of saying to me, 'If you finish it before the summer, the problem is,' he said to me, 'without a shadow of doubt, this will be referred under Article 26 of the constitution by the president to the Supreme Court to test its constitutionality.' He said, 'I've gone so far legally in this that, you know, there's clearly a possibility that it's gone past the issue of marriage' – you know, the constitutional protection on the family. He said, 'I've gone so far, I've no doubt it'll be challenged, it'll be subject, it'll be referred.' So he said, 'If you pass it before the summer break, it'll be referred immediately, sent up to the Park, the President will call a Council of State, and refer it to the Supreme Court.' He said, 'You'll piss off the Supreme Court judges, all of whom will be required not to go on holidays.' These are all the practical things you have to think of. So I had that decision. Do I go for it? Or do I leave it over until September? In the end I decided to go for it, even if it meant the judges not being too happy with me, and hoping that if they did sit on it, they would say that it is constitutional.

IVANA BACIK: I was in the Seanad by the time Civil Partnership Bill came through from Fianna Fáil and the Greens, and I do remember while I think it had unanimous support in the Dáil, in the Seanad there was a rump of Fianna Fáilers, along with Senator Rónán Mullen, who took a very strongly opposed view to it. So there were people who had not shifted at all. But the middle ground had clearly shifted by then. And by then, I remember David Norris talking on the record in the Seanad about how he felt that civil partnership was no longer enough, and he was tempted to vote against it, that he felt the whole debate had moved on because of the foot-dragging of the government over bringing in civil partnership, the debate had shifted to marriage equality. I think he was right about that. At the same time, you know, I was glad when he and all of us did support the Civil Partnership Bill as a stepping stone.

DAN BOYLE: I think it was important that the debate got aired. I didn't think it did elsewhere. It didn't in the Dáil. It didn't in the wider media either. I think one of the effects of that is that the tail end of a conservative Christian criticism of this type of social policy – I'm not sure how you treat it to be honest. They don't do themselves any favours because they feel kind of isolated, but at the same time, I feel a bit guilty about the illiberalism that's not allowing the debate to play out properly and effectively. I believe in marriage equality, I believe it's going to happen, but I believe it should also undergo a proper process of public debate.

DAVID NORRIS: That bill was amended by some of my colleagues, a very small group of colleagues, sadly including Fergal Quinn, which rather surprised me. I wasn't a bit surprised by Rónán Mullen or Jim Walsh, or even Labhrás Ó Murchú, although on other issues he's very good in terms of human rights, and he's a very fine speaker. Hanafin? He was always a rather vague presence, and he also spoke fairly moderately even when taking an extreme position, and I knew the family, and was completely opposed to what his father stood for, but his father was very gentlemanly, a nice old thing. Des Hanafin. I got on terribly well with Des, liked him, and he was a bit mischievous too.

JOHN HANAFIN: Why I in particular had voted against the Civil Partnership Bill was because it wasn't all-inclusive. I was very surprised that those who were looking for rights didn't look for those same rights for people who were not in a gay conjugal relationship; brothers, sisters, two lifelong friends who had lived together who wished to form a civil partnership. There was no call for them. And the impression was given that we were still trying to hold a view that would restrict people. In actual fact, we would all have supported it in my view, and reading the Seanad reports, if it had been all-inclusive, not wishing to discriminate against anybody ... My concern was I was anxious that it was going to put a gay and lesbian relationship on a higher footing than two friends who had lived together or siblings who didn't have the same values, or didn't have the same benefits and that was a drawback for me.

DAVID NORRIS: Anyway I wasn't so offended by that but I was offended terribly by the nature of the amendments they put down, which were all supposed to be 'conscience clauses', which would allow confectioners or hairdressers or the renters of premises or the printers of stationary or florists to refuse to grant their services if they thought they were gay. I mean, that's apartheid! Absolutely straight from South Africa. And utterly against the Gospels. I try not to bleat about it very much, but I am a believer and I go to church every single Sunday, and it means a lot to me, and I know the Bible inside out, which is one of the Church of Ireland traits, you know, that you always had Sunday school and all these readings every Sunday and all this half a dozen readings from the Bible, so I know it pretty well. And I can quote it, and so I quoted it back at them, and I was very surprised in some of the votes they kept calling for repetitive votes on the same thing. There was a classic attempt to talk the bill down, to filibuster it. I just felt that was pretty awful ... There was another one that said that if a counselling agency felt there was a conflict with his religious ethos, it could refuse to permit counselling for same-sex couples. Well, that's very shocking to my mind. What about the Good Samaritan? The Good Samaritan was from a very different religious context and there was hostility between the Jews and the Samaritans, and yet the Good Samaritan went across the road, helped the injured man, led him to an inn, paid his expenses in advance and said he'd be back in a week's time to see how he was. And yet what they were saying was, if a gay couple break up, we just simply withdraw, stand aside, and say, 'With the help of Jaysus, maybe they'll break up within the next week or two.' That's disgusting. They're entitled to be disgusting inside their own 'religious ethos' in inverted commas, whatever their ethos is, and I'm very suspicious of these ethoses, whether they're Catholic or Protestant or anything else, especially when there's State money involved. Then I think it a form of oppression that my tax money should be used to help fund an organisation that would not give people like me any assistance because of their discriminatory attitudes. Fine if they want to do that, but let them do that with their own money. It was fairly heated.

AVERIL POWER: I remember just thinking it was crazy. I just thought it was a bit nuts … I hadn't expected when people were arguing in all seriousness that they thought the relationship between a brother and a sister was the same as a relationship between a lesbian couple or a gay couple. I just can't relate to that on any level. I can't understand how people can miss the basic fact that there's a difference between an intimate loving relationship and a familial relationship or a friendship or anything else. I just didn't understand any of those debates. I suppose at the time there would have been a little bit of worry that the government might cave on the legislation or they might take on board those amendments but thankfully they didn't. They stuck with it and they pushed it through, and they were only a minority … But that seemed to be getting some traction or at least was in the debate for a while.

JOHN HANAFIN: If we hadn't supported the Equality Bill, they might not understand where we were coming from, but we had. So therefore all they had to do was add two and two. 'Are you against gays?' Well, no actually, definitely not. You know. And that's the reality. The proof is there. If they really want to see what we were thinking, read what was actually said. Because I come from a particular perspective on it doesn't make me wrong, it just means I've a different view.

JOHN HANAFIN, SECOND-STAGE SEANAD DEBATES, 7 JULY 2010: Last week, the European Court of Human Rights ruled that gay marriage is not a human right. Moreover, California, which is associated with Hollywood, flower power and Arnold Schwarzenegger, recently voted against gay marriage. That is the future … Those who regard opponents of the bill as negative are wrong. Truly inclusive civil partnership would include all couples in caring dependent relationships, including same-sex couples, cohabiting couples and individuals in caring relationships which are non-sexual, and give such persons rights that would protect them against economic vulnerability in the event of a break-up ... There is no doubt that the bill should provide protection for religious organisations and individuals who conscientiously object to facilitating events and services where such conflict with their religious ethos. We will recommend that the Government accepts the conscience clause proposed by the two Church of Ireland bishops. It is worded in such a way that the unintended consequences feared by some cannot occur. What do I mean by the words 'unintended consequences'? This morning, I walked through the grounds of Christ Church, a beautiful Presbyterian church on Rathgar Road. I was taught how one should dance properly in a hall located under the roof of the church. It would be unfair to ask to hold a civil ceremony breakfast or celebration in this hall, located as it is within Church grounds, if the Church authorities are unwilling to do so.

AVERIL POWER: I find it hard to take those arguments seriously. So they're either completely missing the point of what a loving relationship is about and what commitment is about and what they would expect between themselves and their wife and themselves and their husband, and the relationships that other people have. So they're either missing that point and they don't get the importance of intimacy and love and commitment in that sense, and the difference between that and other types of relationships that we have with our friends or our families or our parents or everybody else, or they're trying to deflect and just trying to throw in kind of random things. One of the things that struck me at the Constitutional Convention was sometimes, I think, that they get that they've lost the point, that they've conceded some kind of point, and then they're thinking, 'What are the things we can claw back?' Some of that seemed to me in civil partnership legislation – the amendments that were put down were like, 'Ok, so we'll give them civil partnership, but how can we demean it as much as possible? How can me make sure that they won't really be sure, when they apply for somebody to celebrate the partnership, that they won't be sure that the registrar won't turn them down as a conscientious objection? How can we make sure that when they ring a florist that they will wonder if the florist will give them the flowers? How can we make it as difficult as possible for people?' So yes, you give them a legal right to partnership but you put in place every possible obstacle and every possibly uncertainty to kind of try to strip away its meaning as much as possible or make it as uncomfortable as you can.

DAVID NORRIS: I was originally going to vote against it myself … I had found myself in the same situation with the decriminalisation bill. I told them I wasn't voting for it because they tacked in various things, including rather nasty provisions to control prostitution. And I said I do not want my freedom at the expense of other vulnerable people. Because you see this is all to show how goodie-goodie they were, because you let the aul fairies off on an old ramble, but you control the tarts and make their lives miserable. It's a sop to the right wing, and I think that's disgusting. When I heard the things that were said and when I saw the amendments I said to myself, 'I will not go into the lobby with these people who have put down these amendments and vote against the bill.' I couldn't. And I said I will have to go shoulder-to-shoulder with all the different parties because it's a historic day and I will be included. I've registered my protest and I'm going to push on this issue, and I'm going to push for full marriage.

TIERNAN BRADY: David Norris had made a strong speech against at the time and there was a lot of pressure in the lobby – not pressure, gentle discussion with David from all parties. At the time they couldn't understand why he was against this, because they're coming at it from the other angle. And he was right to hold, and explaining what equality was, but taking the sense of 'I can't be for this'.

JERRY BUTTIMER: At the time my biggest memory of that bill was that David Norris was going to vote against it early on, and I remember myself and Joe O'Toole pleading with him, not that he needed pleading in the end, but to ask him to make sure he didn't vote against it. Because he recognised it wasn't the be-all or the end-all, but that it was a stepping stone. It was, as I say, an incremental point on the journey … It would have been more authentic for myself to be out, but I made a decision that it wasn't about me.

DAVID NORRIS, SECOND-STAGE SEANAD DEBATES, 7 JULY 2010: Let me be clear about one thing. There is nothing visionary in the legislation, nor is there anything revolutionary about it. An historic opportunity has been missed. From being among the leaders, we are now among the laggards of Europe in this regard, falling behind not only the Netherlands and all the Scandinavian countries but even Catholic Spain, which has introduced full civil marriage for same-sex couples without society falling apart. This legislation does not grant equality; it merely improves the second-class status of gay people in some practical ways ... The first and foremost important of my reservations regarding the bill is the complete abdication by its drafters of moral responsibility for the welfare of children ... Let us be clear about the facts and cut through the deliberate and misleading obfuscation that has been created by elements within a number of Christian traditions. First, children can and already have been adopted by gay people. They can only be adopted singly, however, which means quite starkly that if the legally adopting parent dies, the surviving parent who has helped to rear, nourish and parent the child is instantly cut off in the legal sense. Much worse than that, the child himself or herself has no connection with the surviving parent and is cast adrift. What is this except child abuse? Let no one say this was done unawares for I and others have made the situation very clear. Even the Roman Catholic Church has abolished limbo and yet the State of Ireland, with this legislation, has brought it back again for a minority of our most vulnerable children ... Gay people cannot marry, but murderers, child abusers, burglars, bank robbers, ex-priests and ex-nuns can marry. I, a member of this House in good standing, have no such right.

But it was Norris' previous use of the term 'dog licence' that really irked those who supported the Civil Partnership Bill.

CIARÁN CUFFE: David Norris was there saying that it was just a glorified dog licence, so you had to engage with a war on two fronts: detractors who said it wasn't worth the paper it was printed on, and realise that within yourself it wasn't what you wanted, but it was an incremental change that would result in greater recognition of same-sex relationships, and I thought that was worth doing. We all did.

KIERAN ROSE: Irresponsible. Bizarre. I mean if you read his speech in the Senate, he said it was child abuse. That's his opening statement in the Senate. And then by the end of it there's a quote, 'the greatest law reform in a generation.' And that's in the space of a couple of hours? And again, somebody who knows, somebody who's highly experienced, somebody who's a legislator who knows, who should know what's possible and what's not possible. And again playing politics with people's lives. That's what it is. Either you know what's at stake and what are the consequences of what you're saying. If you don't know that, you shouldn't be a senator, you shouldn't be in a leadership position. Or else you do know that and you still play to the gallery. Or you're having a mad half hour, or you feel like saying it, or whatever. But that's irresponsible! I was hugely disappointed. I thought he did himself a huge disservice in that. I thought that he had been such an important figure and was such a brilliant speaker and such a brilliant person, and you know shared a lot of the GLEN approach by saying the Irish people are wonderful, praising people to bring them along. He won in his way, he won a majority of Irish people. And then I thought he just threw it all away in the opening speech. Ok, regained it in the end, but like, inexplicable.

DAVID NORRIS: Kieran Rose always made me laugh because in the beginning Kieran and his group, GLEN, which emerged out of the Hirshfield Centre – and it's extremely good and extremely effective. It was a wonderful thing that American fellow Chuck Feeney gave them money. I mean, we always had to make the money by running discos all the time. They never had to run discos and stuff, and that made them very professional, and they've been very, very good, but they all emerged out of the Hirshfield Centre where we all slaved. But in the early days of GLEN – or maybe it was before it was called GLEN, I can't remember – but they were still hanging around in the penumbra of the Hirshfield Centre, they would disagree with somebody like myself for example, because I was seen as a gradualist and a reformist, rather than a revolutionary. And it then turned completely the other way around, you know? They became reformists. But I have to pay tribute to this, they were superb lobbyists. And there were several of them there, one is a former Fianna Fáil – Tiernan Brady – excellent. Brian Sheehan. Those two played a huge role.

BRIAN SHEEHAN: One of the key things was some people were portraying this as a dog licence. And we were trying to say it's absolutely not a dog licence.

Norris began to reconsider his inclination to vote against the bill.

DAVID NORRIS: I would have felt it would have placed me in a kind of revolting alliance with people whose position on that issue I had nothing but contempt for. And it was an advance. There's no question about that … I did change my mind on the day, but it was because of the amendments. It rankled. I was hoping to persuade the government. I had put amendments down. And I was hoping to persuade the government to protect the children. If they had given me that, I'd have immediately said I'd vote for it. But I think to me the protection of children is the primary thing. And the welfare of children. And to leave children adrift in this? I'd heard and met with gay couples, particularly lesbian women and their children, their families, and they were wonderful people, absolutely wonderful people and happy children … Then they took up this business of registrars. And I challenged them. I said, has any registrar contacted you? No. Has the association of registrars? And I contacted them and I knew that they hadn't. They didn't have a bother with it. But they were fighting for other people's conscience according to themselves. It was really horrid. Horrid, horrid, horrid.

TIERNAN BRADY: There was quite a bit of very polite 'Would you not think about supporting this?' going on in the Seanad, and David changed his mind.

DAVID NORRIS: No, I do not regret it a bit. Not in the slightest. They needed a kick in the arse. You see the problem is – I don't want to bring personalities into it, but some of the people in GLEN – was that they got contact with government, and they began to collaborate. So, no, while they were sucking up to Dermot Ahern for example, I was telling him that he didn't have the balls of a titmouse. I said that to him! To his face! I think he said something like, 'You're very hard,' or 'There you go, you're always the same!'

DERMOT AHERN: David Norris called it a dog collar [*sic*] but he knew right well – privately I think he would have acknowledged that this was a move in the right direction. You can see very quickly that there's a significant change of mood.

DAVID NORRIS: Anyway, the 'dog licence'? I'm glad it got under their [GLEN's] skin. It wasn't intended to get under *their* skin, it was intended to get under the government's skin, but if it got under their skin as well and gave them a bit of a kick in the arse, good! But I admire and respect all of them and the work they've done, and they've worked terribly hard. But I mean, as that wonderful curtain line of *Some Like It Hot* goes: 'Nobody's perfect!' Do you remember that one? When he says he swears and he smokes and his mother wouldn't like him and he takes the wig off and says I'm a man – 'Nobody's perfect!' And I completely include myself in that. I can make disastrous – well, I don't know about disastrous, but I can certainly put my foot in it by speaking what I see to be the truth, but if I am discovered to be wrong, I'll change my position. I see nothing immoral in changing your position if somebody's able to demonstrate that you've got things upside down. But I speak forcibly and I don't engage in too much diplomacy.

IVANA BACIK, SECOND-STAGE SEANAD DEBATES, 7 JULY 2010: In the party's view and mine, this bill does not go far enough. It does not represent equality for gay couples. It does not provide for recognition of gay marriage and it has a most glaring omission in that it has only a very minimal reference to protection for the children of gay parents and this is a major flaw … While we support this bill as a step forward, an advance in the rights of gay people, we do not see it as being an ending post. As the Irish Council for Civil Liberties said, this is a staging post and not a milestone. It is only a step on the way to true equality.

RÓNÁN MULLEN, SECOND-STAGE SEANAD DEBATES, 7 JULY 2010: My view, which I do not believe to be bigoted, is that the right to marry is the right to form a stable, publicly supported union with a person of the opposite sex … This is not an argument between people who think that homosexuality is sinful and people who think it is ok. It is wrong to characterise the argument as being based on such polar oppositions. Many people have very strong support for people's right to a private life, for their right to their values and for their right to love whom they want, but they also support the right of society to make certain values known, to support certain ideas around family and so on.

JOHN HANAFIN: What we found was there's a huge intolerance towards our view and in fact it's often overlooked. In fact, during that time we were very fortunate that those of us who voted against the Civil Partnership – because Brian Cowen had been very tolerant and understanding of the view which was quite usual, because if you vote against the party line, you vote against the whip and you're automatically expelled. And there was no guarantee you would ever be taken back, whereas Brian Cowen had indicated to Labhrás that we'd be back in a short while. He met him and they had a coffee or tea and he said to him, '*Beidh tú ar ais i gceann tamaillín*' ['you'll be back in a little while']. So we were very fortunate in that respect.

TIERNAN BRADY: The day it passed in the Seanad was a brilliant day actually, because Rónán Mullen had tried his best to filibuster it and had put through tonnes of amendments, and the Seanad sat until about two in the morning. And each one of the amendments being put forward, each one of them being voted down, and he was trying to get a line vote on each went, which meant basically stall the bill for as long as humanly possible. It was just – it was obstruction for the sake of obstruction, because ultimately the bill would pass. But he was just, 'Here's another amendment, here's another amendment, here's another amendment.' And you could see the speeches from all side of the house going, 'No, no, no, no, we have to move this on, we're in favour of this.' And the speeches got stronger and stronger as the day went on.

CIARAN O'CUINN: The last day in the senate was very emotional and quite extraordinary because you could see it was a fulcrum moment. You could see the Senate and the Dáil and everything sort of catching up with the people, and you could see it before your eyes – it was quite amazing. And even the opponents of it and you know these people – I don't agree with them, but you know one or two of them were crying in the Senate going, 'Look, I don't have any problem with gay people but I just don't want this.' Now, I fundamentally disagree with that point, but still, they did mean it. And everything was out in the open, everything was fine. And it was in that debate you could see the foundations for marriage. You could see it.

On 8 July 2010, the Civil Partnership Bill passed with a vote of forty-eight Senators for, and four against, Labhrás Ó Murchú, Rónán Mullen, John Hanafin, and Jim Walsh.

DERMOT AHERN: My gamble of holding it before the summer paid off, in that it was even better from the point of view that it passed ... Three Fianna Fáil senators voted against it, one of whom was my personal friend, Jim Walsh.

JIM WALSH, SECOND-STAGE SEANAD DEBATES, 7 JULY 2010: The minister [Dermot Ahern] and I have been good friends for many years. A long time ago, I told him I would oppose him every step of the way in regard to sections of this bill but hoped it would not interfere with our friendship. It is my intention that it will not.

DERMOT AHERN: Ah sure, that's politics.

JOHN HANAFIN: The fact that you can look back and say, 'I'd do it again, I'd do the exact same thing again', that would mean that you're actually quite glad that you took the stance that you took, you said what you had to say, and you got an opportunity to say it ... The first thing was I was absolutely certain at the beginning that I was out of the parliamentary party and I would lose the whip and probably lose the seat. Thankfully – and very quickly it became clear that Brian Cowen wasn't like that – he wasn't going to be vindictive. In that instance, we knew quite early on, even though the decision had been made and the Rubicon was crossed and that was it, we were going to win or lose, and the consequences of it – you'll probably lose your seat, not only the whip but the seat. He was quite generous. Brian Cowen was generous in a position of power.

SANDRA IRWIN-GOWRAN: I was thinking how symbolic it was that the State was rubberstamping this bill that was for the first time going to recognise lesbian and gay relationships – my relationship, you know?

DERMOT AHERN: In the end, I was completely taken aback. The President didn't even call a Council of State meeting. I mean, I was absolutely astounded over it. Now, I'm friendly with Mary McAleese, personal friends. We've gone on holidays together, our families, when she was President, when she broke her leg skiing that time. And, I mean, I was very surprised.

CIARÁN Ó CUINN: For all the talk, there are these issues that people think there are huge opposition to, but when you get down to people individually there was very little opposition. The greyhound bill was about fifty times more difficult. All these other bills on stupid little things were much more difficult. There was no real opposition to this. There was no real tough work.

GERARD HOWLIN: Come the time, there was genuinely a good, solid ballast of people who were open for it and up for it. And that coincided with a period where people in politics and TDs were just so acutely pressurised. They didn't have the capacity, the will, the energy, or anything to take on another issue, to take on another battle.

STEPHEN COLLINS: It's funny. In Irish politics you find that something doesn't happen for a long time. And then when it does, there's not that much debate or opposition to it.

22

THE DIVISION CONTINUES

'Ours is always going to be the less populist;
incremental change is never going to be the populist approach.'

– Tiernan Brady

GRÁINNE HEALY: To be fair, I don't think GLEN ever just said they just wanted civil partnership. I think GLEN have always said, 'Our ultimate goal is … but this is as much as we think we can get at the moment, so …' It's not that they've had a sudden interest in marriage equality. I think, to be fair to them, they had always held that and, as I said, our view was: because it wasn't equality, we simply weren't publicly going to settle for that. And that has caused difficulties between the two organisations.

TIERNAN BRADY: Look, I think there was probably a lack of understanding about how difficult it was to get civil partnership over the line, and the real political fear from the politicians about civil partnership, never mind civil marriage. Civil marriage wasn't on the political table. The Greens had a policy in favour of it, very clear, they knew it wasn't achievable. But that was it. So that was four TDs or five TDs out of 106. You know, there was a lot of Fine Gael TDs who had to be dragged to the table when it came to civil partnership and a few Fianna Fáilers as well, and again people fearful of it. I always put it this way: civil partnership passed the Dáil with the vote of every single person in the house. No one voted against it in the Dáil, but not one TD welcomed it on local radio. So they were prepared to vote for it in Dublin as part of a broad consensus step forward which they knew was the right thing to do, but they were terrified of the impact that would have on their constituencies.

Some organisations lost sight of a political reality, and we lost sight of [the need] to explain that political reality, that this wasn't a simple case of 'No, no, no, we'll have the marriage box please' – this was 'We have to fight to get *this* box, civil partnership, over the line.'

EOIN COLLINS: I think the division to me came in two ways. One is, I think, the quest for marriage suddenly became possible and international and people could see it. There's a huge amount of young people coming out for example. It became a huge rallying point and a very important and empowering thing for younger people. I also think that marriage brought a lot of people out that hadn't been out, older people out who hadn't been out when we were working in the '90s and early 2000s. It brought out a lot of people who, I suppose, were new to gay politics in a way and were really, really empowered by marriage as the goal. I think that was very healthy and I think the Zappone-Gilligan case really brought things together as well on that. These were two older women expressing the equality argument for marriage very strongly. So I think that's what happened. There was an enormous raise in expectations, a huge raise in expectations. It was hard for us to kind of, you know, come in, because in a way when you're coming in to that environment, you're kind of throwing cold water on people's aspirations and on their expectations. So it was a difficult thing. But I think that kind of movement for marriage did help drive a civil partnership model that was close to marriage. I think that was very important.

MAX KRZYZANOWSKI: It's a fundamental miscalculation on GLEN's part, if you ask me. It manifests in other places as well: it's the perception that there is only one tone of voice that the entire community should be speaking with at any one time … I remember drawing strength from the likes of Rory, from Senator David Norris, from Tonie Walsh and from other people when they went, 'I'm not prepared to accept your categorisation of me as second-class citizen.' So GLEN, I don't think, appreciate the value in that. Or maybe individuals in GLEN do, but certainly the overarching impression that I've gotten is that they really only have one listener in mind and it is a strategic thing, and I just think that is reductionist and also unnecessary. We have to have a community with a plurality of voices. We have to be available to the different opinions within our community.

RORY O'NEILL: It actually got quite scrappy at times, didn't it? Sort of heated. Again, I was in two minds about that. At times I thought it was a bit depressing that there was in-fighting going on, sort of. I've never really liked the sniping away at GLEN, for example, because I think they're doing what they and many other people think is the right thing to do. And their ultimate goal is the same as everybody else's and they've just decided this approach is a better way to do it. And it's perfectly reasonable to take that position. So I never liked that. But on the other hand, I've always thought, even though it would slightly depress me and you'd go online and see especially younger people going on about GLEN or whoever it is as if they were terrible, terrible, awful people – on another level, that sort of excited me because so little politically excites or motivates the younger gays. I'm always banging on about that and I feel like such a schoolmarm, but it's true. It really is true. So that on another level excited me. At least they were getting angry about something, angry about something other than the price of a pint in The George.

KIERAN ROSE: I think there's an important thing about being able to disagree with people and to maintain a friendly position on things. I think that was lost as well in the civil partnership debate. We were never personally offensive to people, but people were personally offensive to us. On the Gay Pride parade, for example, 'Fuck GLEN' was one of the t-shirts. And that didn't come out of nowhere. That was not like an idiosyncratic thing of one particular person or one group of people deciding to put that on their t-shirt. It was the outcome of a certain vilification of GLEN. A very personalised thing.

MAX KRZYZANOWSKI: They don't have a mandate. They have a niche. And they've been very successful. And let me put this on the record, I'm hugely appreciative of an awful lot of the equality work GLEN have done. They've done long-term work of enormous significance. They've also been good collaborators on a whole range of projects. I think, like anybody else – like me, like Noise, like all other groups – they have their weaknesses and they have their strengths, but because they had that longstanding history, and because they are very close to government, and they've developed relationships with people in government and the civil service and things like that, that's a really useful thing that they've done. And they have been very informative on employment equality legislation and other things that have happened that are invaluable to huge swathes of Ireland, not just even the LGBT community. They've helped inform legislation that has been of benefit to Irish society. You do tend to develop your frame of reference from the people you work with, and the people around you, and they've a quite deep knowledge of how to lobby, and how to petition, and how to try to advance what they see as the best legislation, or the best policies for the LGBT community, but, as with Noise, the 'T' was pretty silent in GLEN, and some would argue it still is. It's non-existent in their title but they have done some work. They have been unreliable partners to the trans community. And they certainly could have benefited from the kind of transformative process that Noise underwent [in relation to trans work].

TIERNAN BRADY: I think in organisations, we always have to make a choice, and it's a really difficult choice because there isn't a right answer on this. You either work on the progress and take the larger incremental approach, bedding down success, building on success, or you hold out the purist approach. And in a way you need both, you know. You have to have both because that's how you get things done. But one organisation can't do both. You can't be the provocateur and the conciliator all at the one time. And I think that was a challenge for us, and we ended up taking this approach because we thought this was the way to deliver marriage quicker. And Marriage Equality took a different approach. You know, ours is always going to be the less populist; incremental change is never going to be the populist approach. It never is anywhere.

EOIN COLLINS: I just felt it was so unfair that people seemed to have constructed an argument that there was a choice between marriage and civil partnership, and GLEN were going for civil partnership because they didn't have faith in the argument that marriage was full equality. That was just simply untrue. And I heard that again and again: 'If only GLEN would come out for marriage.' It was just so exasperating because you had a sense that we are for marriage, but we are trying to ask questions about, well, if we don't accept civil partnership, will we get marriage sooner? And our view was that civil partnership was going to be not only delivering something for lesbian and gay people now, that it was substantial, it was marriage-based, but it would actually would increase the momentum for marriage. That's something that we believed. People just didn't listen to that argument. I felt personally as though it was a hard one, because we had been working so much. I suppose a lot of it as well was that our work was behind the scenes and it was hard to talk about, and there are communications issues around that and people can't see what you're doing all the time. But it was definitely very hard, personally, I found to deal with.

GRÁINNE HEALY: There have been incidents and things that happened, things that were said, meetings that were had that didn't go well … It has always been my wish that GLEN and Marriage Equality can work together. In practice, that hasn't worked out. I think that's because of GLEN's *modus operandi*; there is a certain arrogance in their belief that their way is the only way, and therefore, when Marriage Equality, instead of saying that 'this is a stage that needs to be shared' and having a number of organisations pushing. So, for example, I feel LGBT Noise had a role to play. It wouldn't be my role, but they had an important role to play for the particular community audience that looked to them. Marriage Equality had a role to play, and I still feel that what we actually got in the Civil Partnership Act was hardened, a much hardened document, than what GLEN would have gotten if Marriage Equality hadn't been on the stage. So again, I don't know. Maybe because I'm 54, there's something about being around a while, and you kind of think, you know – this is not about Kieran Rose or Brian Sheehan. They're fine men and they do great work. I don't have any personal animosity towards them, and I want to work with them and I've always wanted to work with them. But the difficulty is one of the things that has come back is GLEN going in and talking to some of the politicians whom I would know personally who have rung me to say, 'You know GLEN are badmouthing Marriage Equality in here?' And I'm saying, 'Well, I'm really sorry to hear that.' And they're saying, 'I just have to say you're saying X, and they're coming in and saying Y.' So you know, I've had to go and say that to GLEN, which is not an easy thing to say. And they haven't denied it. My thing has been that I would like us to be able to work together on this project. We are now in a position with ICCL that we are now working together. It's not easy, because there has been a history. And also because GLEN continue to consider that they have the field marked out and that they know the right way forward, and that in some ways Marriage Equality are just interlopers and they'd be much happier if we just disappeared. So that's not going to happen. I think we will continue to work together. I think we will get this across the line.

KIERAN ROSE: I believe in progress, I believe in delivering real change for people in their ordinary everyday lives as soon as possible. And I take that very seriously. And I don't play politics with people's lives. And because I know people who have benefited from that … That's worth being harangued by what I would say are zealots. Those people who said 'civil marriage or nothing' had nothing to offer to those people – and wouldn't have for 2015. We could lose; we hopefully will win. People are benefiting now from this – people's relationships – people can have human rights to live together and to love one and other and take care of one another. If the campaign was carried on by people who wanted to stop civil partnership, that would not have been possible. And I'd love to ask them to check their conscience. Could they stand over that?

BRIAN FINNEGAN: It's been presented as black and white, you know. There are factions, and I've heard many people say, 'By getting a civil partnership you are buying into apartheid, buying into a law that enshrines our inequality.' And then you've got people who are the more moderates saying, 'We're buying into this as part of a process going towards [marriage].' So there's a real black-and-white thing on the Marriage Equality side. And in a way it doesn't serve them very well, I don't think.. They're more about spin. They're more about, 'We'll take that and we'll spin that into a message that will bring us towards our goal.' I mean, my job generally is not to take a strong line. My job is to allow it to play out within the pages and, you know, my line has always been marriage equality, but I have never taken the 'marriage equality or die' kind of line … I could say to people, 'I don't think you should get civil partnerships. By taking up civil partnerships, you're telling the government that it was perfectly ok to do that.' And it wasn't. It wasn't. But that's a hard line to take, you know? I don't think I'm a hardliner anyway. I think politically things happen incrementally and I think that there needs to be a radical movement and there needs to be a political movement that is very strategic, and there needs to be push and pull within that political movement so that it can actually be teased out within the movement. I suppose there's an unhealthy relationship between Marriage Equality and GLEN. I think that it's a healthy balance to have those players all there. Because also for us who are observing, who are not actually playing the part, it allows us to have the debate … I think the more that people get visibly civil partnered, the more photographs that there are of weddings, people are falling off from that intense kind of drive [so as] not to be sitting at the back of the bus. And I think that civil partnership would have been a major step towards it, because it demystifies it. So we're on the road towards it, it's just how it's politically and legally going to play out is the question really.

KATHERINE O'DONNELL: I was sorry for the guys that they got such a backlash. I've spoken with some of them and it was quite heartbreaking to work so hard for so long, so strategically and so well to have been so pounded and pilloried among the community. I felt really weird for me – I've such a long and strong critique – to feel such sympathy for them, but I really did. I think they were treated badly. And from what I can see, it took a toll personally. And I hope they get the thanks sooner rather than later for what they achieved.

EOIN COLLINS: One thing I have to say is despite some bitterness, none of us every really fell out at the end of the day. I think that's a nice thing. There's a sense that people get on and whatever. I think it's great. It's like the Maoist one: let a thousand flowers bloom. I remember the Pride in 1992 and myself and Proinsias De Rossa, Kieran Rose were walking on it and I remember it seemed big at the time, and the one next year where we could all fit in literally into the courtyard of the Central Bank plaza. But we felt huge. And now seeing Pride, where it's just so ginormous. That's one thing I want to get across: it's just amazing how quickly things changed. Sometimes people don't realise things shifted. It's extraordinary. And I think the quest for marriage has been a really important one in that shift.

AILBHE SMYTH: While I admire the work of GLEN, for example, in relation to the civil partnership issue, and I do think they worked very, very hard on that, that would not have been my chosen route. Their argument as I understand it has always been that civil partnership is a route to marriage. Whereas I felt it was an unnecessary route to go. I think you're always better to go for 100 per cent. Certainly my own background in left-wing politics and human rights issues, I'm not prepared to go for less. If I'm going to be out there fighting for something, I'm going to fight for 100 per cent. I'm always going to fight for rights, and indeed probably for revolution. My politics have never been reformist politics. Inevitably I would have been always drawn towards Marriage Equality's politics rather than those of GLEN. That being said, I do admire GLEN for the work that they do on a very broad spectrum, and would certainly always stay with that and continue to respect and admire their work and to support their work. On the issue of marriage and civil partnership, I'm for marriage. I just don't want to do it myself, by the way, but I am for everybody's right to marry.

COLM O'GORMAN: I feel very, very strongly from my own professional perspective that if any organisation is seeking to advance the human rights of any group of individuals or population, it's incredibly important that their positions are fully informed by an engagement with that population and with those people. So rights holders' participation, and active rights holders' participation, is incredibly important. And ensuring that your campaign and your calls are representative, and reflect what that rights-holder group actually want, as opposed to your assessment of it, even if you're a member of that group, is absolutely vital. I think it's fair to say that there was a disconnect between the case that was presented for civil partnership and the lived reality for LGBT people. Now, I don't know if that was GLEN's fault or even their responsibility – GLEN are GLEN, you know, they were an organisation doing a piece of work, and their structure is their structure, and their constitution is the way that they're constituted, but I do think that there needed to be more of a considered engagement with the LGBT community in all of its diversity, you know? And it's not white, middle-class, male, single, with concerns about pensions and inheritance and income tax and property. Those are very real concerns for people, but they're very limited. They deny the reality of huge numbers of people. Absolutely women, and men who aren't concerned with that. Again, it's been really interesting in the context of the whole debate that we've had on prejudice [in early 2014] that you know one of the things that I think was most valuable about what Rory was certainly saying, and it's something I feel very strongly too – prejudice is nobody's dominion. Look at this community. Look at how this community treated lesbians. Look at the view of lesbians in this community. Or transgender people particularly. There's no point in imagining or pretending that the LGBT community would be very different from wider society, and that power and influence wouldn't be almost automatically in the hands of educated, middle-class, middle-aged men. That's the way the world has been. And it's changing thankfully, but it's the way the world has been.

ELOISE MCINERNEY: The last thing I ever wanted was there to be divisions because I always firmly believed that we needed to present a united front. If we started arguing among ourselves, then what's the hope? We have to be together. We are a community and we have to show that we are a community. I think inevitably anytime you've got politics, you're going to have elements of discordant division – that's just the way human nature is and that's what's going to happen. People are going to have different strategies, different opinions on how things should be done. And you have to somehow just find a way to compromise, I suppose, to find a way to get through that. I think it was a shame this created a sense of hostility, and certainly was disappointed when people became quite abusive, say online, against GLEN. Certainly I was quite disappointed by that and would have hoped that people could have maybe kept the tone a little bit more measured. There was disagreement and disagreement is always going to happen – that's just normal.

GRÁINNE HEALY: I don't know if we'll ever all end up being bosom pals having Christmas drinks together, but that's ok. That's not an important thing.

SANDRA IRWIN-GOWRAN: LGBT Noise started and that created an opportunity for LGBT people to get involved. The Marches for Marriage – and I think it had and has its role. But I think at the time, I think, it created an expectation that we could have marriage but we were settling for civil partnership. And I think that was quite damaging because I think it made some people apologetic then when civil partnership came in … So I think there was a big chasm there. But I don't think it was with everybody. I think it was with certain groups, and people that were involved in those groups. And certainly most people that I would know and come in contact with since would have seen that, God, when we got civil partnership that was actually a huge leap forward.

KIERAN ROSE: Obviously we lost that PR struggle or we lost that communications battle. We did try and do a bit of it. We did have briefing meetings in the Central Hotel in Dublin – what's in and out of the [bill] and what our position was. And we did it around the country. That doesn't communicate with a huge number of people. We were communicating through the media, national media. Yeah, we were a small organisation with limited resources. Do you concentrate on the Dáil and the minister and the officials in terms of your limited hours? It took the shine off civil partnership, and we lost that. GLEN lost that. It should have been part of our strategy. And whether we could have done it, because emotional arguments are much easier. It's much easier to say, 'We want equality or nothing. We don't want second-class citizenship,' and all that kind of stuff. As they say, once you're explaining, you're losing. And I think that's probably one of the worst things. I got the sense that sometimes people nearly had to feel they had to apologise for having a civil partnership. They had to kind of say publicly, they said, 'Well, we of course want civil marriage.' So it took the gloss. It should have been seen by everybody – all lesbians and gay men – as a phenomenal victory, which it was, and a fantastic achievement, not for GLEN but everything that everybody had done – every person that had come out in their school, or factory, or to their parents. It should have been seen as a victory for all of that, and now let's go on to civil marriage. But it was almost like a civil war or something.

23

THE AFTERMATH OF
CIVIL PARTNERSHIP

'It felt very anti-climactic.'

– Fiona de Londras

GRÁINNE HEALY: The day the civil partnership legislation came through, I remember being on the radio with Eamon [Ryan] from the Green Party and he was saying, 'This is great.' And I said, 'We welcome this because it does bring in certain rights and obligations, but what we want to know from the minister is when are we going to have equality?' And he laughed on the radio and said, 'I'm with you, and I think we will see it.' So that was our way of continuing to hold the equality ideal while working towards it. So I think there was a lot of – even within the political parties, there was a lot of – not confusion, but certainly GLEN were saying, 'This is it', and GLEN were saying, you know, 'The community are supporting us on this, we're representing the community', and we were arguing with GLEN. We were saying we're going around the country standing up on platforms with GLEN, and the community are fucking savaging them.

DENISE CHARLTON: I remember the dinner with Frank Sharry, and Kieran Rose at the time was asking a question about the movement, and he was saying it was a phenomenal movement and Kieran saying, 'We've arrived, we've got civil partnership', and just really understanding for some people that was arrival and for others it wasn't. And that's ok.

BRIAN FINNEGAN: I'm from Sligo and the *Sligo Champion* had a civil partnership couple on their cover. That really stands out to me. I couldn't walk down the street in Sligo when I was a kid without being abused for being gay, so I never imagined in a million zillion years that that representation would be there in a celebratory way.

EOIN COLLINS: When the bill was passed, the Finance Bill on taxation, we worked with the Revenue Commissioners to make sure, and we got actually really good traction with them. They ensured, for example, that the children of civil partnership could be in the top scale for inheritance tax, schedule A or whatever it's called. Again most of the tax elements then were very close … Suddenly everyone who had these problems all started getting their visas, which was to me incredibly moving. I remember this Filipino woman who was a nurse in the Mater. She'd been in Ireland five years and her partner couldn't even visit her because they were afraid it would be considered immigration intent. She hadn't seen her partner for a few years, she couldn't afford to go back and as a result her partner could come over to Ireland. The two of them got a civil partnership. We were at it in Capel Street. And the partner could live and work in Ireland. I remember this Cuban guy and his boyfriend and they were in such bad straits and suddenly he got his stamp for him. And they were just fantastic, absolutely fantastic. State agencies worked really well, the Revenue Commissioners were really good and Social Welfare were good as well at getting things done. And then we worked with the Registrar General then to make sure the services were accessible, and he had been on the Colley Group so I knew him very well. It was ironic that despite all that was said about registrars wanting exemptions, none of them did. They loved doing civil partnerships.

BERNARDINE QUINN: Initially, four or five years ago, Moninne Griffith came down here and we had a nice conversation about marriage way back at the start of the campaign when there were kind of tensions within the community between marriage equality and civil partnership. There was a very strong drive, I suppose, not to entertain the prospect of civil partnership and to insist on marriage from the word go. That was followed on in the advice from the experts from Spain who came over here to present their experience … From a service-provider point of view, my concerns were we had two terminally ill people here and civil partnership would have been enough to secure their partners for them … So there was concern that anything is better than nothing.

FIONA DE LONDRAS: It felt very anti-climatic, even though it did some things that were important and helpful. It always struck me as not making sense that we had just created another tier of relationship recognition rather than the easy thing to do, which is opening up marriage, deleting one subsection of one act and seeing what happens. I was disappointed this was the option that was taken. I'm not disappointed there is a civil partnership option – I would like that to be one, but also marriage. I understand the pragmatics of it, but one can be pragmatic and still be disappointed.

JERRY BUTTIMER: We've seen society accept civil partnership. It's become part of the lexicon, it's become part of the tapestry of community life. Where you hear people say, 'I'm going to a civil partnership', as if they're going to a wedding, even though it's not a wedding in the way we recognise it. So I think it's been positive. And I think if we had gone down the constitutional route and lost, it would have set the case back I don't know how long – I can't quantify that. There's part of me that says we should perhaps have gone down that route, but there's another part of me that says if we want to bring change, if we want to make sure the lives of all of us who are lesbian, gay, citizens are improved and enhanced, then we should do what we're doing by having the referendum and then we can make sure the constitution of our country reflects that. And that's probably in hindsight the wisest move to do. And I know there are some who want to take a charge and fly full at the courts, but my fear would be if we lost in the courts, what would happen?

SANDRA IRWIN-GOWRAN: I had a civil partnership in April. We waited a few weeks after the first ones because I was heavily pregnant at the time. Our second child was [born] two weeks later, so we didn't want to be the first lesbian shotgun civil partnership! … During the ceremony, I was kind of struck by how emotional it was because again it was this civil registrar, State employee, I suppose giving us the recognition of the State. Both my partner and I were pleasantly surprised by how emotional we were around that.

DAN BOYLE: We took an attitude that the incremental approach which was not without criticism; I mean, people wanted to go straight to marriage equality. Although that was an approach that different countries in Europe took as well. Some went straight to it, some took the two-step approach. We felt that civil partnerships being seen to be undertaken in public would help a wider public debate, would help enthuse the concept of marriage equality.

LINDA CULLEN: It meant fuck all to me, frankly. It was a very unhappy day for me. We became civilly partnered – we did because we needed to around our kids, we felt, because while it didn't give me any rights, it showed intent. And Feargha and I needed to rationalise things around property. Because we had children, we felt we had to do it. So, sorry, it was a happy day, we tried to embrace it, but it was a very sad day. I found it a very sad day. Because it isn't equal. For me it was just a big glaring thing: you are less. I felt that's what was being said to me all day ... I felt a bit heartbroken getting civilly partnered. I'm getting a bit upset now, but I did feel heartbroken about it, and I'm sure Feargha felt the same. I think it's a mistake to think that the amount of people getting civilly partnered means that it's a great success. It does not. People are doing it because they really feel they have to. They've been in relationships for years and years, they have property together or don't, whatever – ageing – and they need to do it. Pretty much all of my friends who have been civilly partnered feel the same as I do about it.

TIERNAN BRADY: I think civil partnerships created a massive visibility. Decriminalisation slowly created a visibility of people. Civil partnerships slowly created a visibility of couples, which again took it to a new level.

COLM O'GORMAN: Our kids really wanted us to get married. So did we. Don't get me wrong, absolutely we did ... When civil partnership became a possibility, we really looked at doing it. We wanted to do something at home, we wanted to do something for family, we wanted to do all of that stuff and we wanted the protections that would give us as a family as well. But that was challenging for me because I was very critical of civil partnership as a lesser model and as a way that actually managed to write in levels of discrimination into Irish law in a way I thought was unacceptable ... But we decided that we would find a way to make it work, make it acceptable, get what we could from that, kind of go, 'Ok, well this is what we want, we can't have what we want but we've been offered this – is this enough of what we want in order to do this?' And I think we kind of decided that it was. So we'd even confirmed possible dates and all the rest of it. We went down to Enniscorthy to meet with the civil registrar at the health centre. This was 2011. So we were going to do it in October 2011. We were sitting with her and she was very lovely and we brought in our ID and that kind of stuff and it was reasonably high-spirited and giggly because it's quite an exciting thing to be doing. But as we sat there more and more, and it's not just about the space – I do think there are issues in Ireland with the level of joy we wrap up around civil marriage in part because of how it's been limited to certain spaces. In parts of the country up until relatively recently if you wanted a civil marriage, you had to do it at the health centre, not in the kind of space you'd want to use to celebrate your relationship and your marriage. That had changed, so you now had choices around hotels, but they were still reasonably limited. I wasn't hugely excited about where we'd have to have the civil partnership – in the quiet function room of a hotel somewhere in Gorey at best. But the clincher for me was when we were sitting there and taking down information and she was talking about, 'Where will you live after you've been married? Oh hang on, I can't say that. Where will you live after you've been …' and she was trying to get her head around the language 'civil partnered'. And I kind of went, 'I don't want to be civil partnered, that's not what this is, actually. I want to marry this man, that's what this is.' With all of the meaning marriage has had to all of those who came before me going back as far as we could possibly go back, that's what I want to do. This is about ritual, this is about more than a simple legal contract, it's about much, much more than that. When Paul in a moment of madness not long after we met asked me to marry him, it's because he wanted to get married. And when I said yes, it was because I wanted to get married. So we just walked out of there and I knew we weren't going to do it. It wasn't going to work.

LINDA CULLEN: Sometimes I think people need to sit with a thing for long enough to really get it. I think Marriage Equality has been a huge mobiliser and motivator in the change. Huge. Because they've gotten people out there. They've gotten people to talk. 'Marriage equality' is just the term now. Everyone knows it.

BUZZ O'NEILL: I had a huge problem with civil partnership. I've certainly softened. But I would have been vociferously opposed to civil partnership, not because I thought we were getting anything less – it's proved that we were getting a huge amount less – but it's just because politically at the time

I could see what was coming down the line. I just thought that if he brings this in, we're stuck with this for fifteen years. I knew Fianna Fáil were on their way out, pretty certain Fine Gael were going to be in there, and I just thought, 'We're going to be stuck with this. And no Justice Minister is going to have the political will to get involved with this' … I was like, 'Hold out for the real thing' … The age profile of the first civil partnerships were 45+. So imagine living as an illegal closeted gay in Ireland in the '60s, and being with that partner for the last forty years and you're hitting 70 and 80 and you can finally have your day out? Who wouldn't jump at that? And who'd deny it? I'd be a right cunt if I was trying to deny them that. I just felt that where we were politically it was wrong to accept it. And his [Dermot Ahern] famous line, 'This is not a stepping stone to marriage.' But hey, who knew we were going to get the most liberal, middle-class Jewish Minister for Justice [Alan Shatter]! Hooray for him! He's having a nightmare with a load of other stuff and, as a Minister for Justice it turns out he's pretty crap, but as a Minister for *social justice*, he's been incredible.

Alan Shatter resigned as Minister for Justice in 2014 amid a flurry of controversy, and was replaced by Frances Fitzgerald.

MURIEL WALLS: For every person who went to our wedding – and we had 200 – they talked to their friends and their family and the person in the shop and the person in the supermarket or the tennis club or everything else, and it just was a ripple. We were at a civil partnership a couple of months later – two friends of Rosemary's, and they were together thirty-five years. And they were like children that day. They were just so happy. It was infectious, and the staff at the hotel just kept saying, 'Aren't they wonderful!' Such a magnificent day. Nobody wanted to go home, we were all just delighted. It was just joy when there wasn't much joy in the country, I can tell you, 2011 and 2012. And the way the newspapers took it up and just normalised it all. It became a 'Have you been to a civil partnership?' type of thing.

EOIN COLLINS: As a result of all of those civil partnerships across the country – I mean, I had been at two of them, one of them must have had 800 people at it, older people and whatever. The impact of this, it's like when you take just one couple who do this civil partnership, how many people have they invited to take their relationship seriously? Your work, your family, your friends, and in your neighbourhood. It's like all these little bombs going off all over the country. Happy bombs! So I feel it did help move the momentum for marriage.

KIERAN ROSE: Our strategy has delivered radical progress. You now have civil partnership throughout the country. Whether you like the term or not, lesbian and gay relationships are 'normalised'. It has brought civil marriage sooner.

BRIAN SHEEHAN: Every single country that has marriage – except for South Africa because there's an exception there – every single country at the time had moved from civil partnership or civil unions to marriage. There was nobody [who had] ever gone a direct route to marriage. So [that's] the trajectory of change.

COLM O'GORMAN: I really do think drawing a clear line from civil partnership to marriage equality is incredibly flawed, and I have not seen that evidenced. It might *seem* obvious – doesn't mean it's true.

NIALL CROWLEY: There was the theory that you get civil partnership, then you get civil marriage. It struck me at the time as a really bad theory. It's the thing of you could get stuck at civil partnership and that just was too dangerous in terms of actually achieving equality for lesbian, gay, bisexual people, that it was an anti-equality position essentially. I also felt that in terms of the reaction to our own report, it suggested that at the time, even in 2002, that the popular mood might be in a different space, and actually there was a possibility of going straight to civil marriage, and there were examples of countries going straight to civil marriage. I think Spain was one of them. I can't remember exactly. I think around the time Spain and Portugal were making moves as well. It certainly did seem to be possible. So why go the roundabout route? In a way it seemed very pragmatic, very unambitious and very risky. Now, the result is that we got civil partnership and now we're getting a referendum on civil marriage. So to some extent it doesn't matter anymore. I wouldn't be getting wound up about it really. It's a theory and I don't really buy it, but the fact is we are now at the point of a referendum on civil marriage for a mixture of reasons, possibly because we went through civil partnership, definitely because we had those cases, particularly the partners seeking the adult dependence allowance and then Katherine and Ann Louise's case. And also because I think [we had] one of the most extraordinary and inventive and innovative campaigns in terms of Marriage Equality. They were, in terms of campaigning, light years ahead of anyone else. There's a lot to be learned from their work, I think. It was really astute and strategic as well.

EOIN COLLINS: I know Marriage Equality said when it came through that it would set the quest for marriage back, and I don't think really that the facts would bear that out. I think it actually increased the momentum for marriage. Then also, while we're waiting for this, while we're having this debate on marriage, we also have people with strong rights already, that people do have something that they can avail of and I think that's very, very important as well.

COLM O'GORMAN: They're right in that a referendum on marriage equality will follow the enactment of civil partnership legislation. But I think it's a little bit much to draw a line between the two things without evidencing that line. If you want to talk about impact, well then some real research needs to be done into how did we get to a point where we have a referendum on marriage equality and what role did civil partnership play in that? I'm sure it played a role. But the other piece is if we had have had civil partnership without the demand coming up the inside of that and behind that for full marriage equality and pointing out the very significant flaws in civil partnership, where would we be? So you know, if those who were saying, 'This is not enough' and 'This is not acceptable' hadn't been saying it, would it have been enough? And would we have marriage equality? Would we have a referendum? I'm not sure that we would.

EOIN COLLINS: I remember being on the radio arguing with Colm from Amnesty International, and we were arguing about marriage and civil partnership, and I remember the interviewer saying, 'So, are you just saying that you know civil partnership is a compromise in order to get you along the road to marriage in the end?' And I said, 'Yeah.' And it kind of did summarise for me what we had been doing.

TIERNAN BRADY: My gut always was: how do you create human rights? Which is what we're trying to do; we're trying to establish the right for lesbian and gay couples to marry as a human right, not just a civil right. And that's about taking each step – and this is only my own strategic analysis, there is no truth here, there's just lots of different opinions. Taking each step, bedding it down, building it … it doesn't just get you closer, it gets you to the next step faster as well, because the success of the step that went before gets you to the next bit quicker.

KATHERINE ZAPPONE: I think Ann Louise and I are both on record disagreeing really with the strategy – and it was a strategy – to move for civil partnership legislation. I would have argued we felt we were moving into the twenty-first century. A lot of other countries started with civil partnership and then moved to marriage, but look, we have their history to learn from, why do we have to do it that way ourselves? Furthermore, once they get marriage, they get rid of civil partnership. It is the establishment of a discriminatory institution. So I mean, I think we both felt that very strongly, believed that, still think that. Obviously we saw very clearly how it unfolded, why it unfolded, whose interests were being pursued, and identifying that. At the same time I suppose I thought anyhow it would be counterproductive to be out there slamming it, so to speak, in terms of the overall importance of building the possibility of where we were going. I'm on record in the Seanad on the one hand making those statements in relation to it is a discriminatory institution, and on the other hand we have witnessed and we have been present for people's civil partnerships – we do understand at a human level what that means to them. We also know, at least many of the people we're aware of, that they would have waited – they decided for different reasons that they weren't going to wait; they were going to do it; it meant something to them. All the while they were doing it within a very limited context. That should not have to be the case. Why do we have to do that? Because some politicians aren't ready yet? Are you kidding me?

AILBHE SMYTH: While I think quite a wide range of lesbians and gays were also pro-civil partnership, the awareness and educational dimension has now definitely become 'But marriage is what we want. We'll take civil partnership for the moment, but it is very much to ensure we have our rights,' and so on and so forth. But marriage is a very key desire … I love going to civil partnerships and they're great fun, but I think there is now a very real awareness that it's not the full shilling, and when marriage comes along – well, we'll do the marriage registration thing as well. So I think people are no longer thinking, 'I just need to get civilly partnered, that will be fine.'

TIERNAN BRADY: I absolutely understand the analysis [of momentum potentially slowing], but I don't agree with it. To be honest, without sounding like a real politician, I've always had massive faith in the LGBT community. We're all conscious of the strength of feeling towards marriage. I didn't think for a minute civil partnership was going to dissipate enthusiasm; I thought it would build it, I thought it would show people what's possible. I thought civil partnerships happening in Ireland would be things that would mobilise and motivate people.

AVERIL POWER: I think civil partnership will help to deliver marriage, and I'm not sure we would have got marriage without it.

NOEL WHELAN: What changed the pace first was the reality of civil partnerships happening in this country. As I wrote, the fact that they're seeing civil partnership photographs in their local newspapers – they were on the front pages of the local newspapers when they were the first, and now they're just included in the wedding photograph pages.

As civil partnership became part of Irish society, another general election saw the complete trashing of Fianna Fáil and the Greens, and the Labour Party and Fine Gael entered into a coalition government in 2011. Two openly gay Labour Party TDs were elected, John Lyons and Dominic Hannigan, and another Fine Gael TD, Jerry Buttimer, came out.

JOHN LYONS: I remember getting a number of letters in the first few weeks of being elected from all sorts of people from all sorts of places in Ireland and beyond Ireland. But the one that stood out was a middle-aged man from somewhere around Terenure who wrote to me and he was kind of congratulating me on getting elected, being one of the first openly gay TDs, and he said to me, 'There are a lot more people walking tall today because of you.' And it didn't even resonate with me at the time, but I remember when it did resonate with me. I was walking down Molesworth Street past the passport office, and a penny dropped. I was going to some LGBT event that I had been invited to. The penny dropped about what that letter meant at that stage. Before I knew it, without being consciously aware, I was beginning to get involved in LGBT issues.

24

WHY MARRIAGE?

'I was in England for a couple of years and then I came back, so it would have been maybe 2004, 2005. I was in the front lounge with my friend. Somebody who was, I guess, a student, late teens, early twenties, and it was the early days of LGBT Noise going around and we got into a conversation about it. I started putting forward the arguments, the radical feminist critique of marriage and why anybody would want it and it's a patriarchal institution. And I was struck by her response, which was kind of a dismissal of "that old stuff", "surely we're beyond that old stuff now". And I was really struck by what had been at one point the radical arguments had now somehow become kind of conservative, old-fashioned arguments.'

– Michael Cronin

One of the debates that never really gained mainstream traction in or outside the LGBT community was a critique of marriage itself.

ANDREW HYLAND: Within the community there was two sections. There was the LGBT community, and it was about starting a conversation with them. It was starting a conversation so they would want us to represent them, want us to talk on their behalf, which very much happened. We're a grass-roots organisation, and we wouldn't have become what we are without that constant dialogue throughout the years. Then there was the feminist movement, and within the feminist movement there was, and rightly so, opposition to marriage. I've a master's in equality studies based on feminist theory, feminist economics and so on, so I totally appreciate and understand where that comes from. Over time, it was more talking to people [about] why we believe as a community we should have access to marriage, and we're not saying it's an ideal to live up to, but it's something people should have access to, and, within that, how do we as a society look at marriage?

KATHERINE O'DONNELL: Marriage is different all over the world. Not only in every jurisdiction, but in Tibet a woman can marry husbands, in Utah a man can marry many wives … in Nigeria wealthy women can marry other women once they've had their children. There are lots of different kind of ways of doing marriage. But here it's been relatively recent, I'm an eighteenth-century scholar so I can tell you it's quite recent, this new form of marriage. And every single decade we've had marriage, it's been changed, sometimes very significantly, like in 1996 when divorce came in. So it's a contract between a man and a woman that's under constant renegotiation. Of all the kind of contracts around, it's the one that's revised most often by law, it seems to me. But what it allows that couple is quite a lot of privileges, and until very recently, until feminism kind of took hold of it, a man was allowed a huge licence over his children and his wife, even to the extent of being allowed to rape her or being allowed beat her. Again, this is quite recent, those things have changed, and feminism can take a lot of credit for now a more egalitarian marriage, but that institution or that contract or that family formation gets an awful lot more privilege than other types of families and that's really where my critique is. They get a lot more material goodies, a much greater slice of the pie, but again, more importantly, and most hard to combat in some ways, is they get a huge amount of cultural affirmation that translates eventually into capital. There's been very interesting economic studies done in the United States comparing the happiness, health indicators and material prosperity of single men vis-à-vis married men. And there is a married dividend. The married man does earn more and gets promoted more against an equally qualified, same race, same ethnicity, same cultural and educational background. So that's what I don't like too, that there's so much more cultural affirmation of that type of family. And I would like to think that the resources of a State in material terms, in cultural terms, values all kinds of family formation. And I think that the system too is quite confining at times for the people who are in it, quite constricting. It's a very narrow definition of how to live out what are increasingly longer and longer lives. We tend to try to make it a honey trap for people too. But it can be quite entrapping. I'm a cultural critic, so you're always suspicious when there's a huge amount of cultural activity promoting something. There's a lot of anxiety around this idealised union, and a big industry and making believe how perfect, and lovely and wonderful it is, which again can be very isolating for people in that union.

MARIE MULHOLLAND: I'm not opposed to gay marriage. I think everybody should have a choice. I think they should be able to take the option that most suits them, benefits them, and makes them happiest. What I'm totally opposed to is the pursuit of gay marriage to the exclusion of everything else. And not just the exclusion of other options, but the exclusion of other voices and other critiques. And the silencing of that.

RORY O'NEILL: Well, when it first started being discussed here as something that might be achievable or whatever, I did hear quite a few voices who were just against marriage full stop, because that's the kind of people I hang out with! And so that was definitely an issue at the beginning. Certainly for me, it was something that I very quickly put aside, even though when I was younger, I would be quite pish-posh about marriage per se. Then two things really happened. One was seeing friends of mine getting civil partnered in other countries first and how much it meant to them and going along to those ceremonies and for the first time thinking, 'Oh, I can see why somebody might want to do this.' Maybe I just have not been lucky enough to ever meet somebody to feel that about. For example, my friends Niall and Nigel, their civil partnership ceremony was so amazing and beautiful it really did make me emotionally change how I felt about it. But also, on top of that, on a pure fairness thing, no matter what anybody feels about marriage, to say that this group of people can do it and this group of people can't is just intrinsically unfair. So I used to say in those early conversations with people who were against marriage, 'Well, that's fine. Be against marriage, and persuade people they don't need to get married, or change the system, or whatever it is, but don't sit back and let it be ok for one group of people be able to make that choice when another group of people that you're part of aren't able to make that choice. It may not be a choice that you want to make – and that's fair, you know, fine – but lots of other people do want to make that choice. So they should be able to make that choice.'

ANDREW HYLAND: When I started to talk to friends of mine, there was that kind of sexual liberation idea – maybe it comes a bit from queer theory as well, definitely from feminism – that marriage as an institution is patriarchal, and why would we want to buy into that? That it's a heterosexual norm and we don't want to be part of that. I never really agreed with that from the start in the sense that I always felt that the gay community should have access to marriage. Whether people subscribe to it or not is an individual choice.

IZZY KAMIKAZE: There were novelty weddings; I remember those as well. I do remember there were two women in Galway who had a big 'getting married party', and it was a party – it was an excuse for a party. They'd been together for many years. They almost immediately broke up! Which may have formed some of my notions about what was likely to be the outcome of this kind of carry on! I'm making no claims in this to represent anybody else, this is totally my subjective memory … The vast majority of lesbian women I knew in the '80s certainly had a heterosexual past. Many of them had been married and had children. So obviously, recognition of families or the kind of problems people talk about now around non-recognition of families, let's say, those things were problematic from time to time for people. So those kinds of things were talked about. But I know an awful lot of women who spent twenty years legally married to somebody that they could not divorce from. They might have split up from twenty years beforehand, but they couldn't legally separate themselves. I think the notion of marriage did not have an awful lot of appeal to that generation of women. They would not have seen it as a means of more equality.

But dissenting voices were in a bit of a bind. Vocalising opposition to marriage within the community became unfashionable. There was a sense that everyone had to get on board, and that the opposition that needed to be fought was the form of those who opposed marriage on an equality level outside the community.

MICHAEL CRONIN: My three main concerns can, I suppose, be summed up as follows: (1) How can we find a space in the current public conversation for a perspective that is critical of the marriage campaign but from a queer, gay-affirmative and anti-homophobic perspective? As Pantigate demonstrates, once the referendum campaign gets going, that will become even more difficult, probably impossible. (2) How can we manage to engage in a political discussion while acknowledging that this is an issue in which people are so deeply invested emotionally and affectively? For instance, I find it very uncomfortable and challenging to express my opposition publicly as someone who, firstly, is a potential beneficiary of the change, and, secondly, am opposing something that is deeply important to individuals who I respect and love, and opposing subcultural organisations that were very important to my own formation. (3) How can we develop a perspective on this that acknowledges that this is simultaneously a victory and a defeat? It is a progressive development that will make our society more inclusive, tolerant and affirmative of loving relationships and different families. But it will also entrench inequality – between the married and the unmarried, the secure and the precarious – and is another indication of how the utopian hopes of 1970s gay liberation and lesbian feminism have been thoroughly defeated.

And so, the catch 22: of course the vast majority of LGBT people in Ireland wanted access to marriage on an equality basis, but holding a critique of marriage itself became problematic, and eventually, rather mute. Wider society and the media began to view marriage as a unified goal for LGBT community, while critics of the movement and the institution of marriage admit to self-censoring.

SUZY BYRNE: I remember being at Lesbian Lives in the early 2000s where people were criticising the way in which the debate was taking place, who was leading it, that it was very male, and that it didn't look at the diversity of relationships within the community. There was a narrative of what I would have identified as 'the Good Gay' … gay and lesbian couples that are monogamous, buy houses and fit in with everybody else. It became very conservative. I'm firmly in favour of marriage equality, but I want to see other forms of relationships recognised. But there's an awful lot of conservatism and tut-tutting – not just in Ireland, it's happening internationally, where everybody now sees marriage equality as the thing to go for because it fits into a model of the family. And I very naively maybe thought we would have a range of relationship formations recognised. The Irish Council for Civil Liberties produced a document that Fiona de Londras, Marie Mulholland and people in the ICCL worked on, which had a range of relationship recognition options in it. We don't talk about those things anymore.

KATHERINE O'DONNELL: When I say I was an interested bystander when it kicked off, I was an interested bystander, somebody who was going to make critiques. And I did at various junctures along the way in kind of a very quiet way to lesbian-only or lesbian and gay events around a critique of marriage. But only there. I had decided that I wasn't going to be publishing anything or I wasn't going to be speaking out in any kind of media fora … I needed to realise that, you know, I'm all for democracy and this seemed to be a big democratic wish, certainly of younger gays and also I would say people who had been closeted for a long time, and this was a way they could come out. And so I wasn't going to undermine that ground. And I could also really understand that psychologically it was going to be extremely important for those people. I always warn my students that whenever you talk about 'those people' you're in danger of saying something awful, and here I am patronising. But it was going to be extremely important psychologically speaking for younger lesbians and gays to feel that they had equality with their brothers and sisters in their own families. That seemed to me to be kind of a very important thing to have won. So I was just going to step back from literally queering the pitch. Even as I had an awful lot of reservations. Even as I knew that my generation, my community, my moment was now going fast. The kind of community I had been part of and the vision that I had of what that community could be, was disappearing with the marriage movement, and I really felt it was time to let that go.

There were initially some 'official' conversations about marriage.

KATHERINE O'DONNELL: A Pride forum in 1999 or 2000 – I can't remember who I invited or what was said, but I do remember [what] the whole tenor was. I remember making a joke, something like, 'Yes, I'll support you and your marriage, but please don't ask me to the wedding.' That was kind of what I remember the gist of it. And I remember one particular couple, very bravely, Karen and Karen. And the younger Karen, as she was called, put up her hand and said, 'I really want to get married. I want to marry Karen.' And at the time when she said that, it punctured a lot of our kind of cosy, lefty, hip, queer critique. I was very impressed by her. It was almost brave to put up her hand and say, 'No, I want to get married.' And I – you know, I felt my heart kind of responding and saying, 'Yes, I would be very happy to see you marry.' It just wasn't going to be something that I could kind of personally get behind I suppose. And I remember going away and thinking a lot about it and thinking, 'Ok, my personal preferences are leading to certain kinds of prejudices perhaps, and we are now starting to see much more visibility of people.' People like me, who had hit our heads very, very hard off homophobia, had done a certain amount of shattering, opening a space, and there were all kinds of other people not of our political analysis who were taking up the kind of identifying positions of being lesbian and gay. So I thought, well, Karen is my sister too.

RORY O'NEILL: Somehow it felt very arrogant for some gays to say, 'I'm against marriage and therefore we shouldn't have it,' when there are plenty of other gays who do want it. You may disagree with them, but it just seems really arrogant – my way or the highway sort of. And in the beginning I definitely heard those arguments at lot. And I have some sympathy with those arguments, because I felt that being gay sort of released you from the rules your straight brothers and sisters have to put up with … And that somehow gay people, I thought, were always able to forge their own ways of being happy and make their own decisions about relationships and all that, and prove that there are other ways, that there isn't just one way. So I have a lot of sympathy with that argument, but when it really comes down to it, it's the sort of the equality issue that kills me. There are people who want to make that decision, and I might be one of those if I met somebody that I felt that strongly about, and they should be able to make that decision. Especially when you have a whole society – every fairy story, every Disney story, every everything, every fucking 'Marley and Me' – all about the married couple. You can't sort of pile that on gays and sort of say this is how your life is going to be when you're a kid – you're going to be a princess, you're going to walk down an aisle, you're going to have this – and then pull it out from under them. So there was definitely that kind of conversation ten, fifteen years ago a lot. But you know, in my own mind, I've passed that ages ago.

MARIE MULHOLLAND: I think the other thing is, and I'm perfectly up for the criticism, the thing that really exploded within me was how on earth can these women call themselves feminists? Because they would give no critique of marriage from a feminist perspective. There was nothing being discussed.

AILBHE SMYTH: I really had to work quite hard I think, and in a sense I started off developing a position which when I think about it now is extremely cumbersome – that sometimes the way politics happens is not always clean and clear, 100 per cent politically correct and so on and so forth. I developed a position which was: I do not believe that marriage, patriarchal marriage as it has been constituted as experienced by so many people, is necessarily a fantastic institution for women. I think it favours men rather than women. And I think up to a point that's still the case. But I do obviously fully recognise that people need to marry – I'm talking about straight people now, because it is used as a baseline, social-organising institution in our society so that so much follows from being married or not married so to speak. So there are all kinds of very practical issues, not all to do with children; some have to do with inheritance and healthcare and ownership of property, and in lots of ways also simply the recognition of you as a couple, all passes through marriage to a very large extent actually. Your social status, your standing in a society tends do go through the marriage institution. Our attitudes towards marriage have I think changed a lot over the last thirty, forty years anyway. But basically I was recognising that I have a critique of marriage as an institution because I don't think it favours women, I don't think it enables women to achieve our potential. But at the same time, I do recognise that people need to get married and while I would far rather abolish marriage perhaps as an institution altogether, the reality of our society is that we need it. We need to be able to do it because socioeconomically that's the way we're set up. Many people would argue that it's more than that – I'm not absolutely sure – but as a reality it is very, very difficult to dislodge it. Divorce rates all over the post-industrial world tend to show that, when you've got 50–60 per cent divorce rates, people still remarry. So it is very difficult to circumnavigate marriage as a key or central basis for social organisation and particularly where families or children are concerned. And I have to say to myself, well, since that is such a central institution, it really is not acceptable that gays should be excluded from this simply because of our sexuality. Because of every other aspect of our lives we claim equality, and so it's logical for us to claim equality in that regard. So while I would not wish to activate that right for myself, I completely understand and recognise the right of lesbians and gays generally to be able to do that on the same basis as straight people. I don't think there should be any differences in any part of our lives.

DENISE CHARLTON: I remember going to Sligo to speak … And a lot of the women there would have been anti-marriage, really anti-marriage, very strong, feminist. I remember thinking, 'Oh my God, how am I going to explain this?' And I did the journey of working as a feminist, being involved in Women's Aid, not seeing marriage as an institution that was in anyway helpful to women, but then, you know, really coming around to the point of view where actually that's for people to choose, whether they want to engage in that institution – and gay women will probably do it very differently, in the same way they do partnerships. I don't know for gay men, but I assume the same. When I understood that it wasn't just about love and the big white dress – the actual rights that went behind it were very significant, and the State was denying a whole group of people those rights, that's what really convinced me. Once I was convinced of it, I'm still not sure about the institution of marriage for a lot of women – I think it is very unequal – but at the same time, if the State provides a huge amount of rights through a certain mechanism, that mechanism should be open to all. And then for me, it became very personal around the right to parent, and my children's right, a legal right, to both parents, and that really is a kind of motivator for me rather than marriage as an institution.

In 2009, the NLGF published the 'Burning Issues' report by Dr Seán Denver, Orla Howard, Olivia McEvoy and Ciarái Ó hUltacháin. Equal rights at work emerged as the most important issue for LGBT people surveyed, followed by bullying/violence against LGBT people, then marriage equality, support for younger LGBT people, supporting people coming out, health/mental health services for LGBT people, building networks for LGBT people, support for older LGBT people, gay and lesbian parenting, and tackling poverty amongst LGBT people. Women under 36 ranked marriage equality as their top burning issue, followed by bully/violence and equal rights at work. Men under 36 ranked bullying/violence first, then equal rights at work, followed by marriage equality. For women over 35, marriage equality was their fifth burning issue, after equal rights at work, bullying/violence, support for younger LGBT people, and support for people coming out. For men over 35, marriage equality didn't figure in their top five burning issues. Marriage equality did not feature as a top-five burning issue for transgendered respondents. Still, in the report's survey findings, marriage equality was listed as 'Priority 1':

In question 4a, marriage equality was raised overwhelmingly by individuals as the most important priority for action by the LGBT community. The issue of marriage equality was raised by 486 respondents, in almost 20 per cent of the 2470 open-ended responses. When the weighting of this open-ended question is taken into account – respondents provided answers listing their first, second and third most important issues, ranked in order of importance – marriage equality registered as the most important issue for over 25 per cent of respondents.

This was followed by 'Priority 2', 'Full equality in general', and 'Priority 3', 'Lesbian and gay parenting rights'. The report concluded:

The Burning Issues Survey is the first national survey to gauge the attitudes and opinions of the LGBT community in Ireland. This seminal scoping study of the Irish LGBT population has been conducted to contribute to the current public debate about same-sex partnership and civil marriage rights in Ireland and to provide a mandate for the future work of the NLFG. The survey findings indicate that equality at work, personal safety and supporting both young people and same-sex parents are of vital concern to LGBT people. Moreover, the results clearly demonstrate that achieving access to the institution of civil marriage is the top political concern of the LGBT community. Full equality under the law is demanded by LGBT people, with only a small number of respondents identifying civil partnership rights as satisfactorily meeting their needs.

BRIAN SHEEHAN: The Burning Issues report was constructed, I would argue – and maybe this is unfair – but it was constructed in the middle of the civil partnership/civil marriage debate and the questions were loaded to make sure it came out to support civil marriage, and it didn't. The issue that over-35 women, under-35 men, over-35 men, all rated the highest priority was equality at work. Under-35 women rated – I think it was families. And marriage came down the line for people, actually.

IZZY KAMIKAZE: If you look at the stuff, it's really set up in such a way, they're looking for people to say, 'Marriage! We want marriage!' Looking for a mandate to be demanding marriage. But from what I remember – and I'm not in any way specialised in this, it's not even one of my main interests – I flipped through it at the time the way people did, but from what I remember, the only group where there was a clear majority demanding gay marriage and where it was their number one priority was young women. Now young women are women who have not yet had any experience of marriage [and] are the ones who tend to have the most romanticised idea of what marriage is about, but men of any age weren't at that point demanding or seeing marriage as their number one issue and older women weren't seeing marriage as their number one issue. It was purely that group and I do remember finding that aspect of the survey quite satisfying. It really confirmed that the same things were important to people that were always important: violence, discrimination in the workplace. Those were the things that were the actual burning issues that were identified by that. And there isn't anything like enough work happening on those things, or enough resources going into those things. Marriage is about what marriage has always been about. I think it is a class thing and so on, that that's what's being pushed, because marriage is very important to people who have property, to people who have pensions, you know? It's not that important for a lot of gay people that I know.

UNA MCKEVITT: I guess the weird thing is, in a way it doesn't feel edgy anymore. That's a really terrible thing to say, but there's no economic opposition to marriage, to gay marriage, so it will probably happen. There's no reason, nobody's going to lose financially from it, so the stakes aren't maybe as high as other issues like the work/life balance for women and things like that. It's just not as interesting for me. But I still think it's essential. It's just a shame anyone gets married. It is always a strange thing, the co-opting into this ultimately patriarchal system, which is what marriage is.

KATHERINE O'DONNELL: These marriages are going to break up, at least some of them. And so another form of magical thinking as well, that again comes out through particularly public debates; people seem to think that by being allowed to marry they are going to find the prince that's going to keep them happy forever afterwards. That's actually a very idealised notion of what marriage can provide and give.

TONIE WALSH: The drive for marriage equality is all about equality at the end of the day, when you strip it all away and if people are brutally honest … I've always been more intrigued by how ordinary LGBT people are just getting on with the business of their lives because I actually think in many ways that's infinitely more subversive. It's the old feminist mantra; the personal is political.

MARIE MULHOLLAND: I remember having dinner a few years back with an old friend I hadn't seen in a very long time. She'd be older than me. She had been a single parent back in the '70s as an out lesbian. She had a really, really hard time. We were chatting about her son who was now a grown adult about to get married and all the rest of it. I was asking how he was doing and I said, 'God, when you think what you came through, and look at him; he's a credit to you. I know things were really tough.' She came from rural west of Ireland, her family rejected her and everything else, and that was just for being pregnant. When the gay thing came out it was even worse … I said, 'What do you think now when you look back on it?' And she says, 'Well, you know, I spent twenty-five years being ostracised for being an unmarried mother. Now it looks like I'm about to be ostracised for being an unmarried lesbian.' For me, that summed the whole thing up.

GRÁINNE HEALY: Marriage is the portal for the recognition for us as human beings, as our families actually being families. So it seems to be such a simple, straightforward thing, but actually its significance is enormous, both personally and politically. That's why this one is going to be an important one to win and one that I'm determined to stick with it until we get it through.

IZZY KAMIKAZE: It must be five years ago, they introduced a debate, a one-off debate, into the Cork Women's Weekend as a one-off thing. I thought that was very interesting. Katherine O'Donnell to the best of my recollection chaired it … One of the things that I would have said there – and I take responsibility for this – is younger people in the community are not really aware of the history. And I don't think it's on to blame them for that. How are they going to be aware of the history if we don't fucking tell them? That's our job. So I remember one younger woman standing up at that debate that day, maybe 23 or something, and saying, 'I've been out since I was 14 and getting married is the first thing I've ever been told in my life that I can't do because I'm gay.' And I was thinking: there's the fucking culture shock. Ok! Well, I can see how it could feel important to you in that relatively cosseted situation. Like, you obviously didn't grow up somewhere where you were having stones thrown at you every time you stuck your head outside your front door. You obviously have a very supportive family, probably the kind of people I used to go marching with thirty years ago, and all of that. So you've got the illusion that that's the battle to fight now, that that's all that's standing between you and equality. And it is an illusion.

KATHERINE O'DONNELL: I gave a talk at Cork Women's Fun Weekend around critiques of marriage. And I ended by quoting this kind of young 17-year-old who had been given the back page of *GCN*, and I found what he said really annoying and I was pointing out why I found it annoying. A friend of mine came up to me afterwards, another lesbian who's also an academic, and just said, 'Oh, you just lost all the young women; they're raging with you.' And they were, they were furious, though none of them would chat with me about it, because I had mocked this guy. And I suppose they were right. I could have been more sympathetic towards him in some ways. But I was really annoyed because I felt – I'm trying to get over this – but I felt, you know, I had done so much. This is going to show me up to be the prig I am, but anyway! I had done so much for him. And he wasn't recognising me as a forebear or ancestor or a mother. He was trying to fit in with, obviously, you know, a sweet boy from around here who's going to a fee-paying school and he wanted all of that, all of that privileged world, and he wasn't identifying at all with any of the things that we had built and made. And I was thinking, 'Well, how would he know? He's not encouraged to think in that way. He's not encouraged to explore the fact that there's been a wealth of a gay movement that had all kinds of alternative ways of being gay and alternative ways of living in the world.' It hasn't just been a movement around sexual freedom – it's been an awful lot more interesting than that. How would he know about that? And that's what makes me sad, that actually there's a big generation split. And I'm not elderly, but I'm a different generation certainly to the 17-year-olds, and certainly to the 20-year-olds and even to the early 30s in some ways. And there has been no transfer of knowledge. There's been no engagement. There's been no passing on anything. There's been no place where we could meet each other as generations of queer people, generations of gays and lesbians, and I feel really sad about that, that we never managed to build a culture that could have been transmitted and changed by the younger generations and that there just seemed to be this rupture and he wanted to be just like his brothers, rather than have anything to do with the kind of world that I was imagining I was building for people like him. So I've had to just get over that.

And it's my fault more than his that that stuff wasn't passed on. And even if he'd known about it, he probably still would have picked the brothers anyway.

DECLAN BUCKLEY: When I was really young, my view of life because of what I was seeing was [that] in order to live as a gay person, what you had to do was you had to keep it to yourself. You hid. Sometimes plainly in view. So many gay people actually chose to get married to mostly unwitting members of the opposite sex and they ended up in these sham marriages, straight marriages when they were clearly gay. When I was younger you wouldn't have done that. Nobody my age would have, it was the tail end of that kind of behaviour. In order to live your life being a gay person, what you might feel what you had to do is reject society, and go into a kind of a gay ghetto. So you were actually ditching society, rather than giving the ultimate price in order to be part of it. And now it seems to have come the whole way back again, where we're actually giving up our individuality, we're giving up the gay identity in order to be this kind of homogenised marriageable people. We're conforming in that way. And obviously there's the intellectual, philosophical discussion of what marriage is, but that's not something that happens in bars. You don't have that conversation, unless it happens in a conversation like this and you get into something that's, 'Well, this is what the opponents of gay marriage are saying – what do you think about that from a philosophical point of view?' But I don't think that's the level most gay people are even approaching the issue. They're approaching the issue as, 'Why can't we have this?' It all taps down to this, 'We're different than you, we're lesser than you; give us an even playing field,' even if giving it to us is actually more of a sacrifice from our point of view than it is from 'society' because what we're giving up is some sort of – without sounding like a total tosser – some sort of enlightened view of the world. We've learned a lot about ourselves through the struggle of coming out without others being amenable to it. We've also learned a lot about ourselves and each other in this gay community which is so cross-cultural, cross-social sectors. And when you compare it against the 'normal' heterosexual society, we have a different balance between the genders as well. So there's a lot of different things that we've learned as a community that is in danger of being taken away, even just in terms of knowledge, when we – if we – what we do if we're 'good' enough.

If we're 'good' enough to get gay-married, then we become the same as everybody else. And the only people left outside marriage are anybody who has radical feminist views on the whole idea of what you're getting into, people who've got extremely left-wing views, people who are maybe as usual the unmarriageable types – all of the people in our community who are lower down the rungs. Because it's all about normalising. The people who are privileged enough to get privileges quickly forget about the people who don't have the privileges and I think that's sad. If we end up in a situation where we lose our empathy which we gained from a sense of lacking. Again, it's very disassociated. We want the right to say, 'I'm mad about whoever and I want the world to know that.' That's kind of a very emotional-based thing. The rational discussion is: is this a good thing for us?

UNA MCKEVITT: How people are treated depends on how they're viewed and what rights they're entitled to. That's how we regard people. So in order to be regarded as people that aren't 'less than', we should have the same as everybody else. However, I don't think it's gay people's jobs to come up with an alternative to marriage. I mean, the government have come up with civil partnership, and that's the alternative! But I think marriage is a very problematic institution that, you know, it organises society. I wouldn't want to be organised that way, myself.

AILBHE SMYTH: I do think it's up to us as lesbians and as gays to really work to create marriages that don't fall into traditional heterosexual patterns. And that's a tall order. It's always a little bit like saying lesbians and gays have to do a bit better than straight people. I know that's a tall order, I know it's probably a romantic expectation, but I would still have it, that we would find ways of being married and doing being married that would be more open and are – I suppose, that seek a different kind of, more of an equilibrium between partners and relationships.

BRENDAN COURTNEY: The irony is, part of it I would never have cared about because personally I wouldn't believe in marriage. I don't believe that one person needs to be bound to someone legally for the rest of their lives to participate in society. But that's not what it's about; it's about equal rights. But going back to what Tonie said, something about that we used to march about our difference and now we're marching to conform? Well, that's my personal belief as well. I don't know if I'd have a celebration of my relationship in that way, having seen people go through protracted divorces. And I know plenty of straight couples who've been together for years and who've never married. It's an odd personal thing, but that doesn't matter because the point is I want the same rights. And I want to be able to do it if I change my mind! And the protection of families is very important for people, that's the crucial thing.

IZZY KAMIKAZE: The central thing for me about marriage – I don't have a problem with it, but it's essentially a private thing between people. I don't think it's the State's business. I say that as someone who's been in a relationship with someone for 17 years, someone I hope to die with. Relationships are obviously wonderful things, but they're private things. It shouldn't really change your civil status in society as a single person or a married person or a married-for-a-second-time person or a person with children or a person without children or a couldn't-care-less person or a person in more than one relationship. It shouldn't change your status.

PHILLY MCMAHON: It's been annoying and galvanising, and focusing and depressing. It has made us pull together in a positive way. I don't want to get married or believe in the institution, but I support the right of anyone else to do that. But because we all have to be on message to convince the majority, we don't get to have an open debate about what marriage means for queers. For me personally, all the things that I wasn't allowed to do pushed me to the more interesting and subversive corners of society. It made me question everything. That was the making of me. I want equal rights – but I think the more heteronormative or mainstream we get, the more we lose of our own carved-out culture, queer culture. I can't really criticise the movement. I'm always in awe of ordinary folk who stick their neck out. So many people have done that in this campaign when they just as easily could have stayed at home. It felt like many disparate elements finally came together to head into the referendum. I think Panti has galvanised people too. Of course her [Noble Call] speech wasn't about marriage, but it all feeds in. Like the rest of the population, we want to be able to stop talking about it. There's no joy in spending years trying to convince decent-thinking people that you should have the same rights as them, and many of them disagreeing.

BUZZ O'NEILL: I can't speak for anyone but myself, but I was best man at my brother's wedding. And when he asked me to be best man at his wedding, that's when I came out to him. So when we talk about legal equality, for me personally it wasn't that. It was just parity. That he was getting married to an amazing woman who he loved and he wanted me to be part of that. And I felt that I was letting myself down by not being straight up and honest with him about who I was and what I wanted. And basically what I wanted, what I want, is exactly what he's got. That's what it means to me. I just want to be the same as my brother, apart from his dubious football-supporting allegiances. And that's it. Equality, equality, equality, equality. We don't want anything more than anybody else. We just want the same.

IZZY KAMIKAZE: Of course I think that if gay people wish to get married they should be able to get married. I don't think anybody is going to argue about that. If the State is providing a service of any sort, it should provide it equally to all – that's a relatively easy thing to sign up to. I don't have a problem with that. But is this the thing that should be being sold to the community as the means of delivering full equality for us? Is this where all of the community's resources or almost all of the community's resources is going? Is this where the focus should be? I don't think it is. So I decided, you know, I'm not going to stop anyone else from doing what they want to do, but I'm not going to get involved in it. But the fact that it's going on at all has flushed all the homophobes out of the woodwork as well, so I do find myself on Twitter and this kind of stuff arguing ... If the right wing are getting terribly worked up about marriage and attacking gay people and pulling out homophobic stereotypes and all the rest of it, you've got to engage with that to some extent. I'm willing to engage with it. I am quite a brave person. I am someone who was prepared to get out and march on the streets for gay people when there were twelve people who were prepared to do it. So of course I'm going to fight that fight. I am somebody who has suffered a lot of homophobic abuse, assaults, spitting, attacks on my home, all the rest of it, over the years. So of course I'm going to fight for gay people, of course I'm going to defend gay people when they're under attack, but my feeling is particularly in this country, as I say, I think a narrative was imported. And if you look at the gay marriage arguments, they're all the same arguments that are being used in other countries that don't have the same legislative or cultural background as Ireland.

MICHAEL BARRON: As a married man, I actually do have a lot of sympathy in many ways with the criticisms of marriage as an institution, but I think by getting married, you transform it, the institution of marriage itself. Two mad-looking fellas, myself and Jaime, going off to South Africa and getting married is different, you know? And that does have an effect on what marriage is for everyone. That's happening all over. In terms of a monopoly, see actually, I've said this – I don't know if it's necessarily a criticism of the movement or the people involved or how well it's been done at all – it's just that in ways there is a limited amount of airspace for issues. And I do think marriage equality has had probably a disproportionate space within that for sure. I do think – again, no criticism of the people involved, who I think are wonderful – but there are issues of severe marginalisation in the community, like LGBT refugees or travellers, young people experiencing mental health issues, all these things, you know, that marriage doesn't speak to. They're kind of harder things to get aired, to get funded, all of these things … You know it's popular, it's a really big international movement and all of those things for sure. Actually in the States, if you look at the funding though, it is kind of serious as well, the disproportionate funding that goes in – that doesn't actually happen here – the disproportionate amount of funding that goes into marriage in the States, versus the money that goes into supporting homeless teenagers, for example, there has been a shift. That actually doesn't happen here, marriage equality is quite underfunded. I do worry about that a little bit. I worry about the idea that it's a panacea as well. I had a conversation with the Freedom to Marry organisation in New York; I went to meet them a few years ago. They do wonderful work, but they were going as far as saying that bringing in marriage equality will end homophobic bullying in schools. And we're kind of going, 'Ah now, seriously, that's really not going to happen.' It's a piece of a jigsaw, it's not the whole thing. But I can understand the impulse, it's a campaign, so it's run like an election and the objective is to win, so you have to throw everything at it. But maybe if we're careful along the way that we don't overstate it as well because when it comes in there will still be all these others issues that will need to be fixed as well … It's funny though, because saying that sort of stuff – even that now in a mild way people can experience it as criticism, and it's absolutely not meant as criticism at all. It's just kind of like, 'Ok, let's keep trying to think of the bigger picture as we go through this', as well.

BERNARDINE QUINN: We're calling marriage equality 'equality' as if the day that there's a bill stamped saying lesbian and gay people can get married that we'll have full equality. Yet in Meath, there isn't one single support service for a young lesbian or gay person to attend; there isn't one qualified full-time youth worker to work with young LGBT people; there is absolutely zero trans services, where the trans services in Dublin are mediocre at best. There's something about 'marriage equality' – that we'll all be equal when marriage comes in, when a kid in west Kerry doesn't even have a telephone number of a helpline that he can ring for support. This was raised by our young people to Mairead McGuinness and to Mary Lou McDonald when they were here, just to say, thinking that your work around marriage equality – that that's not all. The allocation of finances to LGBT work in this country is tiny compared to what is given to most other services. There's something about calling it 'equality'. It's another step on the ladder and it's a hugely important step … But it isn't all. There's another battle after that, and that is to get services to west Donegal, to Mayo, into the Midlands, to get real, solid support in these areas so that a young LGBT person has something in every county, trained qualified people to talk to. In some areas where those services aren't available, where there isn't training for schools, where there's nobody that a kid can talk to, to say that they think they're transgender – I don't want to sound negative – I think marriage equality is going to be fantastic for a lot of lesbian and gay people. I think if you were 14 and coming out today, your story is going to be so much more different than when I was 14. The prospects of you considering yourself what every other young person considers themselves of 14 when you think about your future and what you're going to do: you're going to meet the person that you love, you're going to get married, going to have kids, going to have the house and the picket fence. That will be an option for a kid. When I came out, those dreams were put very firmly away. I was never going to get married, I was never going to have children, I was never going to make my family proud, my dad was never going to walk me up the aisle. All of those kinds of things were not even an option when I came out. As a matter of fact, there was a better chance that I was going to have to go to London, I was going to bring huge shame on my family, I probably would end up not speaking to half my siblings and my parents, having to go away and fend for myself. That was my option. I think that option has dramatically changed. People can live in their home towns easier now … Anything that makes a young person's life easier, and gives them more opportunities, is fantastic. I think that a young person, 14, 15, only starting to discover themselves, they've got a whole other suite of options. They can talk about, 'I'll eventually marry my partner.' I think I'm only after saying that for the first time in my life, that there will be an option to marry my partner.

BRODEN GIAMBRONE: The struggle for marriage equality affects all LGBT people … However, that said, it is clear that across the globe the marriage equality movement has monopolised the discussion on LGBT rights and often distilled it to marriage as the defining feature of the movement. In many countries, these movements are led by privileged gay men and lesbians who promote it as the last vestige of inequality. This is mirrored back to us in the quote from US VP Joe Biden, '[marriage equality] It's the civil rights of our day. It's the issue of our day.' Or the quote by Tánaiste Eamon Gilmore, '[Gay marriage] is the civil rights issue of our generation.' When marriage equality is positioned as the last stronghold of inequality and the great leveller of the rights of LGBT people in society, there is a failure to acknowledge other significant issues within the LGBT community … From my point of view, marriage equality is an undeniably pressing issue for the LGBT community and a fundamental right that we must all get behind in achieving. However, it is not the defining civil rights issue of our time. It is one of many that we face as a society that must be fought for and won. By positioning marriage equality as the last vestige of LGBT inequality we run the risk of depoliticisation of the LGBT community once it's been achieved. As in, we've won, we're done, let's go home. It's clear that the trans community must stand with the LGB community on this issue but there must be a recognition that trans rights are also human rights and must be supported, promoted and financed. Marriage equality should be seen as part of a struggle on many fronts and not the sum total of what we need to be free and equal.

AILBHE SMYTH: I would see it as very understandably valid criticism and I think it is something that as a community we absolutely have to watch out for and seek as far as possible to guard against. But I don't think it's entirely accurate either in that if I just think along that period we were fighting very hard in the NLGF to maintain *GCN* when the crash came, that was very much part of our community movement and try to make it as diverse as possible. BelongTo has done all its fantastic work during that same period of time in relation to young people. And so it's partly true and partly not true. Because it's a very big issue and a very key one, it has of course been a very dominant issue, but the reality is that the work on the ground, whether it's though BelongTo or through for example Dundalk Outcomers or through LGBT diversity or whether it's through the different ways in which the more cultural dimensions, whether it's GAZE or *GCN,* have also worked. Our community are involved in very many issues but it's not surprising. It would be surprising if marriage hadn't become that dominant because the reality is that the majority of people want that issue to be done and dusted and finished once and for all. While I have sympathy for the criticism and we do have to be very careful to ensure wherever we're working to think about a broad range of needs because that's what we work on, it's not surprising that the media like it as well. In a way now, at this stage of the game, we're pushing open doors.

BORIS DIETRICH, UCC CONFERENCE, 2014: There is a danger, after the marriage equality legislation was introduced … There was some kind of complacency. People thought 'Ok we've reached full equality, now we can sit down and relax.' And of course there are a lot of issues in relation to sexual orientation, gender identity, that you need to address. Discrimination still takes place. There is violence against gay men and lesbian women. When you talk about young kids at school, there is harassment, there is bullying. The suicide rate of young LGBT people is much higher than other young people. So there are a lot of issues to address, but somehow in the first few years after the introduction of marriage equality, everybody was satisfied and there was not really a fire to take on these other issues. So the LGBT community really had to reinvent itself, take on these issues, and now they of course are completely on board and active. Also our straight allies, because I was still a member of parliament talking about these issues, I could really feel that people thought, 'There he is again. He has the civil unions, he has marriage equality, now he starts talking about suicide or about violence in the streets, registration of hate crimes. Can't you stop? You have marriage equality.' And so it really took some time to persuade people to think marriage equality is not the end of the line, it's just part of a system where we need to fight discrimination and inequality.

24

THE CONSTITUTIONAL CONVENTION

'There was just this silence. Everyone just stopped.
It was amazing. It was incredible.'

– David Farrell

During the Programme for Government negotiations after the 2011 general election between the prospective government parties, Labour and Fine Gael, several – mostly broad, social – policies couldn't be agreed upon. In previous years, an appetite had grown amongst the electorate for talking shops, national conversations on the state of the nation, and town-hall formats. In the Programme for Government, a commitment to a Constitutional Convention was given. And in that convention, the 'provision for same-sex marriage' was to be one of the topics discussed.

DAVID FARRELL: All the main political parties without exception had political reform at the top of their agenda in their manifestos in the last election. You had the economy, and next was political reform. From the perspective of the political science community, there were quite a few of us feeding in the idea that if you were going to be serious about reform, it should be citizen-orientated and it should be some kind of process involving ordinary citizens. And the term 'Citizen Assembly' was one a few of us were bandying about a lot in opinion pieces and whenever we were ever able to get on the airwaves to talk about it. And that seemed to interest some politicians, particularly in Fine Gael and Labour. So Fine Gael in their manifesto talked about a citizens' assembly for electoral reform and women in politics, and I think more or less that. But the Labour Party talked about a Constitutional Convention to do a root-and-branch review of the constitution by 2016. So when they formed their government and

the Programme for Government, my understanding is late in the night
when they were up against the clock, they agreed there were a number of
items they couldn't agree on, so they were put into a bucket and 'give it to
a Constitutional Convention'. And one of those was same-sex marriage.

PROGRAMME FOR GOVERNMENT, 2011: Constitutional Reform: We will
establish a Constitutional Convention to consider comprehensive constitutional reform, with a brief to consider, as a whole or in sub-groups,
and report within twelve months on the following: Review of our Dáil
electoral system. Reducing the presidential term to five years and aligning
it with the local and European elections. Provision for same-sex marriage. Amending the clause on women in the home and encourage greater
participation of women in public life. Removing blasphemy from the
constitution. Possible reduction of the voting age. Other relevant constitutional amendments that may be recommended by the Convention.

ROSS GOLDEN BANNON: We were so close to not getting it in the
Programme for Government. And who knows what was the phone
call that tipped it? ... I kind of feel like we got it in by the skin of our
teeth. So we got it in, and it felt like us ending up at the Constitutional
Convention was an effort on their part to kick us into the long grass.
I kind of feel like we turned it into a triumph.

JOHN LYONS: It was the Labour Party that ensured that the Programme
for Government would set up the Constitutional Convention.

DAVID FARRELL: A group, myself included, were pushing and pushing
and pushing, because it was meant to have been set up immediately after
the government was formed, and it wasn't. We were also pushing for a
particular way in which it should operate because the assumption was
a convention would be made up of one-third citizens, one-third politicians, and one-third experts. Our view was that was not ideal, that if we
wanted this to be different it really should be the citizens on their own.
So we managed to get some funding, my little group, from Atlantic
Philanthropies to set up an entity called We The Citizens. And we ran
throughout 2011 with Fiach Mac Conghail as our chair, Caroline Erskine
as the main organiser behind the scenes, an absolutely amazing woman.
And our mission was to try to persuade the governing parties that they

should establish a citizens' assembly with the citizens. If they were going to do a qualitative convention they could call it whatever they liked, but that it should be more citizen-oriented. And we had a lot of data behind us to show that it could work, that citizens could be trusted. And we think we managed to have some success in that regard ... They finally set it up at the end of 2012. So I then contacted Art O'Leary who was designated as the key civil servant to run it, and it was clear Tom Arnold was about to be appointed chair. And I said to them that I had a skill set given my work with We The Citizens, and I'd like to support the work of the convention and that I had a couple of other people who would also be good in this regard. So there was a meeting and we discussed it and it was agreed I would be the Research Director.

A submissions process was established for civil society groups and organisations to feed into the discussion on topics before they came before the Convention.

DAVID FARRELL: The means of encouraging submissions from civil-society groups was through the website. For every one of our items we had submissions from all walks of life. But for the same-sex marriage one it was off the scale ... I think it was the order of a thousand of submissions. I think I'm not exaggerating when I say that. The other ones would be everything from twenty or thirty, up to maybe a few hundred. Nothing equalled in terms of coverage – in terms of everything – the same-sex marriage weekend was off the scale.

GRÁINNE HEALY: When we were in contact with the secretariat there, they were clear that they were not going to be able to allow a huge number of groups in to make proposals. So the decision was made that there would be thirty minutes for and thirty minutes against, and a number of us as organisations were brought in and told, 'You've 30 minutes.' So that's when we said, 'Ok.' We went off, we had an agreement, we said we're going to have to share up the thirty minutes between us, so the fairest thing would be ten-ten-ten. ICCL said, 'We don't think we need ten,' and we came up with a proposal that if we could have some time we would actually like to give some of our time to have the young people speaking. GLEN weren't that mad about having the young people speaking initially because I think they thought, 'Oh Jesus, let's not start talking about children. Let's not.' And we said, 'No, no, we think actually these adult children will be really good; we've seen them, we've had them in with ministers.' I mean, they were the reason Micheál Martin immediately said he would be supporting the marriage equality motion at their [Fianna Fáil's] convention.

On 13 April 2013, the Constitutional Convention met at the Grand Hotel in Malahide in Dublin to discuss the issue of marriage equality. The convention was made up of one-third citizens, one-third politicians, one-third experts.

DAVID FARRELL: Once we've identified the experts, we discuss it with the steering groups. So there's a steering group made up of members of the convention, mostly the citizen members and a few politicians … The experts would write a briefing document, ideally a week in advance, so the members would get access to the document – between three and five pages usually. And so that would mean they would have some homework they could have done beforehand. The weekend starts by the experts each giving fifteen- or twenty-minute presentations based on the briefing document in a plenary and then answering any questions from the floor. We then go into small-group deliberation with trained facilitators at each table where the experts are off to one side in the room and my group's job then is to keep an eye on the discussions and our facilitators are trained to let us know if there are any issues coming up where there's some uncertainty, because the job of the facilitator is not to answer the question; it's to facilitate the process. A hand goes up, we would go and get an expert, bring them to the table, try to make sure they answer just those questions. So that's the sort of general, generic framework. And then later in the day we had the advocacy groups come in and be involved in the panel discussion and answer questions, again with the experts on hand to try afterwards to frame or contextualise any issues that might have come up. Then there's more small-group deliberation. And as we're getting close to the end of the weekend, our group is observing all of this, keeping an eye on it and trying to second-guess how a ballot paper would look. We then draw up a ballot paper, put it to the members and ask them to improve it for us. That's usually a very messy process but it gets results. And we finally got a ballot paper agreed and the members voted.

ROSS GOLDEN BANNON: The actual convention itself was so professionally managed. Even to the point of facilitating beyond necessity to those who were so vehemently opposed to us. I thought it was just beautifully managed, and I don't mean in a negative way – just really well done. I'm not a great one for saying, 'I'm so proud to be Irish!' It's very rare that I'm proud to be Irish. I was very proud to be Irish at the Constitutional Convention.

DAVID FARRELL: We had everything from a Catholic bishop in all his regalia basically very politely but very firmly telling us the position of the Catholic Church on same-sex marriage on one extreme to adult children of same-sex couples just standing up and talking about their lives, perfectly normal lives, that they've experienced as young adults now. And so I suppose the way I framed it in my own head was the anti side were trying to talk from the head, whereas the pro side were talking more from the heart. And the experience I've certainly had from observing this process throughout the year is that it's the latter that seems to work better in terms of moving people … Then we had the discussion from Colm O'Gorman and others, we had what's-his-name from the Iona Institute – David Quinn. So they were all on the same stage together debating the issues in a very frank and assertive discussion, but for the most part pretty respectful. And there were some telling moments, particularly when Colm talked about his weekly life as a parent, getting his children ready for school and taking them to school, and, you know, on the one hand trying to show how normal things were, and on the other hand trying to get across the message that, for him, things are very far from normal in terms of how the State sees him.

COLM O'GORMAN: I found myself kind of stepping out of what I was going to say and saying something quite different because I'm really, really, really tired of having to sit there patiently and smile, and be calm in the face of people telling me that I'm not fit to parent my children because of my sexual orientation. On the basis of no evidence. On the basis of their personally held convictions that are grounded in their religious beliefs. And they're perfectly entitled to those convictions, and they're absolutely entitled to voice them – I'll champion their right to voice them – but it doesn't mean that I have to sit there and not call them out on what they're saying. I won't do so aggressively. But it's not my job to protect other people from their own prejudice, actually. The thing that just amazes me is that anybody could exist in 2014, particularly people who would view themselves as intellectuals, and who are intellectuals in

many ways, and professional people who purport to be significant commentators or social scientists, and that they would be offended by the
mere suggestion that they hold views that are prejudiced.

DAVID FARRELL: And it has to be said there was also an awful lot of activity
from the floor. We had Rónán Mullen as one of our members. The way
this operated is that the politician members could rotate – they wouldn't
necessarily be there for all meetings – and for that meeting we had Rónán
Mullen. And he clearly was very exercised about the issues, so he on
several occasions intervened at some length to try and influence how the
discussion was going. It was a disruptive presence, if I'm being honest.
Very disruptive. And I think he didn't do himself any favours, because
after a certain amount of this, it was pretty clear the other members were
just so annoyed with him, that he got the opposite reaction to what he
was trying to get.

COLM O'GORMAN: It was a bit mad actually because the Constitutional
Convention was happening at the same time as our annual conference.
Amnesty's annual conference was the same days. And I'd been asked
to come down to participate from an Amnesty perspective in a panel
discussion. On the panel discussion was myself and Conor O'Mahony
from UCC, who were supportive of marriage equality and constitutional
reform, Carol Coulter was there as the independent, uncommitted, in-
the-middle person, and on the other side was David Quinn, and a guy
from – what's Paddy Manning's crowd called? – Preserve Marriage. I was
listening to what was being said both from the platform and from the
floor. It's not like people from the floor were being particularly adver-
sarial or negative, but I think I'd just had my fill of this messaging about
just this dehumanising argument that's presented by the other side.
And I suppose I was just very conscious of the fact that in part what
was required and what's required of us as people to win this argument,
it's a bit like that fabulous Marriage Equality video, 'Sinead's Hand'; that
we are actually asking people for permission to love. 'Would you please
respect and value my loving relationships? Would that be ok with you?
Would you mind terribly? Thanks.' It's so bloody offensive. And it's
so wrong. And it's so exposing. In my life I've often found myself in a
position where I am saying things that are very self-exposing because
I believe passionately that it reveals something that we need to face as a

society ... I don't think that many of those who oppose marriage equality are necessarily vicious, vengeful people. I think what they say is hateful but it's thoughtlessly so. I think it's unconsciously so. I don't think they know it. And I think that's what's so challenging about it. I'm going to go back a little for a moment: when I talked about the nature of the debate, I think that's one of the things that we need to recognise. As much as I'm going to be offended by the things that they say when I challenge them on the basis of their opinions, I am absolutely challenging something that is incredibly vital for them and that is the sense of themselves as good, and true, and pure, and even holy. And that their views of the world, which I experience as hateful, are grounded in godliness. If you believe that about yourself, having a mirror held up to that is incredibly threatening. So there's going to be a very defensive and possibly even quite violent and aggressive response to that, and that's part of what we're seeing play out now, you know. And I just said it: I'm really tired – and I became very emotional saying it – of constantly having to expose myself and my family to it; it's just not ok. So I talked about how I felt about my kids and how I knew they felt about me ... It's like, our lives are our lives. They are not different. They are not other. They are our lives. And we share those lives in common with you. Our families are our families. And can we please not do this anymore? I don't want to do this anymore.

DAVID FARRELL: For me there were some tingling moments. And I know there were quite a lot of tears, frankly, in the room. It was impossible not to. I think it was the children when they spoke, just about what it was like to be a child of a same-sex couple in Ireland and how normal they were, but at the same time how exceptional they were in terms of how they might be treated by the State.

CONOR PRENDERGAST: It was a real honour. It was so interesting, such a great weekend, really positive and incredibly historic, you know? There are very few moments since I've been talking about this and involved that I've seen as milestones. You can look at a particular event or a particular occasion and say, 'God, that was a critical moment.' But I think the Constitutional Convention was a critical moment. Just how positive, looking back, watching the speeches, and even there at the time, the speeches of the 'in-favour side', so those in favour of extending marriage rights to same-sex couples. They were very positive speeches. They were quite uplifting. They were all really personal, but there was also that really strong evidence base there as well, which I like because I studied psychology and I'm always interested in that. But the no side was a little more doom and gloom, and it was a bit depressing.

IVANA BACIK: They [children of same-sex parents] gave a superb presentation at the Constitutional Convention; it was just electrifying. People were in tears, you know?

CONOR PRENDERGAST: It was very quick, probably the quickest speech I've ever given. Bang on three minutes. But it was basically, 'Hello. I'm Conor. Lesbians raised me and I didn't turn out with a third arm. Here's another person! Look! She also didn't turn out with a third arm. I know other people who were raised by same-sex people; funnily enough, they're relatively normal, or stable, or whatever. We're a happy family. It's not outrageous to want marriage equality. Let's do it.' That's paraphrasing of course – it was far more eloquent than that! Again, my story is a fairly simple story. It's the regular day to day for me. My mothers raised me. My brother appeared and I was very jealous and annoyed until we both grew out of our teens and then we both realised that we both really love each other as all teenage boys do. And therefore, stop treating families of same-sex couples and same-sex couples themselves like second-class citizens. It's not an outrageous idea. In some ways, it's very like the civil rights movement of the '60s and '70s.

GRÁINNE HEALY: GLEN gave us some of their time to allow the voices of children to be heard that day and that swung it, no doubt in my mind. Yes, we were all good, but when Conor and Claire stood up, I met people in the loo after it and they were blown away by these young kids saying, 'I want my parents to be able to be married.' End of story.

DAVID FARRELL: But the most emotional moment was on the Sunday morning. One of the older members asked to speak. And as far as I can remember he was not a particular one who had spoken a lot to camera and microphone. He was using the phrase 'the gays' the way – you know, clearly he was not accustomed to talking about this issue in public. And he started by saying, 'I've never said this to anyone before, but when

I was a child I was molested by a man; I was abused by a man, and I'd always been against the gays ever since, and I always felt that the gays were people I shouldn't have any involvement with' – I'm paraphrasing here. And he said, 'But now I'm grown up and I understand more. And particularly now that I've witnessed and heard what I've heard this weekend I will be voting for same-sex marriage.' There was just this silence. Everyone just stopped. It was amazing. It was incredible.

JOHN LYONS: If you ask any of the one hundred members of the Constitutional Convention … 'What was your most strongest memory from the Constitutional Convention?' If anybody who was there – if anybody who wasn't there could touch the feelings people were feeling inside those two days, they'd say the Constitutional Convention on same-sex marriage weekend is the one that they'll remember most. There were just amazing things happening there that weekend. Humanity was coming out, pure humanity. It was – wow, just wow, unbelievable.

DAVID FARRELL: Jerry Buttimer and John Lyons were both members that weekend and both made incredible interjections from the floor. Again there was tingling, particularly in the case of John when he spoke from the heart.

On the final day of discussions, a vote was cast on whether those in attendance supported same-sex marriage. There was huge interest within the LGBT community in the vote. This was an opportunity for same-sex marriage to be voted on in an official forum. The result would either be a vote of confidence, support and solidarity, or a moment for the issue to be positioned on shaky ground. The online broadcast was streamed live at PantiBar in Dublin, although the stream broke down and most were left checking Twitter and text messages from those in attendance to get the result of the vote: 79 per cent voted to change the constitution to provide for civil marriage for same-sex couples; 78 per cent favoured directive or mandatory wording in the event of such an amendment going ahead, meaning that the State should be obliged to enact laws providing for same-sex marriage; 81 per cent voted for the State to enact laws incorporating necessary changed arrangements in regard to the parentage, guardianship and upbringing of children in lesbian- and gay-headed families.

DAVID FARRELL: And you could just hear once the result came out, you could actually hear the cheer from outside.

GRÁINNE HEALY: I was surprised at the 79 per cent, I have to say, but it was very evident after the children spoke and because we were able to be in the room, you could hear some of the conversations that were going on.

ROSS GOLDEN BANNON: We were leaving and this very elderly conventioner, one of the one hundred, this very elderly man was leaving. And he was so infirm he had to hold on to the banisters to go down the stairs. And he stopped and he grabbed my arm and he said, 'This is your republic too. This is your republic too. I voted for you.' I was just completely overwhelmed. Completely overwhelmed that a man of his age had come so far and felt so strongly about us being really part of the Republic. I was just blown away. And people had a lot of stories like that.

SANDRA IRWIN-GOWRAN: I think the Constitutional Convention was a huge boost for the figures of 79 per cent, and 81 per cent around children and families, to result from that selection of 100 citizens was quite phenomenal, hugely bolstering.

GERARD HOWLIN: I don't think it was phenomenal. I don't think it's up to very much at all. And I think it was a mechanism mainly established to make sure lots of things didn't happen. And in relation to same-sex marriage, to bring it on to the table in a structured way, given the pre-existing commitment. So in relation to same-sex marriage, I think the convention's job was as a – I say pre-cook something that had been decided and in relation to lots of other things was effectively to ensure they didn't happen. So I have to say, I'm not an admirer of the Constitutional Convention at all.

NOEL WHELAN: The Constitutional Convention has got to be seen in a couple of contexts. Firstly a third of the members of the Constitutional Convention were politicians, all of whose parties, with the exception of Rónán Mullen, had signed up in advance for the introduction of marriage equality. So they were all going in there, already voting for marriage equality and arguing, and I had been at the Constitutional Convention for other issues and having an impact in it. So nobody believes that the mood in the country is the 80 per cent, as it was at the Constitutional Convention.

DAVID FARRELL: I think criticism is fair, except what I would say is that in the detail of the – I don't know what you'd call it – regulation or whatever, the document that was passed in the Oireachtas to establish the Convention. In the detail, it made it very clear that the government was committed to responding to the report of the convention, that after its weekend, the convention writes a report and lodges it in the Oireachtas and the government is committed to responding formally in the Dáil within four months in receipt of that report. And that's something I've never seen before, where the government is committed to actually responding because commonly what you'll have is a report, sometimes an extremely good report, that is submitted and never sees the light of day. It just goes into the long grass. So at least they say they'll respond ... And yeah, some things have been kicked into touch – the report on the role of women in politics and public life, that's evidently been kicked into touch – and that's a big disappointment. So my personal hope that if a third or more of the recommendations that are proposing referendums do go forward to referendums, that's a pretty good hitting rate.

SUZY BYRNE: The Constitutional Convention actually sort of made it like that we have to have a referendum.

CHARLIE FLANAGAN: I believe that the referendum campaign would have been divisive, more divisive than it is going to be if it weren't for the Constitutional Convention. And that was an extraordinary weekend in terms again of that building process. The gaining of acceptance, broad acceptance amongst people. This was a group of politicians engaging with and in many respects listening to members of society and oftentimes politicians are too beholden to focus groups and campaign techniques rather than fora like the Constitutional Convention.

GRÁINNE HEALY: I wrote to Mark in the ICCL and I wrote to Kieran and Brian in GLEN and I suggested that maybe at the end of May the three organisations would have a sit down and see how we could work together to ensure that we got the correct response from the government, because they had six months. So that's when we started working together.

DAVID FARRELL: I don't think we would be having this referendum if it hadn't been for the convention. I think it's forced the hand of the Taoiseach and he's had no choice because Labour were clearly pushing for it, but this brought it so much to a head. I don't think Enda Kenny had any choice but to go ahead and say, 'Ok, we'll have this referendum.' So I think it gave a very important weapon to Eamon Gilmore and his party to push once and for all to have the referendum.

JOHN LYONS: I can remember making a call after the Constitutional Convention to Mark Garrett, who would be Eamon's [Gilmore] chief advisor, saying, 'Look, we have to make sure at cabinet that a decision is reached on this.' And he was as passionate about ensuring this was delivered as I am. So the people who sometimes oil the engine were making sure the engine was going to deliver the outcome, although from the outside there might have been scepticism. I did imagine the odd time, because I'm not always a blue-sky type guy, 'What would you do if this doesn't happen?' And you know, I kind of thought maybe a little bit irrationally about what would I do, because it was an issue that – as I said, I wasn't thinking at the time when I came in but became intrinsically linked to the issue and passionate about the issue. I would have been deeply, deeply upset if the Labour Party didn't show muscle on this one. They've shown muscle on a lot of things that people don't see. But on this thing, they had to show their muscle on this.

After the Constitutional Convention, GLEN and Marriage Equality began a new process of collaboration.

GRAINNE HEALY: We had managed to work so well during that that I invited GLEN and ICCL to come to a meeting to just have a conversation.

TIERNAN BRADY: There was contact pretty much from that point on. What was initially two monthly meetings, or monthly meetings, we tried to continue them on to the point we're at now where we're meeting every fortnight, and we're in continuous contact together on a daily basis in terms of emails. It would have flown from the Convention that worked, and that realisation when we're all in the one space and we're finally fighting on the same platform against our opponents, which prior to this we would have been each other's opponents more often than not sometimes. I mean in the small 'o' rather that the big 'o' sense... We're past the point of where the difference is important enough. The differences are getting smaller and smaller... you get to where you go 'it is more important to win than who wins.' We can fight about who wins all day long, but campaigns that fight about who wins tend to lose.

GRAINNE HEALY: It hasn't been the easiest thing I've ever done, but these things are really important, and you just have to get over some of you own stuff, and I think everyone has tried to do that.

TIERNAN BRADY: For many people especially from GLEN's perspective, there were moments that were very bruising in the course of civil partnership passing, and there were moments where people felt that there was no doubt that they had pursued a strategy and had to do significant lifting and felt battered by the process because of the nature of the two principles, or the two differences at the time. No more than anything, we didn't all run into the room together and all hug… and there are personality issues. And much of that is about bruised emotions and being on the other side of an argument for a long time has an impact, of course it does, but this is the moment where you had to swallow your ego and go, look, this is the generational fight that we've worked towards, now we're at the point where it's about to happen and we have to always make sure that we're pushing down that tendency that's inside all human beings to want to win just to look like the winner, when in fact it's more important to win than who is the winner on this one.

GRAINNE HEALY: I think we all realised that the writing would be on the wall then. We were just going to have to work together to get this one route that is now open to us. To be fair I think everybody pretty much got with that programme as soon as we were clear that was it was going to happen.

25

CALLING THE REFERENDUM

'In respect of today's decision, I support that very
strongly and will campaign for it when it comes.'

– Enda Kenny, 5 November 2013

*On 5 November 2013, the cabinet agreed to hold a referendum on marriage equality
before the summer of 2015.*

STEPHEN COLLINS: The fact that Fine Gael as such are in favour of the
proposition and the Taoiseach would speak for it would indicate a huge
shift if you look back over where this would have been ten or twenty
years ago.

TIERNAN BRADY: Politicians hate referendums and rightly so, because
referendums are wild animals – you don't know where it's going to go.
And it can swim off down avenues that you had no idea.

BRIAN FINNEGAN: I think it's a dark, dark thing to cycle to work and see
a poster or a billboard saying that you are dangerous and bad, because
that's what's going to happen. There will be funded – mostly through
America – funded organisations who will have big campaigns saying that
gay people are damaging to children. As the father of a 22-year-old, I find
it deeply upsetting. And so I think it'll be really interesting. I dread it, but
it would be very interesting to see whether that took effect and it could.
Ireland only voted for divorce by 1 per cent – 1 per cent. And the previous time it failed and there was massive, massive campaigns, big funded
campaigns during divorce referendums, the first and second divorce

referendum saying that chaos was going to ensue in Ireland. And people voted based on those messages. These messages are strong, and they're powerful, so that message that gay people are damaging to children is actually fundamental … It goes into the psyche and it goes deep into people, that prejudice. So I would be really frightened about that prejudice being stoked, you know? I would hate to see that prejudice being stoked.

MICHAEL BARRON: I just think it's outrageous that it has to happen at all, that we have to have a referendum on our basic rights. In terms of impact, I would worry about the impact on young people, particularly, who are struggling to come out, or are out and dealing with families. They're going to hear a huge amount of homophobia on television on radio. Their parents are often going to get involved in that homophobia … that continuous wear and tear of homophobia. Young people get it in school every day of the week, all the time, so on the radio and in the papers all the time as well, it's going to be tough.

FIONA DE LONDRAS: We have lots of things that are very good about having a referendum on the constitution. The fact that the constitution should reflect our values, and so on, but what's the flip side? What's the cost? When we have a referendum like this, we literally have to stand in front of our friends, family, neighbours and say, 'Recognise me.' The risk is that they say no. And that causes problems; that's hard; there's a massive social cost to that. And me or you, we can do it, but we're used to it, this is part of the give and take of our everyday life. We are not the typical person who needs this. We're the atypical person. So I think about the 14-year-old in school who's listening to this stuff on the radio. Or the 65-year-old closeted farmer in the middle of Cavan. And people are talking about us, and it's our lives and it's part of our lives we have no control over. That's a massive cost. Most things are not about a core attribute of a person. That cost has arisen when we had an abortion referendum, when we had that egregious citizenships referendum, that must've been what it felt like for people then too. But where there was another option, I cannot fully comprehend why the government would have asked us to bear this social cost. Now, the social benefit that comes afterwards in enormous, because we've all these vulnerabilities we've exposed ourselves to, and our fellow citizens say, 'You're equal,' and that is good. And it will give a level of democratic legitimacy that a Supreme Court wouldn't give. But my God, it's going to cost.

GERARD HOWLIN: It's a fact that Irish people in successive referenda on all sorts of issues have been incredibly conservative, with a small 'c', not an ideological 'C'. 'If in doubt, vote no' is one definitely huge factor, so there's a high threshold to persuading people one by one. And there's also that people understand when they vote in a referendum that [it's] unlike in elections where they change governments very effectively but change patterns of power hardly at all. And you can see that in the 2011 election, where we had the third largest turnover of parliamentarians in any general election in any western democracy since the Second World War, to ensure the continuation of the policies that had been put in place by the government that was trashed to a degree unprecedented in the history of the Irish State. In a referendum, whether it's more powers for Oireachtas committees, whether in the past it's been abortion or divorce or whatever, people understand that this is their one opportunity to give or not to give a significant new power, and they really have to be persuaded to give that consent or assent, I suppose. And they have proved very cautious and conservative with a small 'c' about doing that. So for all of those reasons and the fact that there isn't a single vote in a single box for this proposition, I think a lot of caution [is needed]. This is not nearly done and, you know, there will be an opposition and there will be a public debate, and people are entitled to ask themselves and ask in public if this is a good idea. And that has to be debated rationally and coolly … Votes don't come in trenches, in percentages, they don't come in socio-economic groups. They come in ones. That's the only way you can get votes: ones. Every single yes vote has to be personally persuaded. And if you start from that understanding of how you personally persuade over 51 per cent of the electorate who will turn up on the day – which is a subset of the population, which is quite different from the population, by the way, not particularly fair or democratic, but it's how it's going to work out – where are we now? And I think we've an awful lot of work to do. An awful lot.

AVERIL POWER: When we're looking into the referendum and tactics for the referendum on how to persuade people, I think it is more about giving people opportunities to understand the human impact of discrimination.

JOHN LYONS: When I'm in the smoking area of the Private Members' Bar, which obviously only members can go to because you have to go through the bar to go to it, you're not disturbed by anyone. It's great. There's usually a bunch of lads out there, men, grown men. The odd one has often said to me, 'The likes of yourself and Jerry Buttimer have done more for us around seeing the issues of LGBT than anybody else has, because we see you as one of us.' It's come up the odd time in conversation – it might have been over a drink, to be honest! A drunken man's words are a sober man's thoughts – that's the phrase isn't it? So when you hear things like that you're kind of thinking, alright, by myself and Jerry being here, just being in here, them seeing us as other human beings, I think that does something to normalise people's perception within the political world to think, 'Jesus, what the hell have we been doing here?' You know? I think that has played a little part as well. I'd be lying if I didn't say that, but you almost feel you shouldn't say that because you shouldn't talk yourself up.

STEPHEN COLLINS: [Jerry] is a very popular member of the party, and I know, for instance, talking to one person who would be very much on the conservative side who said, 'Well, I'm a friend of Jerry's. I wouldn't be in favour of this, but I'm certainly not going to oppose. He's a good guy. He thinks it's ok, so I'm not going to be standing in the way.'

NIALL CROWLEY: It's a terrible situation that something like this has to be decided by referendum. I think it should have been legislated for and then see what happens on that. You can't appeal to people's generosity for such basic rights in a way. That shouldn't have to happen.

NOEL WHELAN: My own legal assessment has always been that it was always going to require a constitutional referendum. I don't think you ever would have persuaded a Supreme Court that when the people went to vote for the constitution in the 1930s and put marriage into it that they regarded it as anything except marriage between a male and a female. I think Irish society has evolved and changed and could be persuaded to change that now – but that it was going to have to be changed in a referendum. Once you're stuck with that reality, once you're stuck with the reality that you require a referendum, you need to persuade a million plus people.

26

PANTIGATE

'I'll never forget the fear of being called a faggot.'

– Jerry Buttimer

Aside from champions of either side of the debate, for the most part the Irish media operated in a slightly 'hands-off' kind of way when it came to LGBT rights.

NÓIRÍN HEGARTY: In the *Evening Herald*, and the Independent group, in my time there right through the '90s, 2000s, it was not on the radar. I would honestly say it's only in the last six or seven years that I would even have been conscious of it as a media issue. What you'd get is, there'd be a couple of fancy pictures taken at the Pride march of strange-looking people landing in, but really, there were very few gay people written about. David Norris was the token gay person for newspapers. As I'm saying this, I can't believe I'm even saying it but that's my truthful recollection of it. There was no awareness, and you were limited in terms of who you thought you were reporting for, who you were producing newspapers for – mainstream Ireland. I remember an editor saying he would never put a black person on the front of a newspaper because it wouldn't sell. Now, I don't mean to lob every minority in with every minority, but that was the attitude. Homosexuality was regarded as being outside the experience of so-called 'ordinary' Ireland.

DIARMUID DOYLE: I don't mean to diss the industry that made me a living for thirty years, but until you actually have a row, or until you have a compelling person's story, or until you have a referendum campaign to start the row, the debate tends not to ever take off. You might get an op-ed here or a column there, or a 'wait until you see what they're doing in America now' kind of piece, but in terms of it becoming an issue, I don't recall it ever really being one. Even in the *Tribune*, I don't recall ever writing a column about it because it had come up in the news that particular week. It just seems to kind of worked it's way slowly into the media-political discourse, but I never really noticed it becoming an issue underneath that. And I'm still not sure that it is for the media. But when the referendum campaign starts you can be sure that it will be, because it's going to be unpleasant, all of it.

On 14 January 2014, Rory O'Neill appeared on The Saturday Night Show, *an entertainment chat show on RTÉ One hosted by* Sunday Independent *journalist Brendan O'Connor.*

NÓIRÍN HEGARTY: In relation to the homophobia debate that Panti opened, everyone thought there was an undercurrent of conservatism in society that perhaps wasn't there … I think the media has failed to accurately reflect this and I think the media in general is becoming even more conservative. Through the economic recession, everything is about battening down the hatches. In terms of perspective or how broad discussion should be, there's very little discussion; it's about playing safe. Issues are dealt with in that context. Nobody is going to go out on a limb. I think this development is closely related to the economic situation: keep your head down, keep your mouth shut. Nobody is taking a risk, there isn't room for creative madness. Austerity has bred caution.

RORY O'NEILL: *The Saturday Night Show* contacted me to go on to do a silly drag performance. And afterwards they wanted to do an interview. Essentially what they wanted to do was base the interview on this radio interview I had done with Aoibhinn Ní Shúilleabháin.

AOIBHINN NÍ SHÚILLEABHÁIN: Rory O'Neill was my first guest on a brand new radio series *Aoibhinn & Company* on RTÉ Radio 1 in June 2013. While some people may have seen it as a little controversial having Rory discuss his career as a drag queen as the opening show on early Sunday morning radio, I thought his story was particularly important and relevant in discussing growing up and being gay in rural Ireland. I was new to the role of an hour-long interview and remember being so caught up in Rory's story of realisation and isolation while sitting in the bus home from school that I forgot to queue the music. As Panti, he is a stunning and forceful performer and I was incredibly grateful for his candour in that first interview.

RORY O'NEILL: Beforehand I spent all the time thinking about how I could translate what Panti does into a three-minute thing for the TV. I spent a couple of days working out something to do for the performance part and all that. I never put any thought at all into the interview thing. We did do a pre-interview on the phone like a couple of days beforehand. And it was the usual stuff, you know – how you get into drag, a bit about growing up in Ireland as a gay in the country, living with HIV – the usual shite that I get asked every time! I never gave it a second thought. So on the show I did the performance. They pre-recorded that with the live studio audience, forty-five minutes before the rest of the show, so I would have time to go and change. So I did that, that all went fine. Then afterwards I said I have to get changed and thought, 'Oh god, yeah, I have to do an interview now.' Literally, it was that much of an afterthought essentially as far as I was concerned. And in that forty-five minutes, just to jog my memory, the production assistant showed me the bullet points that Brendan O'Connor would have for the interview, just to remind me what we would be talking about. And it was the same things, the usual stuff, there was nothing about a discussion of homophobia. That wasn't part of it.

During an interview with the presenter, Brendan O'Connor, O'Neill was asked about homophobia in Ireland. What followed was to become known as 'Pantigate'.

JOHN LYONS: The real person who possibly seems to have been left out of this is Brendan O'Connor when he asked the question, 'Who are these people?' Now if somebody's getting paid to do a show, if that's the quality of the questioning he's asking, you know what I mean? I was horrified by that, absolutely horrified.

BILL HUGHES: If the presenter hadn't forced him into naming names, the brouhaha might not have kicked off quite so severely, but it's wonderful that it did. It's wonderful that it did because it lifted the scab, and it said, 'Aha, you're just below the surface.'

AVERIL POWER: I didn't see the programme when it went out live. I just saw a media report about the programme. And then I thought, 'Oh my God, what's Rory after saying?' I thought he was after saying something completely crazy. So then I found the programme on *Broadsheet* or somewhere else online and watched it and then I was just like, 'Now I really don't get this. What is going on?' He was clearly giving his personal opinion. He was asked to name individuals, I'm not sure he would have offered them if he wasn't asked, but he was asked to and he did. And I thought RTÉ's response to that was bizarre.

DAVID NORRIS: [Rory] is a man who is so courageous. First of all, to do all of this drag stuff and so on. He's done a huge amount of good work raising money with the Alternative Miss Ireland for people with AIDS and this kind of stuff. But politically he's often the MC for Pride and this sort of business and what he says is bang on, and he says it without any fear or favour and I like that. I try to do the same kind of thing myself, so I'd be on a temperamental wavelength with him. And then to get all these threatening legal letters. I mean, he's only an individual. I don't imagine he has huge resources.

RORY O'NEILL: I wouldn't even call it an alarm bell. The first time I had a passing thought, which I dismissed, was when somebody said to me, 'Oh, I tried to watch your thing on the RTÉ Player and it's been taken down' – like my sister or something who hadn't seen it. I said 'Oh!' I really didn't give too much thought to it. The show was on the Saturday and I don't know what day it was, but let's say Tuesday, a few days later, I got a call from one of the production people, but not anything to do with that. What she was calling me to say was they couldn't find my details on the system, so could I give them my bank details again for my standard appearance fee. I said, 'Oh yeah, sure. Here's me bank account.' And then at the end of the conversation I said just in passing, 'By the way, apparently it's not on the Player anymore,' because I just assumed it was a technical glitch or something. And I think I even jokingly said, 'Nothing to do with me I suppose!' You know! And she said, 'Well, actually …'

SUSAN DALY: On 14 January, Panti herself mentioned on Facebook, and I think on Twitter as well, that there had been legal complaints about it. Also, a blog called *Rabble* mentioned that the show wasn't available on the Player anymore. We put in a query into RTÉ … What happened then was the thing that actually kicked it off because the statement that we got back from RTÉ was very, very odd. It made reference to the death of Tom O'Gorman, who had worked for the Iona Institute and for the Irish Catholic and so on, and just said that it was out of sensitivity to his family and friends, because obviously he had been killed overnight on Saturday/Sunday, after the interview and not related in any way. That was when our alarm bells went off, because we thought, 'What has this got to do with what Rory O'Neill said on *The Saturday Night Show?*' It had nothing to do with Tom O'Gorman whatsoever. This was a weird fudge, is the only way I can describe it, by RTÉ, around the issue. There was that very lack of transparency at the start, I think, that got us sort of, 'There's more to this.'

RTÉ started to receive legal correspondence from the patrons of the Iona Institute, along with journalist John Waters. O'Neill received solicitors' letters from the Iona Institute (David Quinn, Breda O'Brien, John Murray, Patricia Casey) and John Waters.

The following Saturday, PantiBar was packed for O'Neill's Panti Show. In a highly charged performance, O'Neill detailed what was happening to the crowd.

RORY O'NEILL: I got a solicitor and then he was in contact with RTÉ's legal quite a bit. But I understood that they were going to really keep me out of it and it was just a legal formula and this, that and the other. But of course that's not what happened; they really did name me by name. So there was just lots of stuff that I wasn't happy about on that side of things.

On Saturday 25 January, Brendan O'Connor, the presenter, read out an apology on the show which was as follows:

> Now, on the Saturday Night Show two weeks ago, comments were made by a guest suggesting the journalist and broadcaster John Waters, Breda O'Brien and some members of the Iona Institute are homophobic. These are not the views of RTÉ and we would like to apologise for any upset or distress caused to the individuals named or identified. It is an important part of democratic debate that people must be able to hold dissenting views on controversial issues.

O'Neill tweeted on 26 January that he was 'confused', saying 'no idea who the last line directed at. Am I the one with dissenting views or Iona et al … ?'

The settlement caused controversy at the highest levels, giving rise to debate in both the Seanad and the Dáil.

Senator Averil Power raised the RTÉ settlement on the Order of Business in the Seanad on 30 January, and called on the Minister for Communications, Energy and Natural Resources to appear before the Seanad to give details of and the circumstances giving rise to the settlement.

On 6 February, a group of TDs sought and were granted permission to raise the RTÉ settlement in the Dáil.

CLARE DALY, TD, IND: At the core of this are issues of freedom of expression and basic human rights … unless this issue is addressed, the only conclusion that people will draw is that if you have big pockets then you can use them to stifle debate and control opinion, and Irish people don't want to live in a society like that.

MING FLANAGAN, TD, IND: It would be nice if there was no homophobia, but pretending there isn't doesn't make it all go away … That speech that was made in the Abbey Theatre explained it so beautifully, and the fact that we are all homophobic, we are, but it's a case of working on it, and trying to learn about the whole situation, and fighting against it, and, in the end, everyone gets their rights.

CATHERINE MURPHY, TD, IND: John Waters, Breda O'Brien and the Iona Institute can all be described as 'opinion formers'. They have made themselves part of the public discourse, I stress, public discourse, on such issues as same-sex marriage and frequently present gay people's relationships as less than a starting point. For that to go without challenge is, for me, about setting the parameters of debate to their advantage.

* * * *

SUSAN DALY: I think between 26 January and 2 February, we [thejournal.ie] ran six pieces on various aspects of the controversy. Then I think *The Irish Times*, it ran its first news piece on the 30 January. That was following a mention of the debate in the Seanad.

BREDA O'BRIEN: We did not bring legal action against RTÉ. It never went to court, as we knew it would not, because RTÉ had breached basic rules of fairness and justice by encouraging Rory O'Neill to identify specific people as homophobic who were not there to defend themselves. We asked for a simple clarification and apology. RTÉ refused and when it appeared that RTÉ was going to continue to be intransigent, we said that we would be forced to defend our good names through the courts if necessary. We knew that there was absolutely no evidence that anyone in Iona is homophobic. Homophobia is a very serious charge, one which signals that someone has an irrational fear and hatred of people who are gay. If the unjust, unfair allegation was allowed to stand, it would mean that people would be cowed and become fearful of expressing support for marriage remaining a commitment between men and women. Who wants to be accused of irrational fear and hatred? We wanted to keep a public space for discussion open. The BAI subsequently said that 'there are circumstances in which the term homophobic may be applied to "describe the views of individuals or groups once the use of the term is accurate, fair, objective and impartial and in circumstances where the broadcaster and its contributors can properly defend the use of such a description. A decision in this regard rests with the broadcaster".' The BAI said that the apology issued to the members of the Iona Institute, and to John Waters, who is not a member and who acted independently, could not be 'considered to either support or condone discrimination on the basis of sexual orientation or that it would prejudice the interests of the LGBT community'.

AVERIL POWER: What really concerned me was that it seemed to me – and this is what I said in the Seanad – that freedom of speech was just for the people with the deepest pockets. And I thought it was particularly bizarre that the people that were involved were journalists – and were journalists who write things that are controversial, who aggressively defend their right to freedom of speech, and rightly so, but as soon as somebody said something that they considered offensive, straight away they resort not to their pen or to their typewriter to respond in their columns, but to their barristers. I just thought the whole thing was inappropriate. What frightened me, and what made me decide, 'Right, I'm going to go into the Seanad and I'm going to speak on this in the House and under privilege in the House', is because none of the papers had written anything about it. All of the comment was on social media. And online, blogs, *TheJournal* and things like that. It wasn't being written about in the papers. My understanding was the reason it wasn't being written about was people were afraid of being sued by even commenting on it. And I just thought, 'This is crazy. If we're going to allow people to shut down the debate in this way and create fear across the press about criticising them at all, well, we can't proceed with a debate on any issue on that basis. Not just marriage equality, but any issue.' So that was why I kind of got up that morning and I was just really annoyed. The more I thought about it, I just thought, 'This is outrageous.' So I went into the Seanad and called on the minister to come in. I criticised the settlement and then because I had spoken under privilege in the House, most of the papers covered it then, because they could report on it without being sued.

RORY O'NEILL: In the very beginning, I thought it was laughable. And I thought what was going to happen was that RTÉ would laugh at them as well and that would be the end of it. And I still think that if RTÉ had done that, that would have been the end of it. For the first ten days, that's what our plan was. We were writing these long aggressive replies basically saying, 'Fuck. You.' I thought RTÉ would do the same and that would be the end of it. I thought that for a little while. As things were trundling on I started to realise, 'Ok, this is not how it's going to play out', that RTÉ are just headless chickens about it and really unco-ordinated. A lot of the stuff was that RTÉ's higher-ups ignored it for a whole week because they thought this was nothing, or didn't realise how serious it was going to be. So I thought it was just going to blow over and then I started to realise, 'Ok, this is not going to blow over.' And then of course my solicitor was saying to me, 'You have a good case, but the law is an ass, everything in front of jury is always going to be an unknowable, juries tend to side against what they see as big corporations, and in this case my waters would be muddied by RTÉ, who they would see as a big corporation.' Just lots of stuff like that. So it started to become much more worrying. Basically my solicitors were saying to me, 'You have a very good chance that you'd lose in Irish courts, you'll probably end up being bankrupt but you don't really have any assets anyway. You have half a share in a bar – what the fuck is that?' It was just really grim and horrible. And I was also having some sleepless nights and all of that. My parents were upset about it all. It wasn't pleasant. I did sort of feel some pressure from various gay groups and that, that they really wanted me to go for it, which is fine and all and I understand that, but they weren't the ones who were going to be fifteen years later in the European Court of Human Rights.

On 1 February, The Saturday Night Show *decided to host a debate about homophobia in the wake of the expanding controversy. Colm O'Gorman, Susan Philips, Averil Power, and Noel Whelan appeared on a panel, with others voicing points from the audience.*

BUZZ O'NEILL: They asked me to go on *The Saturday Night Show.* I said I'd call them back, had a think about it, a chat about it, spoke to Rory, and he was adamant he wasn't doing it. I waited to see who else was going to be on it. Once I saw Colm O'Gorman's name popping up, I was like, 'Yeah. I'm going to do that. Absolutely.'

The following day, The Sunday Times *reported the massive payout RTÉ had made to both the Iona Institute members and John Waters.*

RORY O'NEILL: Then when the money thing came out, I recognise that was my saving grace because I was really shocked when I heard how much money. I had thought all along, 'Oh, they've been given a token, a grand each or something.' So when I heard it – €85,000 – I was really shocked. And I thought, 'Well, if I'm shocked, everybody else will be really shocked, and people will see that as their money.' So I knew if we could just get that out. That day I had heard on the grapevine from a few gays in RTÉ, so I just started tweeting and Facebooking 'Oh my god, if the figures that I heard …'

On the same night as The Saturday Night Show, *Panti was about to take to the stage of the national theatre, to deliver a 'Noble Call', a piece of oratory that had been running after the production of* The Risen People. *It was the final night of the play's run.*

RORY O'NEILL: That sort of tickled me: you can have your fake debate on homophobia and I'll give my speech on the national stage!

BUZZ O'NEILL: Despite what Glen Killane [MD of RTÉ Television] says, the feeling within staff in RTÉ was just pure fucking outrage. Especially amongst the gay staff, of which the Kinsey scale doesn't come into it when you get into TV! I mean, you know, one in ten in RTÉ are gay? I'd say you might be talking three out of ten. That's a huge amount of people to be pissed off when you're trying to run an organisation, badly.

RORY O'NEILL: Fiach in the Abbey asked me to do it. He asked me to do it just a few days before that speech. It was the last show of that production, after which there had been a Noble Call every night. So there had been a hundred people had done it or something. He asked me to do it on the very last night, partly I think out of a sense of mischief. He's quite like that, and you know, he joked, 'You can defame anyone you want!' So also it fits in with his historical views and narrative of the Abbey, freedom of speech stuff and riots over productions. He likes all of that stuff, so that's why he asked me.

FIACH MAC CONGHAIL: I think in the Abbey Theatre it became a fascinating dialogue – who should be invited each night, why should they be invited, how they should be invited – all that kind of stuff. We've had an extraordinary bunch, all various different people from all walks of life. On the last night, we knew the last night was going to be a significant night, or symbolic in that having somebody. To be honest with you, Rory's name came to me when I had the day off, which was that Monday. I was flying to London and I was with my kid … I asked him because he is a leader, one of our leaders in our society.

On Friday 31 February, the Minister for Communications Pat Rabbitte intervened in the Pantigate controversy.

PAT RABBITTE, STATEMENT ON DEFAMATION LAW: I would also hope that people and institutions that hold themselves out as commentators on, or contributors to, public debate fully appreciate – as most politicians do – that debate can be robust, heated, personal and sometimes even hostile. If you enter the arena, you cannot expect that the Queensbury Rules will always apply. It would be a matter of serious concern if recourse to our defamation laws was to have a chilling effect on the conduct of public debate on this issue, in the lead-in to the forthcoming referendum on gay marriage.

RORY O'NEILL: On Friday night and I'm falling asleep in bed, that's when I started to have actual ideas about exactly what I wanted to say. So I remember before I went to sleep I took out my phone and put in a few key words, then on Saturday afternoon I wrote it. It didn't take long and it wasn't that hard because I knew essentially what I wanted to say. I, you know, tried to learn it quickly, I rehearsed it once or twice in my living room. I thought the speech was good, but you know what it's like: you can think something's good but that doesn't mean that it actually is good. So I didn't really know, but I did think it was quite good … I do remember saying to Philly on the way there in the cab, 'I think I might be able to make one of these actress types cry!', and that would be enough for me.

PHILLY MCMAHON: He was pretty relaxed. You know Rory – he is so laid back. He had been asked to appear on *The Saturday Night Show* on the 'debate' episode and he had agreed in theory, if Waters or O'Brien or Quinn were on the panel. They had said no outright so he didn't think it was wise to start debating with everyone who rolled out that hadn't been implicated.

FIACH MAC CONGHAIL: All through that week my staff – straight, lesbian, gay staff, everybody – was proud that the Abbey Theatre was doing it. I had an instinct about inviting Rory as Panti, but that's all. I wouldn't claim anything else, except my instinct is based on twenty-five years of programming experience and my own work having done lots of queer work in the Project Arts Centre … There was a kind of an excitement, a pride, and I remember this clearly, some of my staff came back deliberately to watch her on the stage on Saturday night and I was glad of that. That in no way matched the impact it had afterwards, obviously. Because of our relationship with Philly, thisispopbaby, and Rory from last year at the Peacock, it was something quite natural for us to do as well. So it didn't feel false. It didn't feel like I was jumping on a bandwagon.

PHILLY MCMAHON: There was something magic and accidental about Panti appearing on the national stage speaking from the heart while a petty debate raged on on RTÉ. He was relaxed, and nervous about what he was going to say. He had written the speech that afternoon and hoped he would remember the words. He certainly had no idea of the potential impact of the speech. We gave out Team Panti badges to the Abbey staff, and took some photos beside the 1913 gear they had in the foyer. I asked Panti if the speech was any use, and unusually for Rory he admitted that he had shed a tear writing it. The sentiment of the thing, and the week's events catching up on him. And like good friends, myself and Ian slagged him about that! Then Panti was whisked backstage and us and the entire Abbey staff crammed in with the full house to hear what was going to be said.

PANTI'S NOBLE CALL SPEECH, THE ABBEY THEATRE, 1 FEBRUARY 2014:

Hello. My name is Panti and for the benefit of the visually impaired or the incredibly naive, I am a drag queen, a performer, and an accidental and occasional gay rights activist. And as you may have already gathered, I am also painfully middle class. My father was a country vet, I went to a nice school, and afterwards I went to that most middle class of institutions, art college. And, although this may surprise some of you, I have always managed to find gainful employment in my chosen field: gender discombobulation. So the grinding, abject poverty so powerfully displayed in tonight's performance is something I can thankfully say I have no experience of. But oppression is something I can relate to. Oh, I'm not comparing my experience to Dublin workers of 1913, but I do know what it feels like to be put in your place.

Have you ever been standing at a pedestrian crossing when a car drives by and in it are a bunch of lads, and they lean out the window and they shout 'Fag!' and throw a milk carton at you? Now it doesn't really hurt. It's just a wet carton and anyway they're right – I am a fag. But it feels oppressive.

When it really does hurt is afterwards. Afterwards I wonder and worry and obsess over what was it about me, what was it they saw in me? What was it that gave me away? And I hate myself for wondering that. It feels oppressive and the next time I'm at a pedestrian crossing I check myself to see what is it about me that 'gives the gay away' and I check myself to make sure I'm not doing it this time.

Have any of you ever come home in the evening and turned on the television and there is a panel of people – nice people, respectable people; smart people; the kind of people who make good, neighbourly neighbours; the kind of people who write for newspapers – and they are having a reasoned debate about you. About what kind of a person you are, about whether you are capable of being a good parent, about whether you want to destroy marriage, about whether you are safe around children, about whether God herself thinks you are an abomination, about whether in fact you are 'intrinsically disordered'. And even the nice TV presenter lady, who you feel like you know, thinks it's perfectly ok that they are all having this reasoned debate about who you are and what rights you 'deserve' or don't 'deserve'.

And that feels oppressive.

Have you ever been on a crowded train with your gay friend and a small part of you is cringing because he is being SO gay and you find yourself trying to compensate for his gayness by butching up or nudging the conversation on to 'straighter' territory? This is you who have spent thirty-five years trying to be the best gay possible and yet still a small part of you is embarrassed by his gayness. And I hate myself for that.

And that feels oppressive. And when I'm standing at the pedestrian lights I am checking myself.

Have you ever gone into your favourite neighbourhood café with the paper that you buy every day, and you open it up and inside is a 500-word opinion written by a nice middle-class woman, the kind of woman who probably gives to charity, the kind of woman that you would be happy to leave your children with? And she is arguing so reasonably about whether you should be treated less than everybody else, arguing that you should be given fewer rights than everybody else. And when the woman at the next table gets up and excuses herself to squeeze by you with a smile you wonder, 'Does she think that about me too?'

And that feels oppressive. And you go outside and you stand at the pedestrian crossing and you check yourself and I hate myself for that.

Have you ever turned on the computer and seen videos of people just like you in countries that are far away, and countries that are not far away at all, and they are being beaten and imprisoned and tortured and murdered because they are just like you?

And that feels oppressive.

And for the last three weeks I have been lectured to by heterosexual people about what homophobia is and who is allowed identify it. Straight people – ministers, senators, barristers, journalists – have lined up to tell me what homophobia is and what I am allowed to feel oppressed by. People who have never experienced homophobia in their lives, people who have never checked themselves at a pedestrian crossing, have told me that unless I am being thrown in prison or herded on to a cattle truck, then it is not homophobia.

And that feels oppressive.

So now Irish gay people find ourselves in a ludicrous situation where not only are we not allowed to say publicly what we feel oppressed by, we are not even allowed to think it because the very definition – our definition – has been disallowed by our betters. And for the last three weeks I have been denounced from the floor of parliament to newspaper columns to the seething morass of internet commentary, denounced for using 'hate speech' because I dared to use the word 'homophobia' and a jumped-up queer like me should know that the word 'homophobia' is no longer available to gay people, which is a spectacular and neat Orwellian trick because now it turns out that gay people are not the victims of homophobia – homophobes are the victims of homophobia.

But I want to say that it is not true because I don't hate you.

I do, it is true, believe that almost all of you are probably homophobes. But I'm a homophobe.

It would be incredible if we weren't. To grow up in a society that is overwhelmingly and stiflingly homophobic and to somehow escape unscathed would be miraculous. So I don't hate you because you are homophobic. I actually admire you. I admire you because most of you are only a bit homophobic and, to be honest, considering the circumstances, that is pretty good going.

But I do sometimes hate myself. I hate myself because I fucking check myself while standing at pedestrian crossings. And sometimes I hate you for doing that to me.

But not right now. Right now, I like you all very much for giving me a few moments of your time. And I thank you for it.

KATHY SHERIDAN: Rory O'Neill kept his head. That speech in the Abbey was amazing. He didn't savage anyone. He just talked about his life.

DAVID NORRIS: I thought to quote Eamon Dunphy, 'It wasn't a great speech; it was a good speech, it wasn't a great speech.' But I was wrong. And the reason I was wrong is because I was so close to it and because I'm gay myself. The audience was for straight people, and by goodness, it hit them straight in the solar plexus.

PHILLY MCMAHON: It was significant for me. It was all my worlds coming together. I felt incredibly proud of Panti standing on that stage, following that play. I had a physical feeling of how important it was to be in that room that night – but I'm a theatre queen, so I thought it could have just been me. I shed a tear. It was a brilliant moment in the theatre. One of the best I've seen. That said, I thought that was it. It was great that the theatre had created a space that TV and radio couldn't, but I thought it was contained to that night.

FIACH MAC CONGHAIL: I think it was an extraordinary piece of rhetoric … What also impacted on everybody is that clearly she was nervous. She was nervous at the beginning and she was self-conscious at the end which was in itself very endearing, very honest, and very vulnerable.

RORY O'NEILL: A few people remarked that they think I look nervous, but I never feel nervous because that's not how I am, but I guess you get an adrenaline rush. I didn't have any water with me, so I had the worst case of dry mouth in the world. You can see me a lot in the video, doing this with my lips because my lips are literally sticking to my gums. I thought when I was giving the speech that it was distracting me and I thought, 'Oh my God, this must look so weird!' So I'm amazed in the video it's not that noticeable, you have to look quite hard, but you can see me [do it]. So to be honest when I was giving the speech that was the biggest thing on my mind, 'Goddammit, why didn't I bring a bottle of water?' And then afterwards, I thought it had gone well. People all said it had gone well, but people say that to you anyway, even if it was awful, people say, 'Oh, that was great!' So I didn't really think that much about it. A couple of hours later, somebody put up a shaky, fuzzy thingy on their phone. And by the next day that had 7,000 views, and it was this crappy phone video thing. I was like, 'Wow!' At that stage, Conor [Horgan] and Caroline [Campbell] were scrambling to get their version up. They had brought two cameras, but they had some problem with the second camera. That's why it took all day and why in the end it's only one camera view, because – whatever, something to do with the format or something. So by the time they got their version up, which was late at night on Sunday, I thought we'd missed our opportunity here because 7,000 people had already watched the crappy one, so there can't be any more than that wanting to watch this fucking speech. You know, it's a ten-minute speech about oppression and homophobia. And you can see it's ten minutes long before you click on it. And you can see that it's a drag queen talking about homophobia. How boring does that sound! So all of the other stuff came as a complete, giant surprise. But also the other parts of the happy accidents were the fact that the show was called *The Risen People* – that adds to it. The fact that the visual is of this shiny lit drag queen and in the shadows behind her are these three or four handsome, downtrodden workers dressed in rags – that all adds to it. The fact that it's called a 'Noble Call', that's an absolute coincidence; it's nothing really to do with anything, but it also adds a sense of gravitas to it or something. And the fact that it says 'on the stage of the national theatre' – all of those things give the video an accidental or unexpected or unplanned sort of gravitas. And I think if all of those things hadn't come together accidentally, I don't think the video would have been as [big].

SUSAN DALY: I got a link in my direct messages on Twitter from somebody who knew we had been covering this, which was a link to the video of Panti doing her Noble Call at the Abbey the night before. When I looked into it, my dinner was almost on the table, and I watched it, and I just got transfixed by it. You could just sense that this was a watershed in how people were allowed speak about this issue. I just thought, 'This is incredibly powerful; we have a platform with over 100,000 people on this site today. I think we should put it up …' Somebody in another part of the media [said], 'You're absolutely insane. You're going to get sued.' That's what I was told. There was this sort of fear as well, and that's something – maybe why established media didn't pick up … There might be a few factors in why people held off, so you just need somebody to get out of the traps and do it and put up the video or report those quotes for everybody else to follow.

RORY O'NEILL: I started immediately getting emails and that started happening the first day. I could just tell from what people were saying that this really means something to these people. And when I started getting ones from abroad and that, that's when I was like, 'Oh, foreigners care about this?' And then all the little things – like even the silly celebrity endorsements – it just adds people to talking about it and sharing it. I don't remember who was the first big famous people to tweet it. Maybe

Graham Norton? Stephen Fry maybe? It just means that other people [started to] notice it or take notice of it. Of course when the Madonna thing happened, I started getting phone calls immediately from all the tabloid press. She actually sent me an email. I felt a bit guilty because I just kind of jokingly put on Twitter a silly tweet, 'Oh, yogurt for breakfast, walked the dog, message from Madonna, wash the dishes, wait, what?' And I actually felt a bit guilty then because I felt a little naive. At first I was feeling bad because, oh my God, will Madonna think, 'I sent him a message and he uses it like that'? Part of me was knowingly doing that because I knew this would again help my case, because at that stage I still wasn't out of the woods and I knew I needed to make as much noise as possible because already making noise was working for me. So there was a part of me that was cynically doing that, but I would never have told anyone exactly what it said, because I felt her's wasn't a public message. She didn't tweet it at me. But I felt better about that about a week later out of the blue, it turned out that *The Independent* contacted Liz Rosenberg and got a quote out of her, and I thought 'Ok, she's fine with it!'

The MEP Paul Murphy raised the issue in European Parliament. Tonight with Vincent Browne *on TV3 played Panti's speech in full on Tuesday 4 February. On Wednesday,* The Last Word *dedicated an hour to discussing the experiences of gay people in Ireland.*

COLM O'GORMAN: Hazel was amazing. She blew me away. She was fabulous that day. So impressive.

MATT COOPER: I still felt that you're able to have the discussion about the issues, but we were trying to do it in a way that removed it away from what could have been legally contentious.

HAZEL CULLEN: I was asked to come in because I have a kind of shocking story of homophobic violence, and so my presence there was really to tell that story and I suppose to be a non-media voice. I wanted to do it because I think that it's important that people see and hear from what you might call 'regular' gay people – gay people who seem like familiar types to the mainstream population, who aren't drag queens or activists, guys who aren't 'fabulous' and girls who aren't 'butch'. Our community is diverse and that's the way it should be, just as all of society is diverse, but I feel like sometimes even the most 'unusual' straight person finds a way to dismiss gay people because of their perceived differences to the majority of the population. I know gay people who don't agree with marriage as an institution, but I don't personally know any gay people who are against gay marriage because they want to 'protect' traditional marriage or because they don't think gay people should have kids.

By now, column inches are clocking up in newspapers, particularly in the Irish Independent *and the* Examiner *on the issue. On Thursday,* The Irish Times *printed an editorial about freedom of speech, discourse, and the use of the word 'homophobia'. That day, a debate is scheduled in the Dáil about the issue, and Jerry Buttimer and John Lyons made impassioned speeches on the floor of parliament.*

JOHN LYONS: Look, the media do what the media do, alright? I mean, obviously we have to look at everybody's agenda – why they do what they do… I think the likes of RTÉ there recently, in their response, to say that they're not trying to censor debate and say, 'Look at all the things we've done' – they've covered ten minutes on *The Late Debate*, the LGBT Noise issue, a follow-up on the whole issue of homophobia on the Brendan O'Connor show. They were three Mickey Mouse attempts in order to kind of say, 'Sure, look, we really do cover issues like this and these are really, really important to us' … It pisses me off big time, the trivialisation of my life. And I'm sick and tired of it.

JERRY BUTTIMER: I remember coming up to Dublin for weekends and being afraid to go into The George, or being afraid to go into the Front Lounge, or whatever the pub was, out of pure fear of being outed or being judged. And similarly in Cork. But there comes a point in your life where you have to be true to yourself and you have to say, 'You know what? I am gay.' I'm very happy being gay. It's part of who I am. I've gone for counselling to talk it out, to talk it through. I've been in relationships with women. And I've been in very loving relationships. And I'm still friends with some of my former girlfriends. And I'll always remember and cherish those times and those years. But there comes a point in life where you have to say, are you being fair to the person you're going out with? And are you being true to yourself? That's a very hard decision to make, primarily because you feel you have to conform to social norms of having a husband or a wife, kids, semi-D – the usual nine yards. And as a consequence of making a decision to come out, I'm conscious that there's a generation of young people who need leadership from those of us in public life, in sporting world, in politics, in music, or wherever that may be, because we must make being gay what's part of being normal in Ireland. And what I mean by that, is that we all live in community. We all go to matches together. We all go to concerts together. We all go to the restaurants and pubs and cinema. And we're no different. Hopefully in time this will all just be a footnote in time.

MATT COOPER: I can understand exactly why RTÉ settled that case. I think legally it would have been very, very dangerous for them to have actually fought that case. I think there's a great possibility that the people who lodged the complaints against RTÉ for that night would have won their case, and that RTÉ would have then been absolutely castigated for having fought a case that legally you couldn't win at great, great expense.

Meanwhile, a controversy about St Patrick's Day parades in New York and Boston banning LGBT groups marching under banners reemerged. Enda Kenny had already committed to marching in New York, but the story of exclusion of 'Irish Queers' from the parade kept rolling. Panti was invited to an inclusive parade in Queens.

RORY O'NEILL: I'm doing these interviews on the fiftieth floor of the Rockefeller centre in these giant radio syndication things. And they're really interested! And they've all watched the speech like ten or fifteen times. And they're quoting *Irish Times'* surveys to me. And I'm like, 'You're like a New York thing and we're looking over fucking Manhattan's skyline and you really care about this!' Because I think there's something zeitgeist-y about it. Partly it's the whole sort of gay marriage debate, but it's also we live in this weird world. As Neil Tennant said to me the night before last, there's two sort of stories. On one hand we have gay marriage in lots of parts of the world. And at the same time, there's Uganda and Russia. But the other thing that really astounded me was I thought the speech was very personal to me and I thought that, for example, the thing about being embarrassed by your gay friend on the train, I thought that was very much me. That I was revealing a dirty secret about me. Whereas it turns out that everybody feels that way. And I didn't know that.

PHILLY MCMAHON: New York was magic. It was like travelling with Princess Diana. The Irish-American queers were open-armed and open-hearted for Panti. The Irish-American thing is so weird, but for the queers it was like Ireland had finally sent a delegate for them. Panti revived the speech (by request) at the Irish arts centre, and in typical American form they were hollering support from the start – 'sing out sister', 'yes m'am', 'preach, sister'. It was brilliant. It felt really important that that happened. She had unlocked something in LGBT people all around the world and we were witnessing it first-hand. On the flight to NYC several people on the flight came up to Rory to shake his hand and say thanks – straights, at that. A young college student sitting beside Rory leaned over mid-flight and said, 'Are you Panti? I recognised your voice. I'm one of the allies in UCD.' It was very sweet. The trolley dollies went nuts over Panti and, more than celebrating celebrity, people were thankful. She had spoken up and said something that many people felt but didn't know it could be named.

RORY O'NEILL: I was having dinner with my old friend Angelo. He brought a friend of his along who I'd know a little over the years; I would have met him but we don't know each other that much. But he's probably a very well-preserved 50, New York City, gay, muscle Mary type – lovely, been around, was a club kid in the '80s – he's that kind of a gay, very super New York American gay cosmopolitan, whatever. And he started speaking to me about the speech over dinner. And he was totally blown away by it in the sense that he wanted to talk about it a lot and what it meant to him and how these things were never vocalised and da da da. And that blew me away, that somebody like him also identified with those things. Do you know what I mean? So there's just something about the zeitgeist-i-ness of it all, that on the one hand you have gays in Uganda and Russia having really awful things happening to them, and on the other hand that kind of gay who, I think, feels that they have to say everything is fine all the time because they're not being beaten and tortured, and depending on what state they're in they can get gay-married and all that. But underneath that, they're putting up with all this low-level homophobia all the time. And I don't know, whatever, by me expressing that at the time I happened to express it in the way I happened to express it, somehow has a significance for people who aren't just Irish. What I thought was a local thing, turns out to not be a local thing.

JERRY BUTTIMER: I'll never forget the fear of being called a faggot. Or being chased. Or being spat at. Or being hit because you come out of a gay bar or you walk out of a nightclub or you walk up a narrow dark lane, or you walk past somebody whom you know and [who] knows you're gay and they call you a faggot. That leaves a legacy and an impression. And I suppose it galvanises you to saying that you'll never again be afraid to say that you are who you are. And even though in my case I only came out two years ago, it was always the classic 'don't ask, don't tell'.

KATHY SHERIDAN: Across the media, the print media can use whatever balance it likes, but the broadcast media is the one that will be most concerning. That's where the thing in February [Pantigate] comes through in the most worrying way. You had people not only taking sides on whether same-sex marriage is acceptable, you had them taking sides on the definition of homophobia. 'What does homophobia mean?' So what voices were being shut down? I thought the whole thing became so desperately confused. Then of course when RTÉ paid up, it made it feel these voices were being closed down. I don't see a problem with the media in terms of fairness. I think there was a lot of fright, and as we know, our own paper [*The Irish Times*] stayed well away from the thing for a week. And that was noticeable. And that, as a person in the media, that would worry me. That chilling effect. That absolutely did happen. Sure, Matt Cooper admitted he stayed away from it. If that happens and the McKenna judgement insists on every single voice being balanced with a voice, then I think we're in kind of dangerous territory.

JERRY BUTTIMER: So, you know, Panti was right: we probably all do check ourselves from time to time. But what we must do, and what we must all strive to do, is make the world we live in is a better place for those who come after us. And those who come before us have built that foundation. We must make sure the roof is on the house and that's where I see myself as being. People like Kieran Rose, David Norris, Arthur Leahy, Ailbhe Smyth, Brian Sheehan and a whole host of others – they, to me, have been the leaders for a long time in campaign. Now it falls to a generation like John Lyons and myself to make sure the roof is put on the house, so the next generation can have that house that's ready to move into, where their world is equal and fair, and where we can eliminate homophobia, and we can have a difference of viewpoints and be allowed to have that, but in saying that I've always made the point that if I discover or I see someone's opposed to what I'm standing for in terms of equality and they say something different that isn't really relevant or correct or that is untrue, then it has to go and be checked and it can't be left unchecked. So, you know, I suppose homophobia exists. We have to ensure young people grow up in a world where they recognise that being diverse and being different is acceptable and that's why Stand Up [campaign] from BelongTo is very important. And equally it's important that we continue to eliminate homophobic bullying from our schools and from our communities and playgrounds. And in doing that, we must stand up to people who have prejudices and show them that having prejudices is uninformed and is wrong and we can change that cultural attitude by making people aware of the values that go with being gay. What I'm really saying is, we're no different to anyone else.

TONIE WALSH: I love how Rory and, separately and together, Panti, have just pivoted overnight this discourse. It's wonderful. It's incredible. I can understand how people have been so blown away and energised by it. It's absolutely wonderful.

ANDREW HYLAND: In terms of what Rory did, it was overdue. I think somebody needed to start that conversation. I think if anybody was the right person to do that, it was Rory.

PHILLY MCMAHON: Rory asked me my advice on what to do. He knew he was right, but it was complicated. I said that if it was anyone else in Ireland, he should make it go away, but Panti had the support to see it through. She had become symbolic at that point. They hadn't just come for the gays and dykes – they had come for the Queen. People were going nuts. The Panti shows felt like political rallies on Saturday nights. I'm sure people got extra laid out of it. The atmosphere was incredible. That wouldn't have happened had it been anyone else. The genderfuck of the whole thing was important too. She was bits of all of us perhaps – although someone will lynch me for saying that! Rory is amongst the smartest people I know, who doesn't run his mouth without thinking, and has spent twenty-five years working these opinions out. He was simply the best person for the job.

Strangely, the story kept rolling in different directions, another incident being rugby pundit Neil Francis making controversial comments about gay people, in his experience, not being interested in sport on Newstalk's Off the Ball *programme.*

MATT COOPER: I was just head in hand. How the hell can he stay stuff which is just Jurassic in its attitude? And my view was that he needed to apologise because what he had said was wrong. But he also needed to apologise for his own sake if he wanted to protect his career, that things have changed and people would just not accept that. And that I wouldn't have been in a position to have let him back on the radio talking about rugby issues if this thing was still actually hanging over him. And I persuaded him and made it quite clear to him. I said, 'Look, you've completely messed up here. You're wrong. You're just not going to be able to stand over these particular comments. You're going to have to come on air, and you're going to have to take a kicking. And you're going to have to take it from me and we're going to get Nigel Owens to administer it as well.' And that's what we did.

DAVID NORRIS: That nincompoop rugby player – whatever his name was – Neil Francis? I mean, I was in bed because it was one of my bad days and I was listening, and I didn't get up until late. I fell out of the bed laughing when he said that gay people weren't interested in sport. I mean, maybe they weren't interested in looking at him, but lots of gay people are interested in sport! And then that they were only interested in ballet and they were all hairdresser fairies or some such. And I said in the Senate afterwards, I wouldn't like to be him the next time I go in for a haircut. I didn't think it was malicious. I just thought it was dreadfully naive. But he did at least establish one thing and he said something that I think was quite important. He said there's nothing more homophobic than a rugby dressing room. Well, it's time they addressed that … And anyway, rugby is the most homosexual thing you could think of. If you think of all of these hairy old men, some of them reasonably attractive nowadays, with their arms around each other's loins and their claws on each other's goolies, their noses up their bums, and then they come out and say they like it because it's a contact sport. In other words it gives them an opportunity to feel each other up in front of 50,000 people. You know, what are they talking about? I think you have to keep your sense of humour and laugh these things off.

DIARMUID DOYLE: The media's role as it always is, is to find a row, encourage the row, report on the row, and then move on to the next row. And that's what happened. Actually, that's not fair, like the row allowed a few decent columns to be written on both sides. But in terms of the papers taking it as an issue to report on? That hasn't happened. It won't happen until the referendum starts, and then it'll happen. What I saw over [Pantigate] was an absolutely fantastic row which newspapers licked their lips at and said, 'We cannot believe this has happened! This is fantastic! Let's go for it. And here, let's get a few of our columnists to stroke their beards, or whatever the female equivalent is, and write some words about it.'

NOEL WHELAN: The media is entirely unrepresentative of the country. The mainstream media argued for all of the European referendums, two of which were solidly defeated by the electorate the first time round … if marriage equality is going to be passed, the man in drag who will do most to persuade the Irish electorate will be Brendan O'Carroll, not Rory.

BREDA O'BRIEN: The weeks after the Rory O'Neill allegations were some of the worst in my life. It is difficult to explain how it affected every aspect of my life, from my professional careers as a teacher and a writer, to my family, who became genuinely fearful for my safety. It was unwarranted, and deeply, deeply unfair. Gay people have suffered a great deal of unjust discrimination. I am not remotely comparing my experience to that, but it did strike me as ironic that some (not all) gay and lesbian people had no problem with demolishing the reputations of others. Paolo Freire, the great Brazilian educator who promoted education as a means to liberation, once said something to the effect that a revolution is only successful if the oppressed do not become oppressors in their turn. I found myself thinking about that a great deal in those weeks.

29

THE OPPOSITION
TO EQUALITY

'"Homophobia" is almost too slight a word –
it's a deeply entrenched othering of lesbians and gay men.'

– Ailbhe Smyth

MARC SOLOMON: Having worked in Massachusetts for a number of years, I presumed that it would be slow in taking off [in Ireland] because our strongest resistance in Massachusetts was from some of the older communities that were largely Irish Catholic, so I presumed that it would have a hard time getting off the ground in Ireland. But it turns out things have gone more quickly than I expected. The whole world is moving extremely quickly, but yeah, I certainly knew of Ireland's history with respect to abortion and the strength of the Catholic Church but given how bad things have been with the hierarchy of the Catholic Church in Ireland, that has something to do with it, people aren't listening to the doctrine of the Church anymore.

BRIAN FINNEGAN: I think it's revulsion. I think it is a revulsion with a sexual act. I think, when it boils down to it, I don't think it's about two women; I think it's about two men. I think it's about a revulsion around a sexual act that is fundamentally there and that those who have fundamental distaste for that plays out into all sorts of arguments. That's my belief. That it is as basic as that.

RORY O'NEILL: I think it's just plain old reactionary conservatives. People who are afraid of change … So the focus of your life is to stop a group of people having something. That, to me, no matter how they say, 'We're not a bigot, we just believe in tradition', that's the essence of bigotry, that you have decided to dedicate your life, to go on TV, to campaign, to argue to stop a group of people having something. That to me, no matter how you dress it up, is hate. That's the very essence of what hate is. You might think, and they might say, 'I don't hate, I love, I'm just trying to protect traditional marriage.' That's all bullshit. Your drive and focus is to stop a group of people that you're not a member of from having something. To me, that's indefensible in every way. I don't understand what kind of person you have to be to be the kind of person that would focus your life that way.

ANN LOUISE GILLIGAN: Somebody needs to change the Church's teaching on homosexuality and it is way beyond its time. The clamp of mind – the manipulation of mind that the Church continues and is allowed to continue with in the different nation states in which it is present. It is outrageous. I really feel this very strongly.

MAX KRZYZANOWSKI: We have rules governing referenda. I don't know whether we have rules governing other issues of broadcast, but it seems to me that there is a creep about this notion of 'balance', which is a fucking nonsense idea anyway. There are some arguments where there aren't finely balanced sides and we saw the damage that was nearly done in the children's rights referendum by a bunch of hysterical right-wing idiots that nearly sunk something – protections for our children that are so horrifically overdue and needed. So I'm wondering if part of the mentality that informs places like RTÉ and radio stations and newspapers is that either you have to have controversy and that sells, or you have to make some sort of show of having balance.

ANNA MCCARTHY: I suppose a lot of the main opposition spokespeople would be of a Catholic disposition, or be aligned with a Catholic group, but having said that, there are some kind of secular commentators, like what's her name? *Sunday Times* – Brenda Power. There are those. I think there's more of a religious influence there than any of them would care to admit. I don't think for them to admit that it helps their case, given the view and the attitude of religion in Ireland now. I think that a lot of the time it comes from a – it is a homophobia, it is. As much as I really don't like to label people bigots or label people homophobes, I think it does come from a distaste of either diversity or having a different social model or concept of family or relationships or parenting. And they just don't like it. They just don't think it should exist and I think they seem to want to do anything they can to prevent that happening, when they don't seem to realise that these relationships exist, these children exist, and there's nothing you can do about it. Short of stopping people from buying turkey basters, you can't stop children from being born. They then want to discourage these children from being born by taking the rights away from their parents, and the rights away from the children, and somehow that will stop this 'scourge'. I wouldn't dare to look into the mind of such problems, but sometimes I wonder is it just some kind of a – just an intolerance of diversity within Irish society. I think a lot of them still feel that whether they simply wouldn't say it, but Ireland still is in their mind a Catholic country and that really, I suppose, if there aren't people obeying Catholic doctrine, then it's no longer a Catholic country, therefore it's negative to them. I don't know. Then other people, I think, who aren't of a Catholic bent but are opposed to it – I think it's more a sort of non-religious homophobia or a distaste or misunderstanding or ignorance of LGBT people, their relationships, the way they have sex, all of that. It's just, I think, a distaste. Then again, there's always the people who just want to have a good argument and who want to gain some publicity for themselves and take the opportunity of the opposite view.

BUZZ O'NEILL: The opposition? Everything to me would have been, 'The bastards. The bastards. Fuck them. Do we engage with them? And how do we engage with them in the media? How do we speak, try and speak politely to them when we're on radio discussion shows or whatever.' … Those were my thoughts pre-Pantigate. Definitely from a PR point of view, I was thinking, 'What's the strategy here? Do we go for their jugular? Do we try and embarrass them? Do we try and show them up? Or do we just point out the plain daftness of their opposition, of their argument?' And then Pantigate came along, and they did all of that for us. They did the most work for a yes vote in this referendum than I think we could ever do … Obviously, and it was a point I made on *The Saturday Night Show*, I've a huge, huge, huge problem with the access that these groups have had. I would go on any radio station and debate gay marriage with the Catholic Church – anyone, from a parish priest to an archbishop – because they're the ones that have officially announced an opposition to it, but they're not the ones that are engaging in the media around the debate. They're sending out their foot soldiers. They're sending out the lobbyist groups. And that really, really fucks me off … I don't want a Catholic marriage. This is a legal, civil issue involving government. It's got nothing to do with the Catholic Church, but fine, they've stuck their nose in, that's grand. So don't just stick your nose in; say it's wrong, tell all your members to vote against it, and then butt out. I haven't heard one member of the clergy on a radio show.

DAVID NORRIS: They should be on their knees, all the Churches, repenting and begging forgiveness from the gay community for the horrors that were perpetrated on them for centuries for which they were responsible. This all comes from religion. It starts with the Old Testament, which has been seriously misinterpreted anyway.

TIERNAN BRADY: If you were talking to TDs, especially outside-the-M50 TDs, they were being bombarded with letters and emails, because again the religious groups and other conservative groups have great networks and they know how to mobilise them. And they mobilise them in the way they thought would have the most effect – scare the bejaysus out of backbenchers. And that did terrify them.

AILBHE SMYTH: 'Homophobia' is almost too slight a word – it's a deeply entrenched othering of lesbians and gay men, which is not quite the same as having a phobia; it's not just a fear or a hatred of lesbian and gay people, although there can be that there – of course, absolutely – but it is also this sense that we are of a species and that's not always accompanied by a fear or a loathing; it can be a way of bolstering your sense of your own species. So it's about power. And it's about having power over people. And I think lesbians and gays, putting our head above the parapet in relation to the twentieth century, the last century when we started saying, 'We exist, we have equal rights.' So I see it as those fighting very, very deeply entrenched, traditional notions that are deeply embedded in society, which are hugely heterosexual and still actually patriarchal – also very white, very abled, and so on and so forth. It is incredibly difficult to dislodge all of those things. It is something else that's so deeply there, that people who have sex in a way that is different from you need to be othered. That sense – there can be a sense of revulsion and loathing of course, but I'm not sure that's quite correct and accurate in a contemporary moment. But there is sometimes something so simple that it's like, 'That's always the way it is and, sure, wouldn't it – would be odd indeed if it were to change; sure, we couldn't change that; marriage, sure, of course it's only for heterosexual people.' There is no logical reason as to why. Turn the world on its head and say, 'Why?' Quite clearly marriage is not only for procreation; marriage is for very many reasons. People like living as couples. They went into the arc two by two by two. Because we have a particularly virulent form of Catholicism in this country, which has had itself challenged since the 1970s by women and then by lesbians and gays. It is just very resistant to hearing any kind of common sense and to recognise any kind of logic to human organisation and human socialisation and to human sexuality.

COLM O'GORMAN: I think they're absolutely entitled to believe that I am of lesser value than them, and that my relationships are of lesser value than them, and to even feel distaste or disgust when they look at me and when they see my husband or my children. Probably my husband and myself more than anything else. I wish they didn't. I think it's kind of sad and rather tragic that they do. I wish for them that they didn't more than for myself. I wish that they'd go away and leave me alone so I don't have to deal with their disgust and their internalised prejudice or shame or whatever the hell it is. But I'll absolutely defend their right to voice it. And more than that, I think it's really important that they do – and I don't mean so that we can expose it; I mean so that we can address it. Because if we don't find the capacity within society to create spaces where we can name our prejudices and explore them, and have them challenged reasonably, respectfully, compassionately, strongly, robustly, powerfully, or whatever, we're never going to get beyond them. So I think it's really important that other people express their views, and that I express mine when we're in direct opposition to each other, including those moments when I'm sitting next to stuff that's outrageous or offensive.

BREDA O'BRIEN: Gay marriage, I believe, will signal legislative acceptance that there is nothing unique and special about being reared by your own mother and father. Marriage will move from being a largely child-centred institution, which the State protects because it promotes commitment between the loving biological parents of children, to an institution which is a State sanctioned stamp of approval on romantic relationships. This is a massive cultural shift. I have no problem with people's committed relationships being recognised, and am happy that their rights should be protected in the event of a breakdown of a relationship. Also, I think it is good, indeed essential, that the law does not exclude LGBT people from the bedside of a sick or dying partner because they have no legal relationship to them... I support recognition of the rights of gay and lesbian people, but I believe that marriage is a gendered institution for a good reason – it helps preserve the commitment of men and women to their own children. I think there is something of intrinsic value in as many people as possible being reared by their own loving biological parents. If we want equal representation of women in parliaments and boardrooms, why do we think gender does not matter when it comes to parenting? Why do we want to re-define an institution that already has 50-50 representation of men and women? At the same time, I believe that relationships between people of the same sex should receive recognition and respect. However, diversity does not mean everyone being treated exactly the same – diversity and pluralism recognise that different situations can be treated differently.

TIERNAN BRADY: Iona have the easiest job in the world to do. They just have to say, 'If in doubt, vote no' …

BRIAN FINNEGAN: Brenda Power [her article in the *Sunday Times* about Pride in 2009] really sticks out in my mind as being a moment when the, I suppose, in inverted commas, 'respectable face of the Irish media', showed their fangs, in my opinion. So I mean they're the things that get people riled up and get them angry and make them go out on the March for Marriage.

AILBHE SMYTH: I remember another one at Electric Picnic was in a tent and it was lashing rain and it was a debate or discussion convened by David McWilliams. It was myself and Colm O'Gorman and Rónán Mullen and another guy whose name I can't remember – actually a very nice man but quite quiet. He was from a Catholic parents' organisation, I think. I remember Rónán Mullen being very, very difficult. I found it very difficult as a woman to get any space in that debate. It was almost as if the three men, or perhaps particularly Rónán Mullen and Colm O'Gorman, were having this conversation. It very rarely happens to me that I don't find a way into a conversation, but I really experienced that then and I actually thought that this was something to do with being a woman in this environment and it just brought home to me at that particular time, rightly or wrongly – it was just a personal thought – that perhaps it's true that marriage of course is also a very gendered institution. And men and women in heterosexual marriage probably go into marriage with different expectations and needs and so on, so that there is something that I don't think we've worked through yet about how two gay men getting married and two lesbians getting married have also got different expectations of that institution. And I think we haven't begun to plumb the depths of that one yet. But it struck me very forcibly during the course of that conversation. And I did, of course, intervene and I was extremely pleased that at the end I got the largest clap! It was also lashing rain and Florence and the Machine were playing in the next tent and I really actually wanted to go into Florence and the Machine!

BRIAN FINNEGAN: They [the media] will allow innuendo, and it is innuendo that says we're damaging to children … and it goes down to a basic sexual thing that we're sexually damaging to children. And they will allow their 'respectable voices' to be heard saying absolutely damaging things that are damaging to society and damaging to individuals, and are incitement to hatred as far as I'm concerned. But yet the Irish media seems to think that's perfectly ok. That's perfectly ok. And it doesn't matter how many of you or me or whoever is going to get to write the odd thing about that subject within the media – it doesn't matter how many of us go, 'No! But no!', we're not the mainstream Middle Ireland voice, and they are. And they're telling Middle Ireland that we're dangerous.

DAVID NORRIS: Certain people have a healthy obsession with other people's sex lives, number one. Number two, there's an attempt to preserve what they see as the traditional Roman Catholic Church. And there's also a kind of, to me, what I would regard as a pathological desire to control other people's lives – and not only their lives, but their deaths … But I don't understand. I'm not a bit interested in other people's sex lives. At the age of 70, I'm not particularly interested in my own! It would take a fair amount to get me going! … I have never in my life thought about what any of my heterosexual colleagues in the Oireachtas do in bed. I don't think I'd be able to eat my lunch if I did.

EAMON RYAN: I don't buy the kind of weakening the family or undermining the family [argument]. I think lots of things undermine the family, but I don't see other people looking to have a recognition of their relationship in that way – I don't see how it in any way undermines my marriage or my relationship. There's lots of other stuff we could concentrate on that has that effect in society, but I don't see extending marriage – I don't see that argument holding.

AVERIL POWER: I don't understand how some people are so motivated to fight against other people's happiness and I'll never understand that on this issue and on other issues. I will never understand that. Especially when some of the people involved have put forward research and have had that research discounted and off they go and find some more research, which has also been discounted. And they seem to be struggling to find things to justify their view. So I don't believe their view is genuinely based on research. I think they have a view and then they go and try and find things to support that view. And I don't get that. I don't get where they're coming from. I don't get where their motivation is.

BILL HUGHES: Marriage equality is putting to bed the last taboo and saying gay people are the same as you. 'No, they're not! They can't do this, they can't do that and they can't get married!' Well, actually now they can. And, as Panti says, look outside – is the sky falling? No, it's not. Get over it. Wake up and be part of it. Embrace it, stop fighting, stop being against it, and stop being so provincial.

DAVID NORRIS: But my God, as I said years ago, they've blessed bombs, agricultural implements and goldfish. And how do they know the goldfish aren't lesbians? With goldfish it's impossible to tell! ... I think it's terribly mean. Why couldn't they give some kind of blessing to two people who love each other? If they're prepared to bless bombs that blow people apart, and goldfish – whose sexuality is questionable – and tractors? Jesus! It's so stupid.

GERARD HOWLIN: I think all voices that are amplified in the media are less persuasive to others than they are to themselves. The media debate, this cacophony of high, loud noise, is a lot less interesting and a lot less persuasive to the vast majority of people when they make their decisions than people either involved in those debates hearing the sound of their own voices or the media wish to imagine. And I think the challenge for the 'yes' side in this referendum is whether people can be persuaded that if they just look around their own lives, people they know – is this a fair shake for people they know in their families, in their street, in their lives, in their community? And I think the more ideological arguments will be far less interesting and have far less traction than those who are intensely interested in the matter [think]. I think the more extreme 'no' side if anything is a plus because it can be quite off-putting. In a sense the more free reign that's given, the happier I'll be because I think it comes across as nasty. Stridency of any kind puts people off.

JOHN LYONS: Some of the articles that people have written who often come from what I would perceive to be a conservative Catholic agenda, which in my opinion does not even represent a minutiae of the population of Ireland, have been given ample opportunity in the broadsheet, particularly in Ireland, to eloquently put what I would describe as offensive language towards me and other people like me. I'm half afraid to even say what I want to say.

30

THE
FUTURE

'We didn't even see it in our lifetime.'

– Muriel Walls

ANN LOUISE GILLIGAN: But you know, to end on a happy note, as feminists, we've all read acres of history and it is history – 'his story'. But, you know, I think in this situation, and in that statement, so often 'her story' has been the atypical narrative of history. But in this case the fact of the matter is: marriage equality is 'her story'. In its origins in this society. And I'm not just talking about Katherine and I. I'm talking about Gráinne Healy. I'm talking about Monnine – I can keep going here – with men who have been utterly supportive …

KATHERINE ZAPPONE: … and happy for the women to take the lead.

ANN LOUISE GILLIGAN: This is a story of women's leadership in this society, who against the odds have brought it to this point … The political is personal and the legal is personal: there are lives that are being profoundly impacted, negatively, every day this doesn't happen because every day this doesn't happen there are young men and young women, especially vulnerable people who are looking at themselves saying, 'Well, there must be something wrong with me that I actually can't participate in an institution in this State that I'd like to. What is wrong with me?', and that, for a vulnerable person, can have a huge impact. So this is not a light or a peripheral issue. And as we said earlier, as a core indentation of patriarchal control of women, it's a huge issue, but just as a societal issue of rights and responsibilities, it is a major issue and every day is a day too long to wait. That's what I'd say. Just my opinion!

UNA MULLALLY: Any further points?

ANN LOUISE GILLIGAN: *Je ne regrette rien.*

DIARMUID DOYLE: When people talk about the increasing acceptance of gay rights, that's because more and more people have come out. They're your sister, your brother, your son, your daughter, and your father or your mother sometimes. So that's kind of happened that the country opened up to that, I think, below the surface. It just became this normal thing and then as it began to happen in other countries there seems to be this acceptance of, 'Yeah it'll happen here, and yeah, it's fine if it happens here.' So you have this huge, at the moment, gap in the opinion polls where 76 per cent the last time I saw it – now, that will probably narrow next year, but I think the debate is running under the radar and parallel with a greater opening up of society. So people aren't as shocked as they would have been if this had ever been raised in the '70s, which it obviously wouldn't have. It's one of those issues that isn't as startling an issue as, say, the divorce referendum was when we had the two referendums where divorce was this shocking thing that has come from the outside world to change our nation, but the nation had already changed before we ever got around to a referendum no gay marriage, so that's why I think people at the moment are pretty calm about the whole thing and accepting of what's going to happen and cool about what's going to happen.

EDMUND LYNCH: I never conceived that the marriage thing was going to happen and I must say well done to everyone for bringing us to this stage.

MURIEL WALLS: I'll be 60 this year, so I remember my fiftieth, and I remember a very heated debate with some friends or colleagues about the whole gay and lesbian possibility of marriage. We didn't even see it in our lifetime. The general consensus was: not in our lifetime. And that's only ten years ago.

DAVID NORRIS: I didn't actually think I would see it in my lifetime. To go from a criminal to having the right to get married is quite extraordinary, but to me the most significant thing is the recognition and solidarity of people who are not gay. That is very, very powerful. Very, very significant. And that to my mind is the most hopeful thing because that shows that we are prepared to live in a diverse society.

In August 2014, the March For Marriage took place in Dublin, with 8,000 people in attendance, the same day the newly crowned Rose of Tralee, Maria Walsh came out in a newspaper interview as lesbian.

A referendum on extending marriage to same-sex couples is scheduled to be held in Ireland in 2015.

Also from The History Press

Irish Revolutionaries

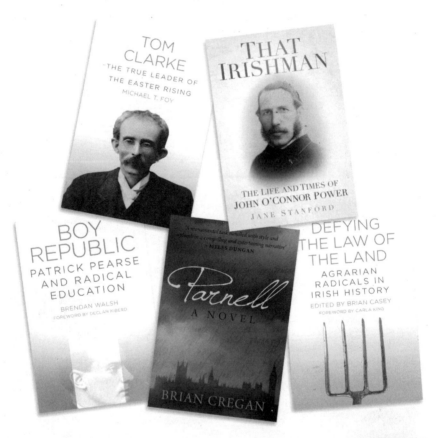

Find these titles and more at
www.thehistorypress.ie